EXPLORATIONS IN MANAGING

EXPLORATIONS IN MANAGING

ALLEN A. ZOLL, III
Management Education Associates

ADDISON-WESLEY PUBLISHING COMPANY
Reading, Massachusetts · Menlo Park, California
London · Amsterdam · Don Mills, Ontario · Sydney

Copyright © 1974 by Allen A. Zoll, III. Philippines copyright 1974 by Allen A. Zoll, III.
All rights reserved. No part of this publication may be reproduced, stored in a retrieval system, or transmitted, in any form or by any means, electronic, mechanical, photocopying, recording, or otherwise, without the prior written permission of the publisher. Printed in the United States of America. Published simultaneously in Canada. Library of Congress Catalog Card No. 73-22646.

ISBN 0-201-08812-6
BCDEFGHIJ-MA-798765

To Lucille,
My wife, associate, and friend.

PREFACE

For a good many years in my education of managers, I have been advocating and practicing the increased use of participation. To me, true learning occurs when the learner discovers personal meaning and relevance of the ideas presented. This suggests that information is useful when it answers a question which has been raised by the learner. But much of what is offered as "education" consists of giving people answers to questions which they haven't raised! Information thus imposed is not very useful. As I see it, the real role of the teacher, or the teacher-writer, is to create activities that assist the learners to make their own explorations and discoveries. If one picture is worth a thousand words, surely one meaningful experience is worth ten thousand pictures.

In a very real sense, this book is an experiment. As far as I know, there has been no other attempt to write a book on managing which provides a series of meaningful experiences, as well as content, to the individual reader. John F. Connors of the Martin Marietta Corporation in New York, and Seymour Levy of the Pillsbury Company in Minneapolis looked over an early sketch of the approach and were very encouraging. During the actual writing, I was able to draw on the advice and counsel of Robert J. Boroughs of The Boeing Company in Seattle. Bob combined a long-term interest in adult education with experience as an executive with another firm to provide me with many helpful ideas and comments.

Mr. Leslie J. Wilson of the Addison-Wesley staff made specific, helpful suggestions from his view as a manager-reader, and Evelyn Wilde provided her skill in grammar and style. Finally, I must acknowledge the many managers, subordinates, teachers, friends, and colleagues from whom I learned much about the managing process.

Seattle, Washington   A. Z.
May 1974

CONTENTS

1 Introduction — 1
   Is this book for you? — 1
   The book's approach — 1
   The book's points of view — 2
   Before you begin . . . — 2

2 Management Practices — 5
   In-basket on management practice — 5
   Commentaries on in-basket items — 36
   Summary — 51

3 All About You — 55
   The future is here — 55
   About you in management — 60
   About your development — 64
   Requiescat in pace (R. I. P.) — 69
   The idea of a self-concept — 74
   Summary — 79

4 Relationships, Up and Down — 81
   Authority figures — 81
   A trust climate — 84
   Taking risks — 87
   Getting feedback — 88
   Performance appraisals — 92
   Reinforcement — 93

xi

xii   Contents

5 Communication — **101**

The illusion — 101
The trouble with words . . . — 103
I'm way ahead of you . . . — 107
Can you hear me down (up) there? — 110
"It's too hot in here!" — 112
Getting feedback — 115
Now that I've told you . . . — 117

6 Effective Thinking — **119**

Case study—the sales manager — 119
Practice application — 124
Case study—the Marston Manufacturing Company — 125
Case study—the regional officers meeting — 129
Summary — 133

7 Managing Changes — **135**

How do you react to change? — 135
Action maze on managing change — 137
Analysis of your action maze activity — 188
Planning for your changes — 192

8 Groups at Work — **195**

All I need is another meeting — 195
Let's look at your behavior in meetings — 197
Other ways of looking at groups — 208
Checklist on working with groups — 210

9 Participation in Decision-Making — **213**

The range of participation in decision-making — 213
Participation in your own situation — 219

10 Organizational Conflict — **223**

Practice application—what should he do? — 224
Dealing with conflict — 226
In-basket on handling organization conflict — 228
Commentaries on the in-basket items — 250
How do you deal with conflict? — 254

11 Motivation — **259**

About "theories" — 259
Applying theories to behavior — 260

	Questionnaires	264
	Some theories of motivation	267
	What are your assumptions about motivation?	276
12	**Some Ideas About Administration**	**281**
	The world of "as if"	281
	Are we talking about the same job?	284
	About authority	286
	How much effort?	287
	Delegation	288
	Don't just do something, stand there!	291
	"Gee, isn't this crisis fun!"	293
	"There's only one little thing wrong . . ."	295
	"He's the guy that cut the cable, remember?"	296
	So, who needs a genius?	298
	Development	300
	"You're fired"	305
	How to "technique" people	307
13	**Managing Your Time**	**309**
	Logging your time	309
	Analysis of your activities	311
	Ideas on time management	321
14	**Problem-Solving**	**323**
	A model for problem-solving	325
	Solving your own problem	340
15	**Your Management Philosophy**	**345**
	Elements of a management philosophy	346
	Identifying your management philosophy	351
	Now that you know your philosophy of management . . .	358
	Epilogue	**363**
	About the Author	**365**

CHAPTER 1

INTRODUCTION

IS THIS BOOK FOR YOU?

This book has been written specifically for the experienced manager in a multilevel organization in business and government. Two uses of it are foreseen: as a learning experience for the individual manager alone, and as a companion text for the learners in a formal course in management. Although the book may well be of interest for students and others not assigned to a management position, the examples and activities provided presume such a current assignment. Also, the beginning first-level manager and the manager in a very small organization may find the content of interest, but a book written for them would have quite different examples, more related to their situations.

THE BOOK'S APPROACH

This book has been designed to present an experiential approach in learning. That is, before, during, and after the presentation of content about managing, you are asked and expected to *participate* in activities related to the content. This interaction with the content takes place through your answering questions, making ratings, analyzing cases, filling out checklists, solving problems, examining and taking action on various materials, exploring an action maze, preparing a log and analysis of time spent, and through your detailed planning for future action.

A key question on the treatment of subjects in each chapter was: How can this content be made *personally involving* to you? Such involvement can make the content come alive and be much more meaningful to you. Ideas which are *self-discovered* through exploration are really *owned*—not just bought and paid for. If you want to only read about ideas in managing, without becoming involved, *get another kind of book*.

"What you get out of the experience will depend on how much you put into it." I don't believe that, and neither do you! But it is a nice way to put the burden on *you* rather than on me. What you get out of the book will depend in large part on our skill in presenting ideas which are realistic and challenging to you in your day-to-day operations, as well as on our ability to create activities which hold your interest. This is where most self-instructional programs fall short.

THE BOOK'S POINTS OF VIEW

One such viewpoint of the book is suggested by the description of the approach to be taken—you as an individual. Reading this book will be an introspective experience, which will help you to define more clearly who you are, what you believe, and how you now act. This is a first step in your making any changes you may care to. It would be presumptuous, even if it were possible, to think that you could become more effective through some force being imposed on you from outside yourself. Instead, increasing your insights about yourself as you are now, coupled with knowledge of the greater range of choices available to you, will enable you to make changes for more self-acceptance and greater effectiveness.

A second viewpoint of the book is of you as a manager. The term "leadership" will not be used here. Everyone can define that term, but no one agrees on what it means. Instead, we will be considering you as a manager. If you are a manager, appointed by yourself or others, you have a job to get done —largely through others. And that is the fact we will start with.

The third viewpoint is of you as a manager in a specific context. Action may be realistically considered only by taking into account the important factors within your situation. The most important of these are: your perception and skills, the manager you work for, and the people who work with and for you. We are all familiar with people who have "learned" new behavior somewhere, have taken it back to the job, and have tried to apply it "full blown" without proper consideration of these factors. Some of the stories about them are funny; some are sad.

To summarize, the considerations stressed throughout the book will be you as a manager, with your insights, an increased range of choices, skills, and your taking action within a particular situation.

BEFORE YOU BEGIN . . .

Most managers have feelings of concern, at least some of the time, that they are not as effective as they might be in such areas as working with others, managing their own time, understanding the working of groups, and so on. But most managers also feel the pressures of job problems, the demands of home and the community, and their own needs for re-creation. It is hard for most managers to invest the time needed to increase their personal effectiveness. As one manager put it: "I'm so busy digging a trench with a spoon that I don't have time to go back to the toolshed to see if there are better tools available!" For those people, the self-development experience of this book is designed to be used in the time they can schedule for their development.

I've tried to make each chapter independent, so that they can be read in any order. But each chapter selected should be read "from front to back," since most are designed to be an "unfolding" experience for you.

As you work through the materials, your conclusions may differ from those stated, and this is fine. You must reach your own conclusions from your own experience. Also, it is expected that you will gain insights about yourself and your ways of operating as a manager which we didn't plan in creating the materials.

If the book is being used as a companion text in a course in management education, a teacher's manual is available which suggests films, group activities, and other experiences which can be used only when there is a group. In whichever use is being made of the book, I wish you well on your trip of self-exploration and discovery.

CHAPTER 2

MANAGEMENT PRACTICES

To be helpful to you in your exploration of managing, we should—ideally—be able to sit at your elbow while you go through your usual daily routine. Then we could discuss some of the specific things you did and might have done. Although we can't do that, we can simulate the experience.

This chapter consists of an "in-basket" for your analysis and action decisions, followed by our commentaries on both the issues and action for each item. You can thus compare your thinking to ours. As used in management education, an "in-basket" is, as the name implies, a collection of letters, memos, and other items of correspondence arriving with the incoming mail on a given morning. Some of the items are from your subordinates, others from elsewhere in the organization, and others may come from outside. You are to decide on the issue or issues presented in the correspondence and decide on what action, if any, you would take as a result of receiving the item.

Administrative aspects of the management job are emphasized in the letters. Omitted are important considerations of the products, detailed financial matters, operating reports, goals and objectives, etc. Although it is unrealistic to omit these factors, their inclusion would make it much more difficult to place yourself in the shoes of a manager in the case. This experience will act somewhat as a preview of the book, since many of the issues are discussed in more detail later.

IN-BASKET ON MANAGEMENT PRACTICES*

Introduction

This will be a different kind of a case problem from what perhaps you are used to. It contains materials which you are to assume have arrived in the morning mail. You are to decide what issue or issues are reflected in each item and what

---

* Most of this material is taken from my book *The In-Basket Kit*, Reading, Mass.: Addison-Wesley, 1971. Reprinted by permission.

action, if any, you would take as a result of receiving the item. You will get the most out of the experience if you think through each item and make notes on it in the space provided. Only after you have finished the entire in-basket should you turn to the commentaries which follow and compare your answers to them.

Your Situation

Assume that you are *Bob Black,* manager of the United States Sales Division of Consumer Products, Inc. Your staff and the sales zones reporting to you are shown on the organization chart on p. 7. Look it over now in order to become generally aware of the organization and your place in it. As the chart shows, you report to Bill Nelson, the Director of Marketing. Upper-level managers, your peers, and key people in your organization are also named in the organization chart.

Instructions

Go through the items of correspondence one by one and make notes about the issue or issues you see and the action, if any, you would take. (Remember, you are Bob Black, Manager of the United States Sales Division.) Then turn to the commentaries and compare your answers with them.

In-basket on management practices 7

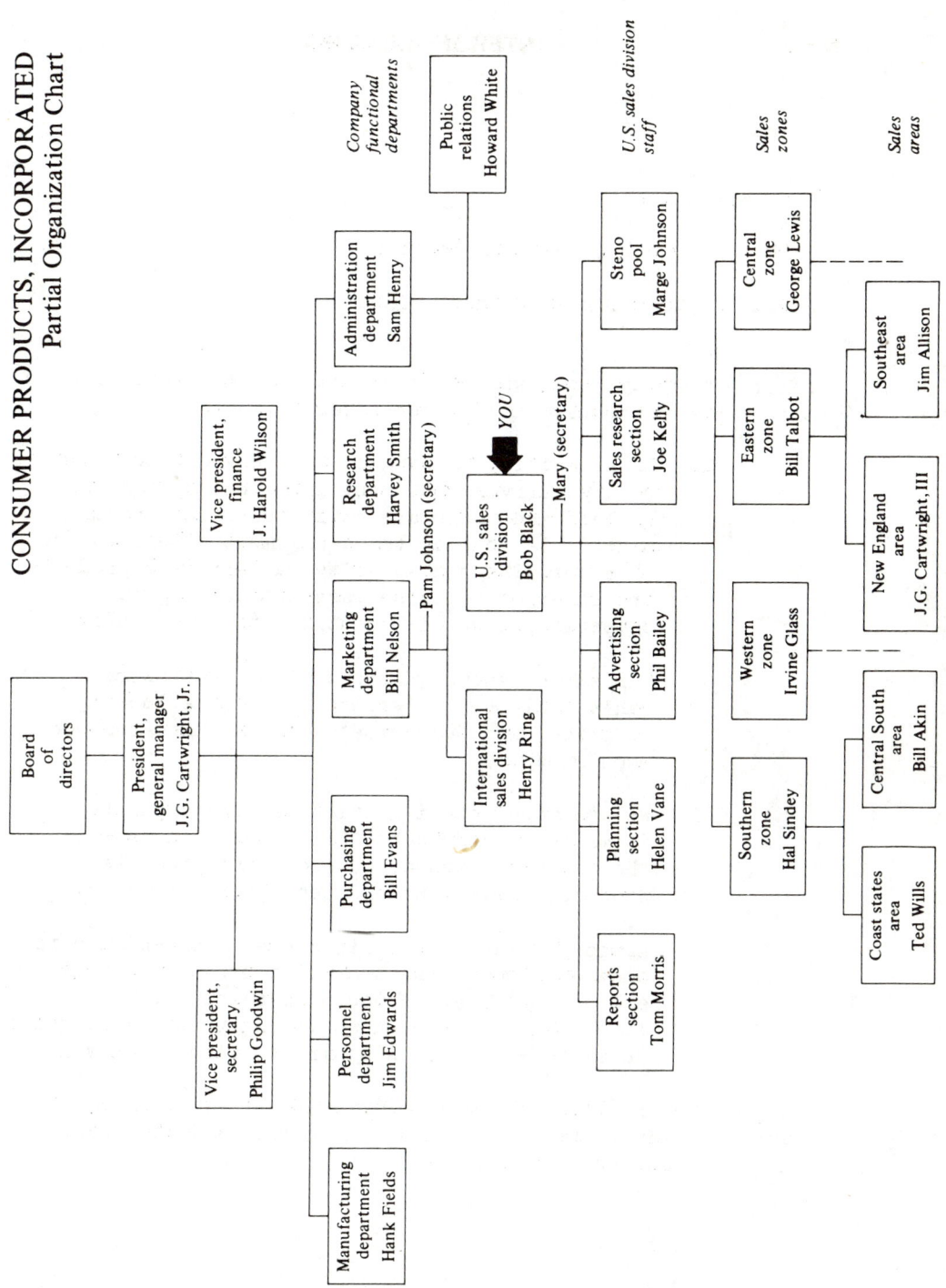

CONSUMER PRODUCTS, INCORPORATED
Partial Organization Chart

MP 1   INTEROFFICE MEMO

TO: Bob Black

FROM: Joe Kelly, Research Section

SUBJECT: Trimming of Product Lines

After a thorough analysis, we have come to the conclusion that these problems exist in our product lines:

1. In attempting to hang on to every old customer we are carrying out many intricate operations by hand and these are consistently losing us money. As long as top management clings to the idea that its high-quality hand-crafted products are superior to those mass-produced by our competitors, we will continue to lose profits.

   Our survey shows that 80% of our customers can't tell the difference. They are looking at price, and our competitors can mass-produce much cheaper.

2. We are manufacturing twice as many separate items as we should be. In almost all cases, the smaller sizes of our consumer products produce small to nonexistent profit margins.

   Although these small sizes are a convenience to older customers and traveling consumers, they are not profitable enough to retain in the line. Again, keeping on making these small sizes seems to be due to a desire to please everyone.

If you concur, I'll notify Manufacturing and Purchasing of this decision to trim our lines and prepare a letter from you notifying the Sales Zones.

JK/LM

ISSUE(S)

ACTION

MP 2

~~Bill Nelson~~ Bob Black
as info.
J.G.

MIDWEST DISTRIBUTION COMPANY

Mr. J. G. Cartwright, Jr.
President
Consumer Products, Inc.
North State Street
Centerville

Dear Mr. Cartwright,

Just a note to tell you how helpful we find the economic analyses coming out of your Sales Research Section. They are timely, and well written.

Mr. Kelly and his staff of economists are doing a fine job, and we appreciate it.

Keep up the good work!

Cordially,

John Williams

John M. Williams
President

JMW/ss

ISSUE(S)

ACTION

MP 3   **INTEROFFICE MEMO**

TO: Bob Black

FROM: Phil Bailey, Advertising Section

SUBJECT: New Unit Head

I thought I would let you know about an idea I'm using to select a new unit manager for Magazine Advertising.

Since there are three men equally qualified for the job, I plan to let these three select the man for the job.

This is real participative management, as I see it, and should serve to make the men more satisfied and happy with management. I'm sure that you agree that this is a worthy goal.

Phil

PB/js

In-basket on management practices 13

ISSUE(S)

ACTION

MP 4 INTEROFFICE MEMO

TO: Bob Black

FROM: Tom Morris, Reports Section

SUBJECT: Need for additional staff

Following is a tabulation of the work load of this office for the past nine months compared to the same period last year.

	9 mos. this year	9 mos. last year
Reports	44	29
Letters	1,189	883

As you can clearly see, we need additional staff. Without two additional people we won't be able to keep up with sending letters and reports to the four Sales Zones.

Unless I hear from you otherwise, I'll ask Personnel to begin the process of finding another staff person and another secretary. The formation of the typing pool really isn't that much help, so we need our own people.

I can probably get a woman staff member for around $2000 less than a man, so I'll try for a woman.

Tom

TM:ga

ISSUE(S)

ACTION

MP 5   **INTEROFFICE MEMO**

TO: Bob Black

FROM: Tom Morris, Reports Section

SUBJECT: Presentation

I have the presentation on the new collection policy ready for the Zone Managers' meeting in two weeks.

I think it's a good one. It gives the reasons for the change and how it will actually help sales in the long run.

I haven't shown it to the other section heads because of the way they tore into the last presentation I previewed for them. But it's ready to go.

Tom

TM:ga

ISSUE(S)

ACTION

MP 6   **INTEROFFICE MEMO**

To: Bob Black

From: Helen Vane, Planning Section

Subject: Needed Procedures

   I think that we should have some procedure to set priorities on jobs from the U. S. Sales Division to be sent to computing. We seem to always be over our budget, and I'm sure that <u>all</u> these jobs don't need to be done on a computer.

   Also, what do you think about getting Bill Nelson's signature on a letter to the Sales Zones regarding delinquent accounts? With money getting tight, delinquent accounts could be a problem.

Helen

ISSUE(S)

ACTION

MP 7   INTEROFFICE MEMO

TO: Bob Black

FROM: Bill Talbot, Eastern Zone Manager

SUBJECT: Change of Responsibilities

Jim Allison--whom we promoted to Manager of the Southeast Area three months ago--is just not making it. So I have decided to shift North and South Carolina to the New England section headed by J. G. Cartwright, III. He is strong enough to handle two more states.

Also, I'm moving Pat Wiley over to be Allison's assistant manager. With this additional help, Allison should be able to get the job done.

bt:ovq

ISSUE(S)

ACTION

MP 8   Personal and Confidential

TO: Bob Black

FROM: Joe Kelly, Sales Research

SUBJECT: - - - -

I wanted to let you know about something I have been thinking about for some time. So, I thought I'd drop you this note and let you be thinking about it. We have a meeting scheduled for next week to go over my career plans. I thought we might discuss what I have been considering then, since that's what my thoughts are all about.

I have been thinking that it might be best for me to leave the organization, and as far as that goes, to leave sales research as a career. I hope that this comes as a surprise, since I have tried to do an excellent job with my assignment here.

But, frankly, I don't think I am making enough of a "scratch" on the world--enough of a contribution, if you see what I mean. We are all given just so many years to live, and I want to feel at the end of my days that I have really made a difference. This would require that I do something other than work for Consumer Products until retirement.

I hope that you understand. Let's talk about it next week.

ISSUE(S)

ACTION

MP 9   INTEROFFICE MEMO

TO: Bob Black

FROM: Hal Sindey, Manager, Southern Zone

Subject: Last Quarter Sales

Here are the gross sales, less returns and allowances, by state, for the last quarter.

State	Sales
Texas	$ 103,964.14
Oklahoma	$ 69,853.47
Arkansas	$ 27,086.59
Louisiana	$ 89,753.96
Mississippi	$ 17,095.85
Alabama	$ 36,967.03
Tennessee	$ 31,076.00

H. Sindey
Hal Sindey
Manager, Southern Zone

ISSUE(S)

ACTION

MP 10   **INTEROFFICE MEMO**

TO: B. Black

FROM: Bill Nelson, Marketing Department

SUBJECT: Assignment

I think that we should be doing some digging on sales of our competitors before Mr. Cartwright's staff meeting next week.

(Pam J.)

ISSUE(S)

ACTION

MP 11 **INTEROFFICE MEMO**

To: Heads of Planning Staffs, All Zones

From: Helen Vane, Planning Section, Central Office

Subject: Meeting to Draft Procedure

cc: Bob Black

    This is to confirm our meeting on Thursday of next week here at the Central Office. The purpose is to begin a draft of a procedure for long-range planning.

    I'm sure each of you will agree to the importance of the subject for each zone, and for the company as a whole.

    I would suggest that out-of-towners plan to stay at the new Hilton Inn, which has just opened, and which is within walking distance of the office.

    See you next week!

Helen

ISSUE(S)

ACTION

MP 12 MEMO

To: Bob Black, U. S. Sales Division, Central Office

Bob, as you know, your predecessor appointed the four zone managers to a special study group to recommend changes in our organizational arrangements to take care of overlaps and underlaps, and our interface arrangements generally.

I guess that our meetings began after you moved up to the central office. Anyway, I was made chairman of the study group. But in our meeting so far (we have had three), the arguing and bickering is such that very little gets done.

Could you arrange for me to have more authority as the chairman? If not, I would suggest that you disband the study group and make other plans for the study to get done.

I. Glass

Irvine Glass
Manager
Western Zone

IG:L

ISSUE(S)

ACTION

MP 13   **MEMO**

To: Bob Black, Manager, U.S. Sales Division

From: George Lewis

Subject: Difficulties with Subordinates

I'm having two difficulties with my people generally, and I wanted to get any words of wisdom you might have to help me.

The first of these is that frequently when I ask my people for data on sales in their areas, or ask them how some sales problem is being handled, and the like--they don't know, and I must wait until they call me back with the info. This makes me feel that they aren't really on top of their jobs. But they are good men. I think that this is improving a little lately.

The second problem is that my area managers are delegating less and less to their subordinates. This causes the area managers to take work home on a regular basis, and the wives are getting ready to revolt! They were complaining to my wife at a party recently.

I'm sure that these problems aren't uncommon. Any suggestions you could give me would be welcome.

George

George Lewis
Manager
Central Zone

ISSUE(S)

ACTION

MP 14

TO: Bob Black

FROM: Jim Edwards, Personnel Department

SUBJECT: Introduction of New Salesmen's Payment Plan

    We have finally reached agreement with the finance office on the new incentive plan for our salesmen. The reason for the delay was some tax angles which had to be worked out. But it's all set to go now. In addition to your suggestions, we were able to incorporate those from our interviews with your zone managers. All the bases were covered with this one, and it will be one of the best in the industry!

    I've asked Howard White in Public Relations to prepare a brochure explaining the new plan for distribution to all of the salesmen. It will be simple, but will explain the basic features of the plan. Do you want these brochures mailed to the salesmen's homes?

    Also, I've asked Howard White to put a feature article in the company newspaper the week before the brochures are sent out. This will create a great deal of interest on the part of the salesmen to read the brochure.

    Do you have any final suggestions before we give everyone concerned the green light?

JE:em
                                                          Jim Edwards

ISSUE(S)

ACTION

COMMENTARIES ON IN-BASKET ITEMS

On the following pages are my comments covering issues and action on each of the in-basket items. They are not to be taken as the "school solution," but to indicate what I was trying to illustrate when I created and included the item. You might well have seen more significant issues and more appropriate actions than I had in mind.

On each page there is space for a "self-evaluation" after you have compared your thinking with mine. Many managers have found it to be helpful to do some thinking about themselves in relation to each item. Here are the sorts of comments which might be listed:

"The issue in this one was too subtle for me. I really didn't see what the writer of the letter was after."

"This one reminded me of a similar situation I once had. I guess I was thinking more of that than the situation given here. Do I do this often, I wonder?"

"I think the action I proposed was better than that suggested."

"I thought the proposal described in the letter was a good idea. But the discussion pointed out some pitfalls I missed."

"I agreed with the discussion given here—'right on the nose.' "

"I had not thought about this issue before."

"I was pretty 'heavy-handed' in my action. Would I be if this were a real issue I faced?"

Now take a look at the commentaries.

Commentary on MP 1

Issues

This analysis is certainly appropriate for a Sales Research staff group to make. However, the change being proposed is a *major* one and should not be made casually. It should be thoroughly explored here, the appropriate decisions should be received, and then the matter carefully explained and thoroughly explored with the sales forces and the distributors. Your sales force may give you the most trouble, since they are usually pushing for more variety, while Manufacturing wants standard items.

Action

Congratulate Joe Kelly on his conclusions from his analysis. Request that he prepare a presentation, for your review, which would then be made to Bill Nelson, your boss. If he concurs, the next step might be Manufacturing and Purchasing, or it might be the Zone Sales Managers. Then to the top policy-making group in the company.

This kind of product analysis should be conducted all the time.

Self-evaluation

Commentary on MP 2

Issues

One of the principles we learn from the behavioral sciences is to "see that the desired behavior occurs and then reinforce it through reward." A compliment seen by all the top brass before it goes to the person is quite a reward.

Action

Pass it on down to Joe Kelly. Or better yet, use it to introduce a coaching session with him.

Self-evaluation

Commentary on MP 3

Issues

With some organizational decisions, it is quite appropriate to turn the information about the decision needed over to the group and abide by their decision. With other decisions, this would seem to be inappropriate.

Phil's goal may be worthy, but it would seem to be unfair to the group to ask these people to make the promotion decision.

Will it be possible for the group to be objective in comparing themselves to their friendly, but competitive, peers?

Is the choice "obvious"? What if the obvious choice is *not* made? What will Phil do then?

Would the person selected have any difficulty in having his authority accepted by the group which selected him?

If the person selected is a failure, who is responsible? The group for selecting him? Phil for letting them make the selection?

Other problems this might cause?

Action

See Phil and discuss the drawbacks of asking the three men to make the selection decision. Recommend against this course of action, but discuss instances in which you think it *would* be appropriate to follow this course.

If Phil disagrees, perhaps letting him go ahead will be a useful learning experience for him.

If Phil agrees, help him think through ways by which he can reverse the decision, or at least change it to a request for a *recommendation* from members of the group.

Self-evaluation

Commentary on MP 4

Issues

This staff group's job is not to produce reports and letters, but *results*. This would probably be a good time to survey the *real* usefulness of these letters and reports to the Sales Zones. Reports frequently have a way of continuing long after their usefulness has ended.

Also, trying to find a female because she would be less expensive is discrimination and against the law. This might be a good time to check on the wage rates for men and women who do the same jobs.

Action

Ask Tom Morris to hold off on staff additions until the Sales Zones have been surveyed. Probably it would be best to have *another* organization under you make the survey.

Ask Personnel to survey wage rates for men and women doing the same job.

Self-evaluation

Commentary on MP 5

Issues

When we ask for criticism on a draft or a presentation, what we usually want is a "warm puppy hug." Every presentation should get a working-over by a devil's advocate or a "murder board" before being presented. Only with dissent can we be sure that the presentation has been examined in depth.

Action

Meet with Tom Morris and try to help him see the real usefulness of criticism. Evidently his ego is quite involved in his creation. It might be useful to have other members of the staff take specific points of view (focus) when seeing the presentation. Such as:

"*You* think of all the reasons they won't buy the idea."
"*You* look for any wrong assumptions we are making."
"*You* look for any objections the distributors might have."
Etc.

Self-evaluation

Commentary on MP 6

Issues

Helen's problem is that she is discussing abstractions rather than concrete instruments. She should be saying: "Here is a draft of a procedure . . ." and "Here is a draft of a letter for Bill Nelson's signature. . . ." Often, the feasibility (or the impossibility) of an idea becomes clear when a draft is attempted.

Action

Perhaps, for now, send the letter back with a note asking for some specific examples of her proposals. At the next coaching session, bring to her attention the helpfulness of a draft.

Placing ideas in concrete form saves the executive's time, and many half-vast ideas die when they can't be made concrete.

Self-evaluation

Commentary on MP 7

Issues

Ineffective people should not be "propped up" or shuffled around in reorganizations. They should be moved to a job where they can make a real contribution to the enterprise, or they should be removed.

Action

Get in touch with Bill Talbot and find out what this "prop" job is all about. Recommend that he start looking for a long-term solution to the problem. If Allison isn't right for this job, develop him or move him.

Self-evaluation

Commentary on MP 8

Issues

Joe Kelly seems to be at a choice point as to what to do with his life. There will probably be more and more managers making very major, and very real, choices about their lives in the future.

It is to your credit (as Bob Black) that you have created a climate of trust so that Joe would risk telling you about his real feelings about himself.

What is your attitude toward Joe Kelly at his choice point? Do you see his searching as a sign of weakness? Of strength? If Joe decides to *stay* with Consumer Products, would his expressed doubts be a strike against him? To his favor? Of no consequence?

Action

No action will be taken until Joe comes in next week. But what will you do then? The situation would seem to call for a great deal of listening on your part and an understanding of what he is looking for, even though he doesn't seem to be able to define it well himself as yet.

Giving Joe advice, or trying to persuade him would seem to be completely inappropriate behavior on your part. It's Joe's life, and he must be the one to decide.

Self-evaluation

Commentary on MP 9

Issues

Remember the old joke: (1) "How's your wife?" (2) "Compared to whom?" Status reports should make comparisons, show trends, and state conclusions. Reports like these should go first to one of the staff sections under you, where they could be charted on a graph comparing them to the yearly sales plan.

Action

Arrange to have these reports on *actual* sales go to one of your sections to be analyzed first. Or have one of your staff people design a new reporting system which compares actual sales to expected sales, so that the zone managers know what *you* are looking at.

Subordinates respect what their manager inspects.

Self-evaluation

Commentary on MP 10

Issues

If your boss gives you an assignment and it is not completely clear what is expected and needed, you should ask. You would make quite a different report if the report were to be used to make a decision instead of to inform.

Action

Ask.

Self-evaluation

Commentary on MP 11

Issues

Oh no you don't! Don't call a meeting to *begin* a draft. Don't "group-think" something which could be thought through by one person alone first. Send a draft out, then call a meeting. Pricing out the meeting (salary × time × people + expenses) will emphasize the effective use of meetings.

Action

Ask Helen to get a draft into their hands before they leave for the meeting. Or have a draft waiting for each person at the hotel when he arrives.

This item is related to MP 6 in that both involve Helen's not being specific with proposals. Discussing with Helen both this letter and item 6, you may be able to help her see more effective practices on her part.

Self-evaluation

Commentary on MP 12

Issues

The only authority which can be delegated is the authority of position. Stated bluntly, this is the power to fire someone if he doesn't do what you wish. A study group such as this one needs the authority of trust and relationship. This must be built up from where the men are now.

The behavior of the study group members may stem from their individual behavior in groups. It seems as if the "support role" is lacking and needs to be supplied before the group can progress. Each group member must feel committed to the goals of the meetings. And it may be that this group has not met often enough for it to become a reference group, toward which the members feel a sense of commitment.

Action

Perhaps you can take over the chairmanship of the meetings for a while. You need to build your relationship with the Sales Zone Managers, and you can help to improve the relations among them at the same time.

Self-evaluation

Commentary on MP 13

Issues

What George Lewis doesn't realize is that his two problems are interrelated. If he, as the boss, were to stop expecting his subordinates to have all progress and answers at their fingertips, they would feel freer to delegate and would use their subordinates more effectively.

If a boss expects his subordinates to "know everything," they tend to try to work on all the problems themselves and be overworked trying to handle everything. And they will tend not to use their subordinates effectively.

Action

You might suggest to George Lewis that he read his second and third paragraphs and think about the relationship between them. Invite him to discuss this further if he doesn't see what you mean.

Self-evaluation

Commentary on MP 14

Issues

If there was ever a way *not* to introduce a major change, this is it. Any new change, particularly one involving an issue as sensitive as the pay of the salesmen, must be planned with some care.

Brochures are not a very good way to communicate, since they are a one-way communication device and cannot answer the hundreds of specific questions which will immediately arise about "my pay." The company newspaper is not exactly looked on as a free press, either.

A notice in the company paper will create interest? Create a riot, probably.

Action

Call an immediate halt to Jim Edward's plans for communicating the change. Plan for a full briefing at each level down through the organization, with printed material as needed. The crucial point of communication will be the supervisors of the salesmen. They must thoroughly understand the plan and be able to answer questions, deal with objections and doubts, and administer the plan properly.

We are a long way from a newspaper story on the change.

Self-evaluation

SUMMARY

Now that you have been through the in-basket items, compared your perception of the issues and actions with ours, and made a self-evaluation, can you summarize your overall approach to these management problems? In which areas did you notice you were particularly strong? In which areas are improvements needed?

Here are some areas outlined and the kinds of questions which you might think about in your summary.

1. The issues: Did you look only at the surface issues, or did you also recognize the deeper implications involved? Were there any surprises in the commentaries? If so, why do you suppose there were? Did you read things into the issues that weren't meant to be there? Was this useful or not? Etc.

_____
_____
_____
_____
_____
_____
_____
_____
_____
_____
_____
_____
_____

2. Your action: Was your action specific or vague? Regardless of what you put down for action, did you have specific plans in mind? Or were you going to do things like: "Call a conference," "Formulate a plan," or "Discuss it with him"? Were there any surprises in the discussion of action given? If so, why do you suppose there were? What can you learn about yourself in reviewing your action? Did you consider only the immediate action in the situation, or did you also think about *prevention* in the future through development of your people, and so on? Etc.

3. Relations with subordinates (look over your planned action): How would you characterize your planned contacts with subordinates? As brusk? Friendly? Supportive? Matter-of-fact? Open? To-the-point? Or what? If *you* were the subordinate in each case and the action was taken with you, what impact would it have? How would the action affect your relations with the boss? Etc.

Summary

4. Relations with peers and superiors (look over your action): How would you characterize your relations with them? If different from your treatment of subordinates, why so? How "open" or "guarded" did you feel you were with them? If *you* were the superior or peer and your proposed action was taken with *you*, what impact would it have? Etc.

_____
_____
_____
_____
_____
_____
_____
_____
_____

5. Overall summary: What things did you see about yourself as a result of this experience with the in-basket? Did you get a feel for your strengths? What were they? Did you note areas where you feel you might improve? What were these? Etc.

_____
_____
_____
_____
_____
_____
_____
_____
_____
_____

CHAPTER 3

ALL ABOUT YOU

The emphasis in this book is on situational thinking—the manager in a context. So let's begin by thinking about you in your present situation. I can't think with you, of course, but perhaps I can help you to think about yourself. Let's do this in three steps: looking at the complexity and rate of change of today's world, looking at yourself now, and looking at your hopes for the future.

I'll raise a series of questions for you to answer. They are for you alone. I'd encourage you to write down your answers—not just think about them. The discipline of writing will help you "put your thoughts in order." If your answers are too personal to leave in the book, write them on separate sheets of paper. (One manager we know even locked up his answers in his safe-deposit box.)

Here are the three areas and the questions for you to think about and answer. The questions are broad, and sometimes multiple, but hopefully they will cause you to think about yourself in each area.

THE FUTURE IS HERE

That we are caught up in massive changes is obvious to you, I'm sure. In his breathtaking book *Future Shock,* Alvin Toffler describes in detail the youth revolution, the sexual revolution, the colonial revolution, the economic revolution, and the most rapid and far-reaching technological revolution in history —the ones going on now.* Unlike what happened in many previous revolutions, which can be dated from the day the first shot was fired, we just all woke up one morning and found ourselves in the middle of all these revolutions all happening at once. Here is a summary of some of the changes we find ourselves dealing with, and the questions for you to answer.

---

* Alvin Toffler, *Future Shock,* New York: Random House, 1970. This is also available in paperback. It's a book which I think you would find fascinating.

1. Experiences with the rate of change

Conditions of: slow rate of change, small moves from the familiar, stability, and order

Giving way to

Conditions of: accelerating changes, constant condition of unfamiliarity, and ambiguity.

    How do you feel about living in a world like this?

_____
_____
_____
_____
_____
_____
_____
_____
_____
_____
_____
_____
_____

2. Experiences with organizations

Conditions of: stability, permanence, power-laden hierarchies, "air-tight" functions, distinct line and staff, one boss

Giving way to

Conditions of: loose-knit forms, semiattached and/or temporary units, transient/ad hoc groupings, project management, matrix management and beyond, out-of-date charts, stability for fleeting periods only, indistinct line and staff, functional mergers, many bosses.

    How do you feel about working in such an organization?
    Why do you suppose you feel this way?

_____
_____

3. Experiences with operations

Conditions of: routine projects, long production runs, planning useful but not crucial, flexibility useful, could afford crisis operations, emphasis on technical problems

Giving way to

Conditions of: nonroutine projects, short runs, planned death of projects, structures and systems for planning critical, flexibility vital, unplanned crises devastating, demands of human problems paramount.

What adjustments will you have to make in this new world?
Can you make those needed adjustments?

4. Experiences with decisions

Conditions of: leisurely decision-making, minor impact of "no decision," enough lucky guesses meant success, past and present experiences a useful guide, social-political environment factors to consider, slow movement of information

Giving way to

Conditions of: rapid decision-making required; "no decision" means opportunities lost forever; enough guesses means catastrophe; repeated, probablistic, long-range assumptions needed; social-political forces key influences; mobile vertical and lateral communications vital.

> How will these requirements affect the life of your organization?
> How do you feel about them?

_____
_____
_____
_____
_____
_____
_____
_____
_____
_____
_____
_____
_____

5. Experiences with the work force

Conditions of: narrow range of life styles, low education level, comfort with stability, low expectations of the work place, influenced by the Depression, security important, predictability

Giving way to

Conditions of: wide variety of life styles, high and increasing education level, comfortable with and expect rapid change, high expectations of the work place, products of our affluent society, fulfillment important, change.

What impacts will the new work force have on your organization? On your practices?

6. Experiences with managing

Conditions of: stable superior, peer, subordinate relationships; long-term relationships; promotion permanent; experience valued, knowledge assumed; knowledge adequate or passable; rate of change could be handled; long-term careers; comfortable, "at-home" feelings with work; personal stability

Giving way to

Conditions of: temporary, shifting assignments; fluctuating roles and relationships; constant adjustments to new people and styles; knowledge over experience; knowledge clearly inadequate; more "walking wounded" obsolete managers; serial careers; irritating uncertainty; more drop-outs, push-outs, lower assignments; more challenge from youth.

This is the key question to you, of course. How will you fit in with this new world?

You can't say: "Stop the world—I want to get off!" So let's go on.

ABOUT YOU IN MANAGEMENT

1. Despite the fact that you are somewhat special because you are reading this book, what we know about human nature and the law of averages tells us that one group of us, of undertermined size, is as far in management, *right now,* as they will ever get with their organization. Some of this small group will move to *lower* positions in the organization in the future. Others will just stay where they are. Another group will make one or two more moves and then come to the end of their advancement. Another small group will continue to move upward to the very heights of the organization. Which group would you like to be in? Which group are you in? Why do you think so?

2. Are you willing to live a lonelier life in upper management where you will be required to make judgments about your friends which will involve their salary, career, and future? Are you emotionally willing to live "in the dark at the top of the stairs"? How do you know?

3. Do you really have the broad view? Or have you merely convinced yourself that you have, and prove it to yourself by sticking to those in your function whose ideas and language are comfortable? Do you really have the broad viewpoint?

4. Do you welcome difference of opinion and encourage independence of mind? Or, are you imprisoned by fixed habits, attitudes, and routines? Do you tolerate drive and conviction on the part of others? This can be a nuisance. The enthusiasts annoy people by pushing too hard. Do you encourage independence of mind? Would the people in your organization agree with you?

_____
_____
_____
_____
_____
_____
_____
_____
_____
_____
_____
_____

5. How sure are you that you are really accomplishing something in your management job? By putting in a hard, fast day with long hours? Do the mail, phone calls, and visitors plan your day for you? Or do you have specific goals and objectives you are trying to accomplish?

_____
_____
_____
_____
_____
_____
_____
_____

6. Can you support the views and decisions of others even though you disagree? Do you take the responsibility for superiors' decisions with your subordinates? At what point do you give up resistance and support decisions by others?

7. What kind of person do you work for? Do you give him loyalty and support, or do you merely tolerate him? How "open" can you be with him? What are the skills he has that you can learn?

8. Are you really concerned with the development of your subordinates? Their development—or yours—is not something apart from getting the organization's work done. What should you be doing about their development?

ABOUT YOUR DEVELOPMENT

1. Often we hope that our comfortable world will just stay still—the "don't anybody make waves" attitude. But the world will never stay still. We are told that we must grow even to stay where we are. Do you really believe this? If so, what does it mean to you personally?

About your development 65

2. Do you want to do more than stay even with your job? Do you want to progress? Do you know yourself well enough to know why? What motivates you? The challenge of more responsibility, more power, or more effect on the future of your organization? Money? Status? The need to be successful? What motivates you?

3. Will you risk failure in order to learn? Mature people often learn less than young people because they are less willing to take risks. We don't like risking failure. Do you keep on exploring your potentialities by learning new skills?

4. Do you really have the desire to stave off your own obsolescence by making the personal commitment this will require? Is the desire strong enough to cause you to seek improved skills and new knowledge and to make efforts to keep you abreast of changing technology? How will you get the skills and knowledge you need to get where you want to be? If this isn't "the convenient time," will that time ever come?

5. How realistically and critically can you look at yourself? Can you see your strengths and shortcomings? Can you comfortably accept your limitations? Can you sort out those things about yourself which you can do nothing about from those you can?

6. Are you willing to take a reduction in grade or pay to get the experience you need to grow? Are you willing to leave your present organization? Does your security come from the organization—or from yourself?

7. Do you know how your organization selects executives? It probably doesn't. Executives select themselves. Are you looking for growth and advancement on comfortable terms, or will it take something more on your part?

8. Now that you are having this personal talk about yourself, with yourself, is there anything else you would care to add?

Now, if you are still speaking to yourself, let's look at another way to approach your long-term goals.

REQUIESCAT IN PACE (R. I. P.)

One effective and interesting way of thinking about what you want for the future is to *write your own obituary.* This may seem a strange thing to do —especially for a young manager with young children. But it is a way of really thinking about what you want to do with your life. Here is a "made-up" example:

OBITUARIES
Retired Executive Passes

"Mr. John Smith passed away at his home yesterday after a short illness. He was 73.

"Before his retirement eleven years ago, *he was executive vice-president* of the Sloan Corporation. According to company officials, Mr. Smith *began his rise to prominence when he researched (on his own time) and sold plans for the company's expansion into the international sales field. He was in charge of testing for the project,* and when it was successful, he was assigned *a key position in international sales.* He later became *vice-president/international.*

"Mr. Smith was *active in civic and service organizations* in the city and *served on many boards and committees* for public betterment. Among other notable volunteer activities was his *work with small businesses begun by people of minority groups.* He believed that 'know-how' was the biggest lack in making a success of these small business ventures. It is to be noted that the failure rates for our city are much lower than in other cities of comparable sizes.

"Mr. Smith attended Tulane University for three years and later *completed his B.A. degree and the M.B.A. through the University of Chicago Extension.* He and Mrs. Smith were *active participants in local college evening courses, taking a wide range of subjects such as geography, foreign languages, geopolitics, painting, and sculpture.*

"When his two boys were younger, he was active in their activities, including *Boy Scouts and Little League Football.* (In working with the Little League, he was able to persuade the other parents to deemphasize winning and emphasize sportsmanship and skill.)

"Mr. Smith is survived by his wife, Edith, and two sons: Robert J., an attorney in Memphis, and Peter L., an oceanographer now working in the Coral Sea."

Note that the items in italics *haven't even been begun* yet by our Mr. Smith. Thinking through what he would like to accomplish in his life, though, helps him set his long-range goals, and now he can begin plans to reach them—at least partially. New goals will come up, and some of those stated will change. But it's a start.

Also, Smith doesn't have control over the vocations of his two sons, but he can help them to explore the world and to find out what *they* really want to do.

In writing your own "obit," you should be honest with yourself and really think about what you want to do and be. It may be that quitting now to open your own business is important to you. Or sitting on a beach in Pango-Pango. Or taking early retirement and buying a boat. But whatever it is, it's *your* life. And all of us have fantasies about things that we don't really want to do. We just "want to want to." Does this make sense?

Writing your own "obit" will take a great deal of thinking and reflecting on your part. It should be done in a quiet time and not in the middle of the usual "hustle-and-bustle" of the office during regular working hours. And look on the first attempt as a draft, not the finished product. After the draft is tried, you will undoubtedly continue to think about and reflect on it. (There is usually an "incubation" period which follows and during which thinking may be unconscious.)

Anyway, let's try it. First of all, what would you have the headline be?

OBITUARIES

Now that you have made a first draft, leave it for a few days or a week, and then go back to it. Look it over again. What changes and additions would you make? Make them. Now does it seem "about right to you" at this point in your life? Of course, it will change as you change and grow and as your interests change. But for now, we can begin thinking about where you are and where you want to be. Make some notes on your answers to these questions:

Have you begun "down the road" toward any of these goals? If so, list these goals.

What specifically are you doing to reach your listed goals?

Which of these goals have you not begun to work on as yet?

What specific things could be planned? When is the right time to begin?

Requiescat in pace (R. I. P.)

_____ _____
_____ _____
_____ _____
_____ _____
_____ _____
_____ _____

What are you now doing which will have to be given up to do the things which are really important to you?

How will you give these up? (Drop them, ease out, learn to say "no," etc.)

_____ _____
_____ _____
_____ _____
_____ _____
_____ _____
_____ _____
_____ _____
_____ _____
_____ _____

What specific plans can you make for beginning the first one or two new directions?

What are the biggest obstacles you face? (Your habits and routines, inertia, biases others?)

_____ _____
_____ _____
_____ _____

One of the biggest problems we have in setting off in new directions comes from our habits and the routines we are caught up in. At work, despite our good intentions, we are met by the incoming mail, the continual ringing of the phone, and drop-in visitors. In addition, there are the high-priority requests from the boss. (If you are the top manager, requests from customers take a high priority and can be time-consuming.) At home, we have the briefcase from the office, containing what we should have been working on most of the day. After a martini or a beer and dinner, we give the briefcase more or less attention and then fall into our comfortable routine of TV and the local newspaper. And then to bed with the feeling: "I just don't know where the time went today!"

It does take conscious effort to break out of these traps. These habits and routines *are* comfortable and are *expected* by the people you work with and by the family. But they can be overcome.

THE IDEA OF A SELF-CONCEPT

When you were making out your "obit," you probably did not list some of the things you might have, because of your "picture of yourself." This can be a limiting factor in your growth, so let's talk about that for a bit.

Our self-concept, self-image, or picture we have of ourselves is a very important part of reality to each of us. Before we discuss the subject, fill out the following questionnaire by completing the sentences with whatever terms come to mind for yourself. Some of the terms you think of will relate to your social roles, some will be concerned with groups you belong to, others will describe activities and qualities. The early terms will be easy; the later ones, more difficult to think of. But fill in *all* of the blanks.

WHO ARE YOU?

I am a _____

I am a _____

I am a _____

I am a _____

I am a _____

I am a _____

I am a _____

I am a _____

I am a _____

I am a _____

I am a _____

I am a _____

Your self-concept is the only "self" you know. To you, it represents complete reality (as mine does for me). Some of the images may not be "true," in that they are not accepted as a part of us by the rest of the world. But that doesn't matter; they are true to us. And there are many things we *could* be, but we don't see these as a part of ourselves, at least not yet.

Our self-image has been forming since that first moment we began, as infants, to become aware of our hands, our feet, and our mouth. As we grew, the cultural and social forces began to have a role in shaping our self-image. We were given either blue or pink booties to wear. We were given footballs or dolls to play with. As we grew, we differentiated more and more "who we were." We experimented with new behaviors, and this reached a peak during adolescence—which can be a trying time for both generations. The wider the range of experiences one is exposed to with some degree of success, the more the facets to one's self-image. In our formative years we may have learned the labels put on us by the world around us. If Billy is told often enough that he is a "bad boy," he may come to accept this and wonder what a boy does to be effectively bad.

Our past experiences have shaped us, and we have arrived at today. Our self-concept represents complete reality to each of us. It persists and resists change. Much of our energy goes to protecting and enhancing our self-concept. Our defense mechanisms act as automatic responses to any threat to this self-concept. It is not changed by outside forces.

Who are you? Suppose we look at how you finished the "I am a" sentences, and then we will know. Your terms, as we mentioned, probably fell into four groups: social roles, group memberships, activities, and qualities. The following are some examples of each:

Social roles
Man or woman
Husband or wife
Father or mother
Brother, sister, uncle, aunt, cousin, etc.
President, group leader, unit head, supervisor
Judge, doctor, lawyer, clerk, salesperson
Citizen, registered voter

Membership in groups
Democrat, Republican
Catholic, Baptist
Mason, Rotarian, Lion, Odd Fellow
Management, union
Nudist club, bridge club

Activities
Golfer, bowler, bridge-player
Sports fan, swimmer, movie buff
Camper, rockhound, sightseer
Homemaker, handyman, tinkerer
Cook, seamstress, gardner
Stamp collector
Gourmet

Qualities
Strong person, talented
Artistic
Handsome, pretty person
Good story-teller
Trustworthy
A good listener

Look over the way you finished the sentences. Did you list some in all four categories? There is some overlap in the classifications; if a person thinks of himself as a "good bowler," he is listing both an activity and a quality, and it is probably related to a group the person bowls with. But this isn't important, as long as you get the idea. By the way, did you list *any* that aren't related to *other people?*

Not all facets of our self-concept are of the same importance to us, of course. Some aspects loom large; others are small. For a man in our culture, his *work* is a pretty important aspect of his self-concept. When we meet a man on a train, at a club, at a party, or somewhere, the first thing we want to know is, "What do you *do?*" And he wants to know, "What do *you* do?" Until these vocational pursuits are established, we are uncomfortable. We have no handle on "who he is," even though this information about his vocation really tells us very little about the man.

Diagramed, a man's collection of self-images might look something like this:

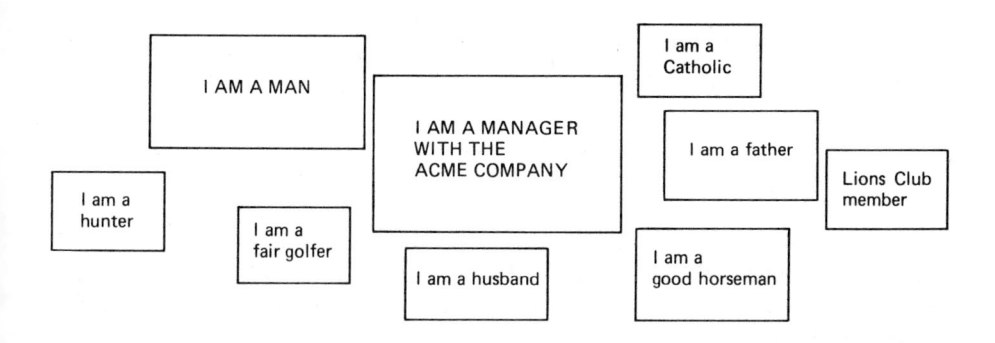

```
┌─────────────────┐      ┌─────────────────┐   ┌──────────┐
│                 │      │                 │   │ I am a   │
│  I AM A MAN     │      │ I AM A MANAGER  │   │ Catholic │
│                 │      │  WITH THE       │   └──────────┘
└─────────────────┘      │  ACME COMPANY   │   ┌──────────────┐
┌────────┐  ┌──────────┐ │                 │   │ I am a father│
│ I am a │  │ I am a   │ └─────────────────┘   └──────────────┘  ┌────────────┐
│ hunter │  │ fair     │      ┌──────────────┐ ┌──────────────┐  │ Lions Club │
└────────┘  │ golfer   │      │ I am a       │ │ I am a       │  │ member     │
            └──────────┘      │ husband      │ │ good horseman│  └────────────┘
                              └──────────────┘ └──────────────┘
```

Today, it is largely true (but seems to be changing) that a woman who is married and has children probably has a much different weighting to the facets of her self-image, even though she, too, may be a manager in the Acme Company. The diagram of her self-images might look something like this:

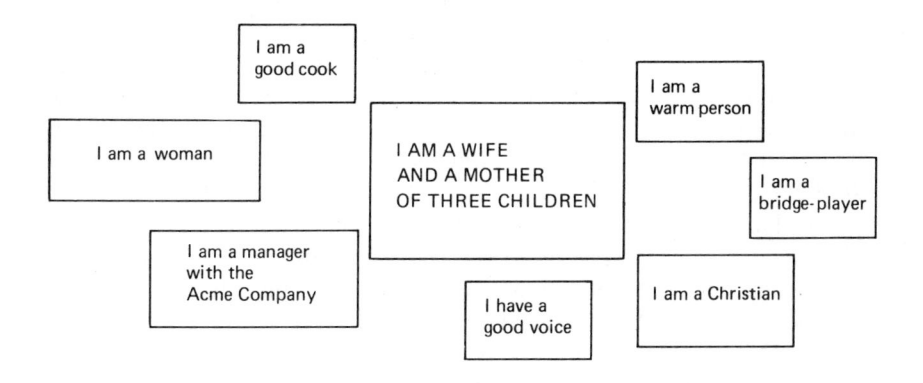

```
                  ┌────────────┐
                  │ I am a     │
                  │ good cook  │        ┌──────────────┐
                  └────────────┘        │ I am a       │
┌──────────────┐  ┌─────────────────┐   │ warm person  │
│ I am a woman │  │ I AM A WIFE     │   └──────────────┘
└──────────────┘  │ AND A MOTHER    │   ┌──────────────┐
                  │ OF THREE        │   │ I am a       │
                  │ CHILDREN        │   │ bridge-player│
   ┌──────────────┐                 │   └──────────────┘
   │ I am a       │                 │
   │ manager with │                 │
   │ the Acme     │                 │   ┌──────────────┐
   │ Company      │ ┌─────────────┐ │   │ I am a       │
   └──────────────┘ │ I have a    │ │   │ Christian    │
                    │ good voice  │     └──────────────┘
                    └─────────────┘
```

Sure, if she works and is the sole support of the children, her job is important to her. But if both she and the man pictured in the previous diagram were suddenly laid off, I think that the impact on the self-concept of each would be vastly different. For the man, removing the central feature of his self-concept would be devastating! For the woman, it might be a bad experience, but the central feature of her self-concept would remain. On the other hand, what is the impact on her when the children grow up and "fly the nest"?

As another example, let's look at the person who has worked as an accountant for the company for 32 years. He lives and breathes for his job. His collection of self-images might look like the following:

```
┌─────────────┐  ┌─────────────────┐  ┌─────────────┐
│ I am a      │  │ I AM AN         │  │ I am an     │
│ rose grower │  │ ACCOUNTANT      │  │ active person│
│             │  │ WITH THE ACME   │  │             │
└─────────────┘  │ COMPANY         │  └─────────────┘
                 └─────────────────┘
```

When he reaches age 65, we give him a gold watch and send him out to a richly deserved retirement. What happens? He is dead in three months. And people say: "Isn't it too bad about poor old Charlie. He was always so active, so full of pep." But the central feature of his self-concept was removed, and there was little left of his "picture of himself." As one newly retired neighbor said to me: "They have taken away from me the only reason I had for getting up in the morning!" (As an aside, a much better "gift" than a gold watch would be working with the Charlies long before retirement to help them develop a richer "picture of themselves" to sustain them in retirement.)

This idea of self-concept also helps us to understand the psychology of an insult. To really "get to" you, I must step on one of the facets of your self-concept. If I said, "You are a lousy orchid grower!" (and you didn't try to grow them), this wouldn't bother you a bit. But if I said, "You are a very poor manager," and your picture of yourself was otherwise, this would probably get a prompt reaction. And if you are a black man, striving for manhood denied you, how can I "get to you" with an insult? That's right, call you "boy."

Well, what has all of this to do with how you completed the "I am a ____" sentences? Hopefully, this gave you a look at what your self-concept is. But that isn't necessarily *you*. Ever since life began for us, we have been forming, reforming, and adding to our picture of ourselves. And often we are limited only by the limiting pictures we have. Have you ever said that you are really not but would like to be: a poet, a writer, a scuba diver, a top manager, a water skier, a well-read person, an economist, a camper, a historian, a good communicator, a civic-minded person, an expert in something, or whatever? You may be limited only by your picture of yourself. And this need not be so.

You begin by assessing your needs, what you are happiest doing, what you are good at, and what your limitations are. Then you set realistic goals which will best fulfill you as a person. And the goals set must be realistic. Each of us is disabled from doing some things. If our limitations are not assessed, our goals might not be reachable, and we would end up being frustrated or living in Walter Mitty's day-dream and fantasy world. Or the barriers may be too great to be overcome by us. When one company president would say, "Don't talk of your problems; talk, instead, of your opportunities," one manager was heard to say, "I can just see me going to the boss and saying, 'Boss, I'm faced with an insurmountable opportunity!' "

It is all too easy to be held back by our own inertia and our limiting picture of ourselves. As Bonaro Overstreet said at a "Future of Freedom" session held in Boston a few years ago:

> It's so dreadfully easy to stop learning, to live off the capital of what we once learned. It's so dreadfully easy to defend ourselves against the challenge to that which we once learned. If we're going to be receptive to the strangeness that resides in other people, we must be learning personalities, we must encounter new unknowns. . . .
>
> No matter how educated we are, no matter how advantaged we are, every one of us lives his life in one little wedge out of the total circle of what it means to be human. And unless we can borrow and lend experience through the medium of exchanging ideas, memories, carings, we are fated to stay imprisoned in the wedge. . . .
>
> If you are going to adventure in life, if you're going to reach out, if you're going through all your days from birth to death experimenting with being human, you're going to have to run risks, make failures, look foolish. . . .
>
> But, if we can listen, if we can communicate, if we can acquire the vocabulary of others, we are privileged by the power of our species to move out of the wedge with our triumphs, tragedies and laughter.*

Now, why don't you go back and take another look at your answers to the questions posed at the beginning of this chapter. And look at your "obituary." On reflection, what changes would you make?

SUMMARY

The important thing to think about is that *you can be more in control of your own life.* You can consciously make more decisions about your life and what you want to do with it. Or you can drift, letting others make the important decisions about your life. I don't think it is too melodramatic to say that we are

---

* Quoted by permission. Mrs. Bonaro Overstreet, a widely known author and lecturer, brings the fresh outlook of an optimistic philosopher to an age in which pessimism abounds. I think you might enjoy her books, some of which were written with her husband, the late Harry Overstreet.

all rushing toward the grave, with the distance getting shorter with each passing moment. It's easy just to drift—until you have the feeling that you no longer have any control at all. A trap is a trap—even if it's fur-lined.

To make more decisions about your life—what you feel you should do with it and what you really want to do with it—can be scary. It may mean taking risks. It may mean really looking at your self-concept and deciding if your ideas about yourself are too limiting compared to what you might try, and do, and be. But it's *your* life.

What road do you really want to be on? What plans can you make to get you on that road?

What would you really like to try, to do, to be?	What specific plans can you make to get you on that road?

CHAPTER **4**

RELATIONSHIPS, UP AND DOWN

When I first began writing this about relationships, the material was divided into two chapters: "Relationships with the Boss" and "Relationships with Subordinates." This became awkward because I was continually saying, "Remember when we were talking about your relationship with your boss, well then . . .," or, "In the next chapter we'll see how this looks to the subordinates." Then it dawned on me that we were talking about the same telescope, but just looking through different ends.

The analogy of the telescope is a good one, I think, so let's pursue it a bit more. When we look up through one end of the telescope to the boss, his attitudes, outlooks, biases, and our perceptions of how we think he sees us are magnified. We are alert to subtle clues to his feelings, moods, wishes, and opinions; his suggestions come on like thunder. Now, let's go to the "boss" end of the telescope and look down at subordinates. Attitudes, biases, the way subordinates see us, clues to feelings, moods, wishes, opinions, and suggestions are all there. But now they have diminished (in importance to us) so as to be hardly noticed! So let's talk about relationships, up and down, together.

AUTHORITY FIGURES

By the time we are grown (whatever age that is), most of us have reached some reasonable adjustment with the authority figures in our lives. Our learning began with father and continued with our successive bosses. If we haven't made such an adjustment, then we may be among those who continually change jobs (leave home) to try to find a situation just right for us.

The authority figures in our lives are usually those who can grant or withhold rewards. Rewards can take the form of attention, service, assistance, recognition, interest, favors, money, and so on. But let's look at a basic reward to a person in an organization.

For most of us in the majority culture, satisfying our financial needs and achieving personal and family plans (the grocery bill, a more comfortable

81

home, college for the kids, better transportation, status symbols, retirement income, that trip next summer) are based on a continuing relationship with the organization, that is, on the continuing income provided. The boss plays a key role here, if he isn't the dominant factor. The boss doesn't have to refer to this, or even to think about it. But the subordinate never forgets it. His behavior toward the boss is selected, consciously and unconsciously, with this in mind. The subordinate's perceptions of what the boss will approve or how he will respond exerts a pretty powerful influence on the behavior of the subordinate. And the boss often is perceived as the one in the relationship who really needs to change. ("If only my boss would take this course." "I wish the boss would read this book!")

Let's see if we can construct a scale which might be used to test your view of how open your boss permits you to be. Like all scales such as this, we can expect the problem of what the terms "mean," what your perception is, and how willing you are to state your real feelings. But let's construct one to use anyway. And let's have the scale reflect some points or degrees along an "open" to "guarded" continuum. (Note that "guarded" doesn't mean being "sneaky" or deliberately lying—it just means being selective in what we would say.) The numbers on the scale are not exactly over the degrees stated in words—the words are meant to merely suggest the range along the scale.

Open									Guarded
1	2	3	4	5	6	7	8	9	10
Completely open with what I think and feel.		Feel able to express my real feelings to him with some care.		Would discuss some feelings and thoughts on this, but not everything.		May drop some hints about my thoughts and feelings, but wouldn't volunteer a full explanation.		Probably would avoid discussion of this with him.	I would probably not talk about this with him at all.

Now that we have the scale, let's look at the ten normal, everyday events which involve your communication with your boss. Rate each topic according to how willing *you* would feel to discuss it with your boss.

Your
rating: The situation:
─────────────────────────────────

_____ 1. The boss has given you a job which you *really* don't want to do. You don't feel that the job is that important in relation to all of the others you must do. But he expects it to be done.

Authority figures 83

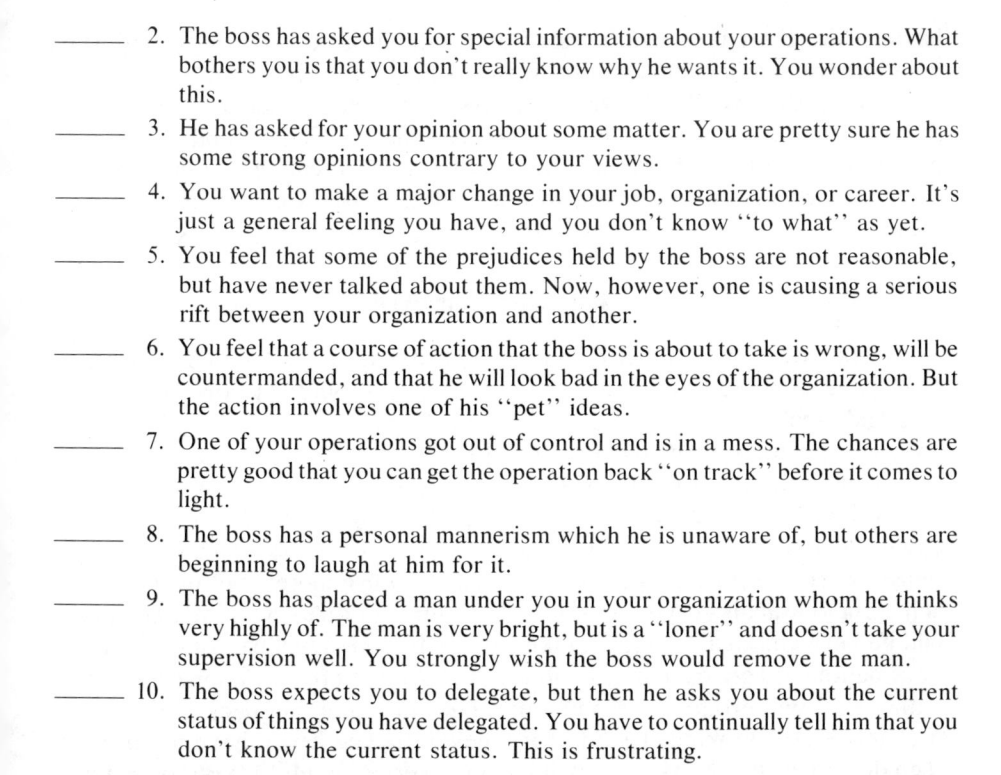

_____ 2. The boss has asked you for special information about your operations. What bothers you is that you don't really know why he wants it. You wonder about this.

_____ 3. He has asked for your opinion about some matter. You are pretty sure he has some strong opinions contrary to your views.

_____ 4. You want to make a major change in your job, organization, or career. It's just a general feeling you have, and you don't know "to what" as yet.

_____ 5. You feel that some of the prejudices held by the boss are not reasonable, but have never talked about them. Now, however, one is causing a serious rift between your organization and another.

_____ 6. You feel that a course of action that the boss is about to take is wrong, will be countermanded, and that he will look bad in the eyes of the organization. But the action involves one of his "pet" ideas.

_____ 7. One of your operations got out of control and is in a mess. The chances are pretty good that you can get the operation back "on track" before it comes to light.

_____ 8. The boss has a personal mannerism which he is unaware of, but others are beginning to laugh at him for it.

_____ 9. The boss has placed a man under you in your organization whom he thinks very highly of. The man is very bright, but is a "loner" and doesn't take your supervision well. You strongly wish the boss would remove the man.

_____ 10. The boss expects you to delegate, but then he asks you about the current status of things you have delegated. You have to continually tell him that you don't know the current status. This is frustrating.

We could go on listing situations, and you could think of many, also. But rating each of the ten situations along the scale should indicate to you that you discriminate in your openness about issues. And the boss and his actions and his relationship with you played a big part in your ratings. Did you tend to be open in everything? Or somewhat guarded in everything? Or somewhere in-between? Were you more open about technical, job-related issues and more guarded about personal issues?

Conditions can affect your feelings of security and your willingness to be open. Some conditions are imposed, such as a group or individual contract, protective regulations, or legal requirements. Outside factors which affect your feeling of financial security may make you more open. Would you have selected the same point on the scale for each topic if, say, you had an outside income of $40,000 per year? Or if you had just received two very attractive job offers? Or if you were only temporarily assigned to your boss and had a "safe" job to return to?

Unusual conditions can occasionally arise which create a "fireproof" condition—such as having a subordinate who is related to the president of the organization. But these conditions are rare.

Now that you have recognized that there are degrees of openness in *your* relations with *your* boss, it's important for you to consider that your boss's behavior toward *his* boss can be rated on a similar scale. And, most important, your subordinate's behavior toward *you* is also on such a scale.

The conditions affecting the openness of the relation between the boss and the subordinate which are of interest here are those which are under the control of the boss and the subordinate. For the boss, it's creating a climate of trust. For the subordinate, it's being willing to take risks. Let's consider each of these.

A TRUST CLIMATE

From your very first contact with your subordinates, they begin to weigh clues from you, some very subtle, about where they should stay on the "open to guarded" scale in their relations with you. If they regard you as threatening, they will spend a great deal of emotional energy in their defenses. If I trust you, I am willing to be more open with you because I see you as encouraging and supportive; I feel that you will not do anything to embarrass me or "put me down," and I know that you have a sound reason for asking me to do something. When I know and feel these things, I can use more emotional energy in achieving our goals. If you do not build a climate of trust with me, however, I will be very guarded in my communications to you; I will carefully screen the information you get from me; I will wait for explicit orders rather than take the initiative; I will produce the minimum, but not "stick my neck out"; and I'll probably start "looking around" for a new job. And if you have my trust and then do something to lose it, it will be very, very difficult for you to regain it.

What the boss should strive for is what I call an "authentic atmosphere," one which is seen as safe because the people in it are helpful, trustworthy, responsible, responsive, and friendly—an atmosphere in which one is able to share control of what happens. (I know that if we added cleanliness, reverence, and helping little old ladies across the street, we would just about have the Boy Scout pledge. But that's what an "authentic" atmosphere means to me.)

I put little stock in lists of "do's and don'ts" because they have such limited effectiveness in helping people change. But a list of them here might suggest more clearly what is meant by a "trust climate."

How to Make Sure that a Trust Climate is *Not* Created

1. Look on expressions of feelings and doubts as signs of weakness.
2. Be sarcastic, but cleverly so.
3. Don't tell the reasons behind your requests or directions. ("Their's not to reason why; their's but to do or die.")
4. When something goes wrong, blow up, hit the ceiling, and look for the "guilty party."
5. Discourage subordinates from coming to you for help. After all, they should be "stem-winders" and "self-starters."

6. Never let them really be sure what's on your mind. This keeps them on their toes.
7. Gossip about and disparage others on the staff when they are not present.
8. Overrespond to casual comments by others about your people.
9. Let them know that you expect them to "stretch the truth" a little if it will make the organization look good.
10. Plan vendettas and other ploys to make other organizations look bad. Draw on subordinates for carrying these out.
11. Always insist on plenty of C.Y.A. (Cover Your ___) letters in the files.

Behaviors that Can Help Build a Trust Climate

1. Encourage subordinates to express feelings, doubts, and concerns. Accept these, and discuss them as part of the situation.
2. Be supportive and protect subordinates' feelings.
3. Be as open as possible about the reasons behind your requests and directions.
4. When something goes wrong, look for what happened, not "who did it." Get full participation from those involved in corrective measures to be taken.
5. Encourage subordinates to look to you as one source for help in getting the job done, but encourage independence rather than overdependence on you.
6. Express your own self-doubts, concerns, and feelings in a natural way.
7. Be candid about the person you are talking to about himself, but never about others. Remember, you are never really "off the record."
8. Take the brunt of criticisms of the organization on yourself.
9. Set honesty as one standard which will not be compromised.
10. Let subordinates see what you really want from them when you ask for their opinion. Indicate if you really want responses such as:
    a) "I think this report (proposal, plan, speech, letter, etc.) I just wrote is great. You read it and tell me it's great, too."
    b) "I've just finished this report. Read it from the standpoint of the intended reader and see what reaction you think he would have."
11. Be open and trusting with others. They will know it when you are (and when you aren't).

"But what you have been describing is just maturity and good management practices," you might say. Yes, I guess it is. When we conduct ourselves in a way which promotes a climate of trust, we can help people move along the scale from guardedness to openness. And to do so will mean that the output from your organization will be better than it would be without that climate of trust. Also, you know more of what's really "going on."

Of Course I Believe...
Lyman K. Randall

Trust you?
Sure, I trust you!
   (I wonder what he's after now.)
Be open with you?
Of course I'm open with you!
   (I'm as open as I can be with a guy like you.)
Level with you?
You know I level with you!
   (I'd like to more, but you can't take it.)
Accept you?
Naturally I accept you—just as you do me!
   (And when you learn to accept me, then I
   might accept you more.)
Self-direction?
I've always believed in self-direction!
   (And some day this company may let us use some.)
    What's the hangup?
    Not a damn thing!
    What could ever hang up
       Two self-directing
       Open, trusting
       Leveling and accepting
       Guys like us?*

---

* Reproduced by special permission from *The Journal of Applied Behavioral Science*, "Of Course I Believe . . . ," Lyman K. Randall, **5**, 1, p. 110. © 1969 by N.T.L. Institute for Behavioral Science. Lyman Randall is director of Passenger Services Training for American Airlines.

It isn't reasonable to expect that your people will be completely open to the authority figure. For example, taking your ratings on the "open to guarded" scale you used earlier (on which you ranked your openness in discussing the stated issues with your boss), what kind of assurances could he give you to have you *absolutely disregard* his ability to remove you from the payroll? After all, conditions do change.

I also think that some deference from the subordinate is useful. In the education of new, first-line supervisors, I introduce the idea of "social distance" to help them think through their new position. If you "play poker with the boys," you stand the risk of one coming in, putting his feet up on your desk, and saying, "You know, I just don't feel like working today." And then you have to deal with that. A complete openness might invite attempts to discuss highly intimate personal or family problems, which would be completely inappropriate.

So that, to me, is what a trust climate is all about. Do you believe it's worth trying to establish?

TAKING RISKS

Earlier, we discussed how the subordinate's behavior is influenced by the "authority figure." Then, in forming the scale for you to make the ratings, I began talking about "how open your boss permits you to be." To a large extent the boss does "permit" us to be open through the level of trust he develops. But the restraints *we place on ourselves* can also be great barriers to open communication.

If several of us were to rank the situations given on the same scale, we would probably place each at a different place on the scale, which would result in a different "average rating" for each of us. There are two reasons for this: (1) the boss (the trust climate he has been able to build, his behavior in the past, etc.) and (2) ourselves (our "hang-ups" with authority figures, our own feeling of personal security, etc.). I know of one subordinate who wouldn't tell his boss that a button had come undone on his button-down collar and was sticking up in the air. (He felt comfortable but the boss looked funny.) "Well, this was silly of him not to mention it." It may seem silly to us, but it wasn't to the subordinate!

Taking risks means being willing to move one step toward openness from the point where we feel most comfortable on the scale—to try consistently to move just one step. If that is successful, the new point becomes your new "comfort point" on the scale. If unsuccessful and you are "put down" because of your attempt, you will naturally retreat to more guarded behavior. But try it again on another issue. (Don't be like a cat. Once burned by a hot stove, it will never sit on a hot stove again. But it won't sit on a cold one, either.)

What does it sound like when we are taking risks? Like this:

"I don't know how you are going to take this, but . . ."
"I'm going to level with you about what I think of the idea."
"You know that I have the goals of our organization uppermost in mind. What I'm going to say is meant to help us reach those goals."
"I think you would want to know . . ."
"I feel a little nervous saying this, but . . ."
"I'm going to be honest in telling you how it looks to me."
"I've never tried this before, and you may not like it, but . . ."
"I think you really want my help, so I'm going to be frank. I'd like your reaction to my being this frank."

Without taking risks, you won't know how open you can be in the relationship, the relationship will stabilize on a "phoney" basis, and you will never be able to get out of your shell and be the person you might be and make the contribution the organization needs. You will usually find that your openness is not only accepted but appreciated. Our barriers to communication are often self-imposed.

GETTING FEEDBACK

Many people propose, and a few do try, to get feedback from subordinates by using a survey of some sort. But getting raw data from a group of subordinates who are sure of complete anonymity *may* be a devastating experience. I wouldn't advise it as a casual exercise. (That's why so many "morale surveys"—or large parts of the responses—end up in someone's bottom drawer or office safe. It's difficult to get that genie back in the bottle!) Here is part of a questionnaire. Thinking about your subordinates as a group, how would they answer it? (You need not really answer the questionnaire; just look it over.)

Agree	Disagree	
——	——	1. I get all the support I need from upper management.
——	——	2. I often bear criticism for mistakes made at a higher level.
——	——	3. I am often judged less on what I do and more on how I look while doing it.
——	——	4. I can't explain company plans to employees because I don't know them.
——	——	5. I usually get as much information as I need from my boss.
——	——	6. I am on permanent probation.
——	——	7. I usually feel comfortable in front of my boss.

Getting feedback 89

Agree	Disagree	
_____	_____	8. My influence is effective only downward to my subordinates.
_____	_____	9. My boss usually understands and appreciates my problems.

    I used this survey in helping groups of second-level managers get some idea about how a sample of first-level supervisors felt about their jobs and their bosses. (The sample of 100 was from among around 1000 supervisors. They were assured anonymity, and the procedures on returning the questionnaire guaranteed this. The second-level trainees were in groups of 20 from among several hundred. Thus, there was *no way* of knowing if any of those surveyed worked for them.) The second-level trainees were asked to answer the questionnaire *as they thought the first-level supervisor would*. Here were the survey results I showed them to compare their perceptions:

Agree	Disagree	
23%	76%	1. I get all the support I need from upper management.
68%	32%	2. I often bear criticism for mistakes made at a higher level.
33%	67%	3. I am often judged less on what I do and more on how I look while doing it.
45%	55%	4. I can't explain company plans to employees because I don't know them.
30%	70%	5. I usually get as much information as I need from my boss.
70%	30%	6. I am on permanent probation.
57%	43%	7. I usually feel comfortable in front of my boss.
18%	82%	8. My influence is effective only downward to my subordinates.
73%	27%	9. My boss usually understands and appreciates my problems.

As you can imagine, these results provoked some "soul-searching" among the second-level managers about their own perceptions (which were quite different on some of the items) and about what they could do to improve relations with their own subordinates. How do you suppose *your* subordinates would answer questions such as these?
    Let me say again that I wouldn't recommend your using such a questionnaire as a casual exercise with your group. Their perceptions may be so different from your's that it can be quite a shock to your self-concept. And the smaller the group, the less the anonymity, and the greater the temptation to try to identify individual responses. Furthermore, once you have raised these questions, the group will expect some kind of response from you, and this might be difficult. However, if you are able to build a climate of trust and encourage individual "tests" toward openness, you will get feedback about the

impact of your behavior, about the perceptions of others, and other data you desire, on an individual basis.

Two people interested in human behavior, Drs. Joseph Luft and Harry V. Ingham, have provided us with a useful way of looking at the area of openness in human relationships.* They use a window frame divided into four parts:

	Known to self	Not known to self
Known to others	AREA I	AREA II
Not known to others	AREA III	AREA IV

Area I is the area of information which is known to both yourself and others—public information. It includes the feelings, opinions, ideas, etc., which you choose to be open about. It also includes things about you which you can't hide very well, such as your age, your looks, etc. (However, you will recognize that many people spend much time and money trying to conceal these things about themselves.)

Area II comprises things known to others, but not to you. These include your habits and characteristics and abilities of which you are unaware. These often have an impact—either useful or nonuseful—in your relations with others. Some examples are: you always interrupt, you have a skill in getting others to want to help, you never seem to be interested in the feelings of others, you always enjoy a good fight, you don't seem to listen, you have bad breath, etc.

Area III is made up of the things that are known to yourself, but concealed from others. Some things in this area are concealed because you don't know how to tell others; some are kept guarded because you feel you may be viewed badly by others if they were known. Some examples are: your feelings, your doubts about yourself, your secret hopes and dreams, the things you know about me which are limiting my effectiveness but of which I am unaware, etc.

Area IV consists of those things which neither you nor others know. These include forgotten experiences which have shaped you, unconscious needs, motives of which you are unaware, etc. These things are normally left alone, but

---

* This frame of reference, named after the two authors, is called "the Johari Window." For a fuller explanation of the four quadrants and its application, see Joseph Luft, *Of Human Interaction,* Palo Alto: National Press Books, 1969.

an experience causing introspection (such as reading this book) can cause a greater awareness of them.

The larger our Area I is, the more effective we can be in our interpersonal relations with others. We can freely pass on our own ideas and feelings, test tentative plans, experiment with new behavior (and look foolish if we fail), express our self-doubts and concerns, and be open with people in other ways. The more open we can be, the more we can bring to bear our full capabilities and the less energy must be spent in defense.

But some people have "windows" which look like this:

I Open area	II Others know, but not one's self
III Guarded and hidden area	

This diagram depicts a person who must spend a great deal of energy in keeping hidden a great deal of information of which he is conscious. The effectiveness of such people is limited, also, because they get little feedback from others about their own habits and behaviors. Although such people have a large "blind spot," they may not want any feedback, for fear it would threaten their self-concept and be too painful to deal with. As a result, these people are confined to their narrow prisons, for they can be open with no one.

How can Area I be expanded? The more trust there is in our relationship, the more willing I am to let down my guard and be open with you. I feel safe; I know you won't hurt me. And when you "level" with others about your feelings, perceptions, and thoughts, you open the way for them to give you feedback about things of which you have no knowledge. And thus the "open" area of our windows can expand, more energy can be used for dealing with important problems, and our interpersonal effectiveness can improve. This expansion of Area I is shown below.

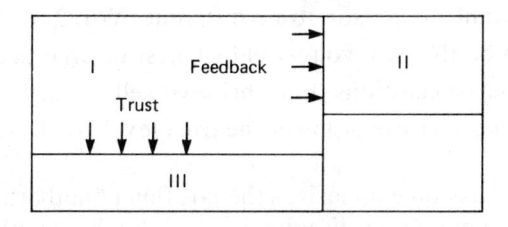

I Feedback →	II
Trust ↓ ↓ ↓ ↓	
III	

We don't just have one configuration to our window, of course. It can differ with each person we are dealing with. With our boss, it might look one way; with peers, another; with our spouse, yet another. If you are my boss, the trust relationship you create with me will play a large part in determining what my window looks like when I am with you.

Now that we have talked about the authority figure, a climate of trust, taking risks, and feedback, how do you use these ideas to become more effective? What would be the impact if both you and your boss read about these things and discussed them? What if your subordinates read about these topics and discussed the ideas with you? Or would this be too risky?

PERFORMANCE APPRAISALS

... and the Trust Climate

The formal procedures being used in an organization may, if followed, get in the way of the development of a trust climate. I say "if followed" because many procedures are adopted but are not followed or are followed only perfunctorily, without real support. Certainly, the superior usually has an important "say" in when and how much additional money is granted to his people, for example. And this is an expected aspect of the relationship. But other requirements can place real constraints on the relationship, such as some of the systems in use which call for formal evaluation of the subordinates. The superior *always* makes an evaluation of his subordinates; this, too, is an expected part of the relationship. But many formal systems of performance rating (or appraisals, or analyses, or merit discussions, or coaching interviews, or whatever) have as their main focus the errors, faults, and weaknesses of the subordinate. Sure, the subordinate's good points are listed first, as most such systems advise, and then the superior says, "But . . . ," and that is when the subordinate starts to listen.

Some questions you might ask yourself about such performance interviews are:

1. How do you account for your feelings about one of these interviews being held with you by *your* boss?
2. How do you account for *your* feelings about holding one of these interviews with your subordinates?
3. Do you really want the person to be different? Why?
4. Can the person be the way you would suggest or urge that he be?
5. What would your suggestions do to his own self-image?
6. Would the discussion raise or lower the trust level you have accomplished, whatever it is?
7. Since such a discussion emphasizes the position of authority you hold over him, would it encourage or discourage his risk-taking with you?

A formal, scheduled discussion aimed at the development of the subordinate might enhance your relationship with him, particularly since day-to-day coaching is often *not* regarded as a real interest in one's career development. The focus of such a discussion would have to be on such things as:

What developmental experiences the subordinate feels he needs;

His progress in reaching the goals mutually established and reasons for difficulties met which were unexpected or very hard to overcome;

Job problems he is having or questions he has;

His feeling about the amount of resources allocated to him for accomplishing his duties (people, money, equipment, space, material, etc.); discussion of your system of establishing priorities to allocate scarce resources available;

Any things you are or are not doing which are hindering his accomplishing his job objectives;

The general performance of the organization and how it might be improved;

The next step in reaching his career objectives and any plans which might be made to move him in the directions he wishes to go;

What things would improve the relationship between the two of you.

This sort of discussion is quite different from that suggested in the usual formal systems I've seen, especially since conclusions of the discussion would not be filed in the subordinate's personnel folder.

REINFORCEMENT

When we do something and are rewarded, we will tend to repeat the act; in other words, the reward acts as a reinforcement. This notion, which comes from Dr. B. F. Skinner, a Harvard psychologist, is called operant conditioning or reinforcement theory.* Stated formally, the main principle can be described as follows:

> *To attach a verbal, manual, or locomotor response to a situation, simply await or arrange the situation so that the desired behavior occurs, and then reinforce it through reward.*

In all formal training we "arrange the situation," but sometimes we can only wait for it to happen (such as trying to get a teenager to hang up his clothes someplace other than the floor!). Then, when it does happen, we reinforce the act with a reward.

---

* Since the publication of Skinner's *The Behavior of Organisms* in 1938, there has been much research and many publications on the subject. The whole field of "programed instruction" stems from Skinner and his ideas. Skinner's most recent application for societies is in *Beyond Freedom and Dignity,* New York: Bantam/Vintage edition, 1972.

Rewards can take many forms other than money—attention, service, assistance, recognition, interest, favors, and so on. You remember the wonderful feeling when you could go home and tell the wife, "I got two 'attaboys' today!"

In addition, there are several other ideas related to the concept of reinforcement.

1. *If one behavior is asked for, and a second behavior is reinforced, the second behavior will tend to occur.* Despite all of our policy statements, procedures, and other stated expectations, what really is repeated is whatever is rewarded. And many times we are not even conscious that we are rewarding the secondary behavior!

Every manager has more balls to juggle than he can possibly keep in the air at one time. And each new policy statement, each new directive, adds more. But we soon learn which balls are heavy and will hurt our toes if we drop them. These are the balls which win applause if we keep juggling them. Other balls are light and will not hurt when dropped—usually no one notices. So these are dropped. In one firm every manager in manufacturing from the second level on up will tell you that the first-line supervisor should *not* spend his time expediting production materials ("chasing parts"), that he should instead spend his time in communicating with his people and doing other noble things. But what does he get rewarded for doing and punished for not doing? Right—getting the production out the door. And what is his most important activity to get this done? Right again—chasing parts!

In another firm, plant managers are rewarded by their results on "the bottom line" (net profit) only. Since net profit can be made to look good through reducing maintenance, development, research, and similar costs, the plant managers do such a good job on the bottom line that they are promoted. However, the result is that some replacement manager in the future finds that he really has a problem on his hands.

You tell me what you reward, and I'll tell you what your people really do.

2. *If behavior is not useful on the job or has no consequences when it occurs, it will tend to stop occurring.* Unrewarded actions simply are stopped.

3. *The further removed in time a consequence is from an action, the less effect that consequence will have on the action.* Rewards should follow the behavior closely in order to have full impact as reinforcement.

One other idea from the psychologists should be noted now: *To attach an emotional response to a situation, simply elicit the desired emotional response in the situation.* For example, when punishment is used as a "negative" reinforcement, we may be simultaneously attaching an undesired emotional response toward us, the workplace, the "Company," etc. How would you teach a superior *not* to give you a coaching session on your own personal growth? You would simply make him uncomfortable (within limits, of course) when he tries to do it. Thus, you might say, "What a waste of time!" or better still, not say anything at all (which is really punishing). How would you get him to hold such coaching sessions *more often?* Right, now you're getting the idea! By reinforcing the behavior through reward when it happens. "Boss, I want to tell you how very helpful these sessions are to me." "It means a lot that you would take time out of your busy schedule to be concerned with my future."

How would you use these ideas about reinforcement in real-life situations? Turn to the next page, and let's find out.

Practice Application

Let's try to apply these ideas to some other work and home situations. *Mark the best answer* in each situation. When you have finished, check your answers with those given in the "Answers" section on p. 98.

1. A father is trying to read his newspaper while his two small children are raising a racket nearby. The father yells at them to be quiet. But the kids get louder and louder. The father finally puts the paper down and gives them attention. What is the father doing?

    _____a) punishing undesired behavior

    _____b) teaching them to raise a racket to get attention

    _____c) not reinforcing conflicting behavior

2. A mother who is reading pays little attention to her small child who is playing close by. But when the child runs off from her, she puts down her book, stands up, and loudly calls the child's name. What is the mother doing?

    _____a) punishing desired behavior

    _____b) expressing motherly concern

    _____c) reinforcing undesired behavior

3. A supervisor ignores regular attendance, but when a person returns from an absence, he gives him a lot of attention. What should the supervisor do?

    _____a) stop giving attention when a person returns

    _____b) more regularly reward good attendance

    _____c) raise heck with those who are absent

4. A manager tells his people *not* to bring him their technical problems—that he is there to manage. But when they *do* bring him their technical problems for advice, he drops everything else and helps them, because he really enjoys working on these problems. What is the manager doing?

    _____a) reinforcing conflicting behavior

    _____b) punishing undesired behavior

    _____c) neither of these

5. A manager of an organization uses the "exception principle," giving attention (not in a punishing way) only to problems and ignoring things which are going well. What is the probable net effect of this?

    _____a) encouraging people to have problems

    _____b) reinforcing "getting the job done"

    _____c) punishing people for having problems

6. A busy manager devotes time to developing his subordinates. But this activity is not recognized or felt to be important by *his* boss. What will the manager probably tend to do?

    _____a) continue to develop his subordinates

    _____b) gradually slow down this activity

7. Immediately following training, manufacturing foremen in one company held exit interviews with each departing employee, as recommended in the training session. Now, six months later, almost all of the foremen have stopped the practice. What is your conclusion?

   _____a) the training they received wasn't good enough
   _____b) more training is needed
   _____c) the problem is not a lack of skill, but a lack of motivation

Practice Application—Answers and Discussion

Here are our answers and discussion on the seven situations presented in the "Practice Application" section. (Don't read these answers until you have selected your own.)

1. b The father is teaching the children that the way to get his attention is to make a racket. Even a spanking can be desired attention.
2. c The mother may think that she is expressing motherly concern, but what she is *really* doing is reinforcing undesired behavior (running off) by giving attention when the child does so. She should give the child attention when the child is playing nearby or running *toward* her.
3. b The supervisor should more regularly reward good attendance. A supervisor *must* keep on talking to people on their return from an absence. He must ask why they were absent, see if the company can help, and tell them why they were missed. But regular attendance should be rewarded for reinforcement.
4. a The manager is reinforcing conflicting behavior. When the manager's people do bring him their technical problems, he rewards this behavior. If one behavior is asked for and a second is rewarded, the second behavior will be the one to occur again.
5. a The "exception principle" may actually produce more problems needing attention. The manager must reinforce things which are going well. Note that the "attention" the people received was not punishing. If it had been, people would start to hide their problems.
6. b The manager will probably gradually slow down the activity. If behavior is not rewarded or has no consequences when emitted, it will eventually stop being emitted. Okay, perhaps he gets enough rewards from his subordinates (or from himself) to continue. But most rewards are seen as coming from the boss.
7. c Since the supervisors have shown that they have the skill to conduct the interviews, the problem lies elsewhere. Training people over again in skills they already have isn't productive. Reinforcement of the desired behavior can be a powerful motivator.

Well, how much did you agree with those answers? If you agreed with nearly all of them, you are ready to start thinking about how you can use reinforcement as a management tool.

On-the-Job Application

Giving praise (or some other form of reward) when desired behavior occurs is pretty fundamental. We all "know" that. So why spend so much time on the idea? *Because we don't do it very often*—not from ignorance, but from "ignore-ance." During our busy days, we conserve energy by giving attention to things which are going badly, and we ignore things which are being done right. But positive feedback about things which are going well can be a powerful force for keeping them that way. In short, in order to do a good job for you, I must know what is expected and get positive indications (reinforcement) when I meet the expectations.

Reinforcement can be turned into an insincere "technique," of course, and like all such ideas, it can make relationships worse. If unwarranted praise is heaped on everybody, and they know it isn't deserved, then it becomes phoney.

Take a few minutes now to think about specific behaviors of your subordinates which you should be reinforcing through rewards. Then think about specific things you will do or say. Use the form on p. 100 (really, just organized scratch paper) in your planning.

100 Relationships, up and down — Chap. 4

Activities to be reinforced: identify the person; does he know what is expected?	Specific plans for reinforcement:

CHAPTER 5

COMMUNICATION

What can I look at with you in the area of communication? We are all experts in communication. We have more experience with it than in any other conscious aspect of living. Our experience with communication begins even before our first word is uttered. We have studied it as an art and science in school more than any other subject. We have all read reams of pages on the subject.

Communication is all-pervading and all-encompassing in our lives. One is a "person" because of it. Love either exists or doesn't because of it. People are sued, arrested, shot, hung, and commit suicide over it. Crippling strikes or labor peace exists because of it. Trust either exists or doesn't because of it.

Although we are all experts in communication, it remains the prime cause of our smallest and biggest problems. Certainly, I have no new, magic words or great wisdom to share with you. But perhaps you would find it useful to explore several simple and nonoriginal ideas which, if *really understood,* can give you a greater awareness in the big area of communication and serve to identify and help you reduce some of your problems in the area.

THE ILLUSION

"The greatest problem in communication is the illusion of it." Think about that. Read the sentence over again. Put the reading down and think about that. Reflect on it. "The greatest problem in communication is the illusion of it." This is a powerful idea. Here are some everyday examples of the idea as we live with it:

"You should not have missed that question on the test. I covered that point two weeks ago."

"Our employees understand our benefit program. It is explained to them during orientation."

"Of course the Chief was in on the payoff system. Right after our biggest 'take,' he told me to keep up the good work."

"He has had the prerequisites, so now he is ready for the advanced course."

"But, honey, you know I love you. I've told you that."

"Sure we changed the specifications because our requirements changed. But that didn't give you the green light to raise your price to us!"

"What stop sign, Officer?"

"Everyone has been informed about the coming change. We had a story about it in the company paper."

"But my wife agreed to meet me right here at three o'clock. And it's past four now."

"The sign clearly warned that trespassers would be shot."

"I've told you a hundred times not to do that."

And so on. Every one of us could add many, many examples of such communication gaps that occur hour after hour, day after day. The "picture in our heads" which we are trying to transmit to the heads of others, so often doesn't get there. And we often think it has, with disappointing results. But the greatest problem here is to *assume* that it *has* and to base our plans and actions on that false assumption.

To assume that we are communicating when we pass the word along through various people, or down through several layers of an organization, would seem to be the greatest folly. Here is an example in an army setting:

SPREADING THE WORD*

Said the Colonel to the Major: "At one o'clock tomorrow there will be an eclipse of the sun, something which does not occur every day. Have the men fall in the company street in their fatigues so that they will see this rare phenomenon and I will explain it to them. In case it rains, we will not be able to see anything, so take the men to the gym."

Said the Major to the Captain: "By order of the Colonel, tomorrow at one o'clock there will be an eclipse of the sun. If it rains, you will not be able to see it from the company street so in fatigue the eclipse of the sun will take place in the gym, something that does not take place everyday."

Said the Captain to the Lieutenant: "By order of the Colonel in fatigue tomorrow at one o'clock the inauguration of the eclipse of the sun will take place in the gym. The Colonel will give the order if it should rain, something which occurs every day."

---

* I was unable to learn the author of this wonderful example of communication downward. I first heard about it in a talk given by Otis A. Maxfield, a consultant in Newburyport, Mass.

Said the Lieutenant to the Sergeant: "Tomorrow at one o'clock, the Colonel in fatigues will eclipse the sun in the gym, as it occurs every day if it's a nice day. If it rains, then in the company streets."

Said the Sergeant to the Corporal: "Tomorrow at one o'clock the eclipse of the Colonel in fatigue will take place by cause of the sun, if it rains in the gym, something which does not take place everyday."

Comments among the privates: "Tomorrow if it rains, it looks as if the sun will eclipse the Colonel in the gym. It is a shame that this doesn't happen every day. But I don't know what this has to do with us."

This example of what happens to a well-intended communication is probably very familiar. But when it happens to us, we don't find it very funny.

THE TROUBLE WITH WORDS...

In *Through the Looking Glass,* Lewis Carroll has two of his characters in a conversation which goes like this:

"When I use a word," Humpty Dumpty said in a rather scornful tone, "it means just what I choose it to mean—neither more nor less."

"The question is," said Alice, "whether you can make words mean so many different things."

"The question is," said Humpty Dumpty, "which is to be master—that's all."

And one of the troubles with words is that we are both "masters"—both the sender and the receivers.

If I looked up from my reading and asked, "What does 'fast' mean?" your first response would be, "Read to me the sentence in which you found the word." By seeing the word in its context, you would be able to define it in terms of its intended meaning, as in fast rope, fast color, fast typist, fast highway, fast watch, fast friends, fast crowd, fast shutter, fast asleep, or Lenten fast. But seeing the context is not always enough. On p. 104 are a set of instructions and a map. There are no tricks involved—it is an honest attempt to communicate. Follow the directions and see where your ending point is.* Do this now, before reading on.

Where was your ending point? At the corner of Bradford and Fifth Streets, as it should have been? Or, was it somewhere else? After seeing the results of trials by many managers and management teachers, I can say that, generally, the ending points selected tend to be on the right-hand half of the map. But not

---

* This is one of the many exercises which have wide circulation within the training fraternity. I'm sorry that its creator could not be identified, so that proper credit could be given.

Map for an Experiment in Communications

NORTH

	1st St.	2nd St.	3rd St.	4th St.	5th St.	6th St.	7th St.	8th St.	
	Magar	Street							
	Johns	Street							
	Bradford	Street							
	Whitehead	Street							
	Deterline	Street							

WEST / EAST

SOUTH

AN EXPERIMENT IN COMMUNICATION

Directions: Using the map that accompanies these directions, follow the instructions given below. Place each X exactly over the intersections of the streets, and proceed with each successive instruction by starting from the last X you wrote, except in the instances when you are instructed otherwise. When you write an X let it stand—make no erasures.

1. Place an X at the corner of Johns and 5th Streets.
2. Walk two blocks east, three blocks south, two blocks west, one block north, and place an X at the corner where you arrive.
3. Walk one block east, three blocks north, one block east, and place an X at the corner where you arrive.
4. Walk five blocks south, two blocks west, three blocks north, one block east, and place an X at the corner where you arrive.
5. Walk three blocks west, one block south, five blocks east, and place an X where you arrive.
6. Walk one block east, three blocks west, three blocks north, and place an X where you arrive.
7. Place another X as far from the west and south borders of the map as your last X is from the west and north borders of the map.
8. Start north, zig-zag north and east, alternating one block at a time and walking five blocks in all; then place an X at the corner where you arrive.
9. Start at the opposite corner of the block southeast of where you placed the last X, walk two blocks west, and place an X at the corner where you arrive.
10. Go three-fourths of the way around a square that has the length of two blocks on each side, starting where you placed the last X and ending south of your starting point. Place an O at the corner where you arrive.

for all; some are on the left, and some are off the map entirely! The same results would probably be found in your attempts to communicate precise and explicit directions to your subordinates. (You know from experience that the same results occur from following the directions which come with equipment from mail order houses!) Would it have helped if the next-to-last sentence had read "ending *due* south of your *initial* starting point"?

One of the troubles with words is that they usually have a greater meaning than the words themselves. Each word is a "bundle of associations" for each of us, and our associations come from our experience. Two women employees quit because their supervisor kept calling them *horses*. In fact, he was trying to stress the importance of "teamwork," the need to "pull together." The two women, however, brought with them their associations from a rural background.

Misunderstanding is less of a concern if the situation is an old, familiar one to both parties and they have been working together (have had the same experience) for some time. We say "they speak the same language." But if the situation is new, or if your experience is different from that of the intended receiver, possible (or probable) misinterpretation should be more of a concern.

We have said that communication is the process of transferring a picture from my head into your head as accurately as possible, and that words are really a "bundle of associations" which make this process difficult. Let's take a look at an example. What "picture" is formed in your head as you read the following?

> After examining the position, John put the newspaper down. He knew that there was an important vacant place to be filled and that an application should be made. He felt he was qualified to fill it.
>
> John realized that he needed to climb at this stage and that the ceiling for the job was high. No doubt about it—he would have to reach out.
>
> Eventually he reached the heights he had hoped for. His application had apparently been good, and he seemed to be doing well at the work.
>
> But, for some reason, he eventually fell down on the job. He had overreached himself, and he suddenly found that he couldn't support himself.
>
> In the end, John was hurt by the experience. He wondered whether the job he'd wanted to do so well had been worth the effort.*

What picture was formed in your head? What I intended was that you see John painting the ceiling in a room and having a bad fall from the ladder. Didn't you get this picture? Read the description again.

Okay, this illustration really was a trick. But we do the same thing unintentionally day-in and day-out without knowing what "picture" is being received.

---

* This example was developed by C. R. (Bing) Grindle, Director of Training and Development, Evans Products Co. Used by permission.

106 Communication Chap. 5

Let me give you a chance to "get even." Let me give you a simple sketch and ask you to describe the situation depicted. (This idea has been used in management training for a long time, so perhaps you have seen it before.) In the space below the sketch, write your description of what the picture "tells" you. Do this now, before reading on.

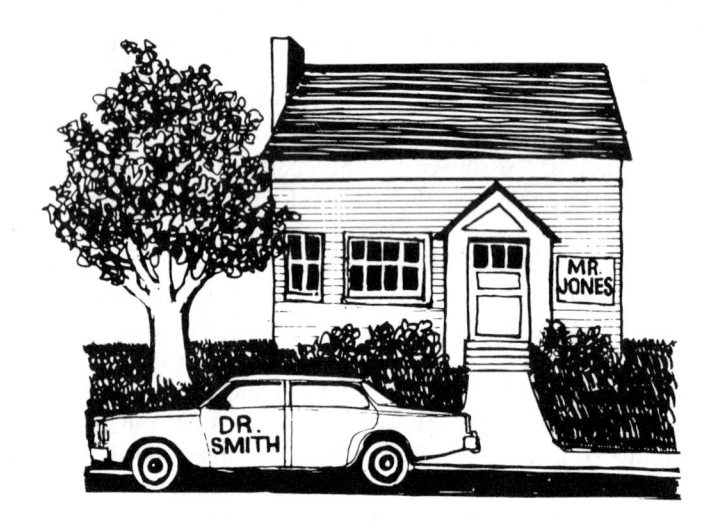

Describe what you see: _____

_____
_____
_____
_____
_____
_____

In your description, did you state or assume any of the following?
1. Mr. Jones is ill.
2. Dr. Smith is in the house.
3. Mr. Jones is (is not) at home.
4. Dr. Smith is a medical doctor.
5. Dr. Smith owns the car.
6. The house belongs to Mr. Jones.
7. Anything about Mrs. Jones.

Any interpretation you made about the bare sketch did not come from "what was there," but from within you. All that the sketch shows is:

A car marked "Dr. Smith" seems to be parked in front of a house marked "Mr. Jones."

Once we go beyond these bare facts, we are making interpretations.

Even if you say the *same thing* to a number of subordinates, you will have many different interpretations. For example, you might say to several subordinates, "Hi, how are things going?" Each subordinate might interpret your remark differently:

Sub. 1: "Well, here's old snoopy again, trying to check up on us."
Sub. 2: "It certainly is wonderful that he is really interested in my progress."
Sub. 3: "All right, already, I know we are behind, so get out of here and let us catch up."
Sub. 4: "What does he mean by that?"
Sub. 5: "Now that's something to remember when I get up there in management. You can't run an operation sitting behind a desk in some isolated office. You have to 'roam the ship' to get a first-hand feel for what is going on."
Sub. 6: "Uh, oh, he knows how I messed things up yesterday."
Sub. 7: "That's what I like about him. Always ready with a helping hand when you need it."
Sub. 8: "???????????????????"

And so on, for as many people as you speak to.

Our listener's interpretations of "what we say" is automatic, natural, and to be expected. Knowing this, and keeping it in mind, should help us keep out of the trap caused by the illusion of communication. I saw an inscription on a plaque on one manager's desk: "I know you believe you understand what you think I said, but I am not sure you realize that what you heard is not what I meant." Perhaps such a sign would help us all keep communications in perspective.

I'M WAY AHEAD OF YOU . . .

All of us are aware that our "thinking rate" is much faster than our hearing or reading rate. If our secretary can take dictation at 120 words per minute, she is a real gem. But all of us think at a rate about ten times faster than this. So, when someone is talking to us, or writing for us, we are way ahead of them. A parallel situation would be taking an excited puppy for a walk. As you plod methodically along, the puppy is running around sniffing, exploring, investigating nooks and crannies to one side and then the other, bounding ahead, and lagging behind to reflect (or something) on whatever seems interesting. He is staying aware of your general direction, but is much busier and covers a lot more ground than you do. Our minds work much the same way.

Let me see if I can illustrate this. Read the following statement through *only once;* then follow the directions. (You can do this in your head, so you won't need a pencil.) Remember, read the statement through only once.

Statement: An elevator with six passengers starts from the top floor of an office building. (It is a self-service elevator; there is no one in it at any time except passengers.) At the first stop, two passengers get off, and no one gets on. At the next stop, no one gets off, but three people get on. At the next stop, two more get off, and no one gets on. Four people get off at the next stop. Next, it stops and three people get on. At the next floor, two people get on. It stops again, and six people get off.*

Directions: Write your answer in the space below.

---

* The statement was developed by C. R. (Bing) Grindle, Director of Training and Development, Evans Products Co. Used by permission.

Have you written your answer? But what was the question? Even though there was no question, most people will make their own interpretation of what the "question" is. It might have been one of several:

How many passengers left after the last stop? (0)

How many people used the elevator during this trip? (14)

After it started, how many times did the elevator stop during this trip? (7)

What was the maximum number on the elevator at any one time? (7)

What was the minimum number on the elevator at any one time during the trip? (1)

We presume that there will be a question, so we tend to make up our own if it isn't stated. Making our own interpretations is a continual activity.

But even if we know that there will be a question, not having it in focus may make us miss the answer because we are paying attention to other details. Let's try another exercise. Read the following statement through *only once;* then turn the page and follow the directions there.

Statement: You are the pilot of a Boeing 747 flying from Chicago to New York City. There are 193 people aboard, including 14 children, 26 married couples, 63 businessmen, and 9 crew members. The plane left O'Hare Field in Chicago at 2:00 p.m. (Central Standard Time) and is scheduled to arrive at JFK Airport in New York at 4:55 p.m. (Eastern Standard Time), one hour and 55 minutes later. The distance is 740 miles.

Now turn the page and answer the question.

Question: What is the name of the pilot?

If you think I didn't give you the pilot's name, read the statement again.

Often, we begin communicating without people knowing why we are "laying it on them." If they know this by having a focus at the beginning, communication can be improved. How do we do this? By saying such things as:

"I want you to handle these requests when I am not here from now on. So, let me explain exactly what it is you are to do when you get them."

"Successful performance on the job will depend on how carefully you perform this activity. Now let me show you exactly what you are to do."

"Since reaching our goal will depend on how well we coordinate our activities, it is important that each of us knows exactly the status of each other's operations. Let me demonstrate the depth we should report."

It will be helpful to provide an answer to the question "So what?" before we begin a communication.

CAN YOU HEAR ME DOWN (UP) THERE?

In the army example of communications downward given at the beginning of this chapter, we saw what often happens. Much of this natural distortion in communication occurs because people at each level of an organization have their own way of looking at the world—in part, because of the nature of their jobs.

It seems to me that one's world changes as one moves up in an organization. One learns to think about larger and larger sections of the organization under him.

You are probably familiar with what is called an "abstraction ladder." An example of an abstraction ladder on a farm is shown below (read from the bottom to the top of the ladder).

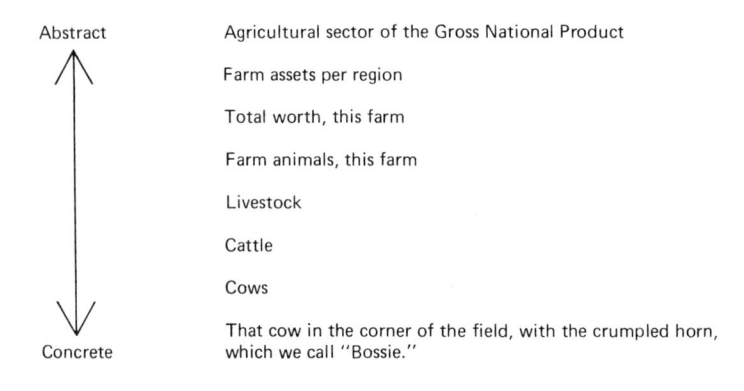

Abstract — Agricultural sector of the Gross National Product

Farm assets per region

Total worth, this farm

Farm animals, this farm

Livestock

Cattle

Cows

Concrete — That cow in the corner of the field, with the crumpled horn, which we call "Bossie."

Can you hear me down (up) there?   111

We are very specific at the lower rungs of the "ladder" and become more and more abstract as we climb upward. Each term becomes more general, encompassing more and more. For example, let's look at a problem occurring in an organization—a behind-schedule condition. From the abstract world of the upper-level managers (who "see" the world as lines on a sheet of graph paper), this condition is unsatisfactory and must be corrected. Sales plans, delivery promises, cash flow, and other important factors are affected when you are behind the expected schedule. This is the view from the vantage point which we shall call "Level D." A partial organization chart as they are usually depicted is shown below:

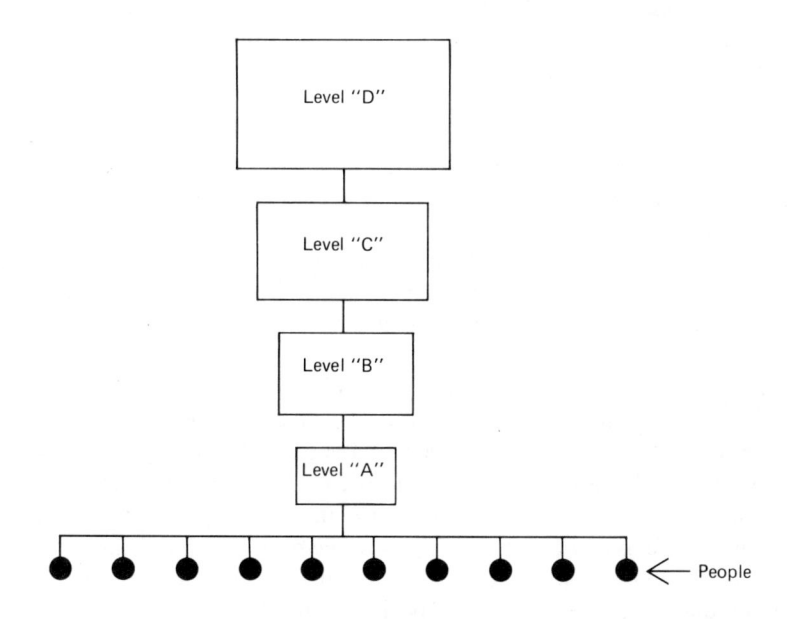

```
        ┌─────────────┐
        │             │
        │  Level "D"  │
        │             │
        └──────┬──────┘
               │
           ┌───┴────┐
           │Level"C"│
           │        │
           └───┬────┘
               │
            ┌──┴───┐
            │Lvl"B"│
            └──┬───┘
               │
            ┌──┴──┐
            │Lvl A│
            └──┬──┘
   ●●●●●●●●●●● ← People
```

Level "D" passes the word down to level "C": "We are behind schedule. Do something about it!" Level "C" translates this into its level of abstraction: "So many hours of overtime are authorized" and passes this word down to level "B." Level "B" instructs level "A" people: "Get five people in to work overtime Saturdays and Sundays for the next two weekends to get us back on schedule." Now, the level "A" manager has a different kind of problem. He has to go to Pete and Charlie and Mary and Bill and the rest of the group to get five people in to work for the next two weekends. And the coming weekend is the opening of hunting season!

The level A manager frequently feels that "They don't understand my problems" ("they" are managers several levels up, or at the home office, or the bureau chiefs in Washington, or some staff group, etc.). And often, they don't. Or, "they" may know full well what the impact of a requirement will be, but know that it must be required anyway.

The level D manager frequently feels that "They don't understand our problems" ("they" are people lower in the organization, or stockholders, or from regulatory bodies, or the public, or the press, etc.). And often, they don't. Or, "they" may understand his point of view, but at the same time may not trust him, or feel he is overlooking the greater values, or feel that the impact will be too great, or something else.

The closer the relationship between levels A and D, the greater the trust and the more the viewpoints are shared. These conditions enhance the quality and accuracy of the communication between levels.

It's hard to live in an abstract world all the time. That's why we see a bent part which is causing problems being passed around and inspected eagerly by the board of directors; it's something concrete in their abstract world —something they "can get their hands on." That's why the Vice-President of Manufacturing goes down to look at a hole in the floor in final assembly. Those moving up into middle management have trouble learning to live in their new, abstract world. They find it difficult to delegate and then not interfere. They really don't trust the manager "down the line" to handle his people right, or to get the work out, or do the other things they know *they* could do. And communications to the middle managers about what is *really* going on begin to get dim. It's a tough adjustment to make.

In some organizations a deliberate effort is made by top management to explain the profit/loss statement to all management people at the end of the year. Such efforts are worthwhile, not because "so many millions of dollars were spent for this and so many millions for that" has any meaning to those at other levels of abstraction, but because in so doing, top management communicates a feeling of partnership—of wishing to share the organization's goals—and trust in, and regard for, lower-level managers. The very act of communicating these things is perhaps more important than meaningful figures. In these efforts, the attempt *is* the message.

"IT'S TOO HOT IN HERE!"

No exploration of communication would be complete without some discussion about facts and feelings. Not making a distinction between fact and feelings is the cause of some of our biggest problems in interpersonal communication.*

---

* Fritz Roethlisberger was a pioneer in what is now called "behavioral science." He was the first to make this distinction for me between fact and what he called "sentiment." This discussion also draws on some of his examples and ideas from *Management and Morale,* Cambridge, Mass.: Harvard University Press, 1941.

It's a simple enough idea. Facts can be objectively verified. Feelings have no meaning without the personal referent. But I communicate my feelings *as if they were facts*. This traps you into thinking that you can change my mind with logic. But you can't.

If I were to say, "It's too hot in here," you might immediately say, "No, it isn't." I would respond, "I don't care what you say; it's too hot in here!" Then you would produce a thermometer and show me that it registered 68°F. That wouldn't sway me any, and I might offer a few suggestions about what you might do with the thermometer. You would get mad and express a feeling about my general level of intelligence. (You would disguise your feelings as facts, also.) What I was saying, really, was, "I feel hot." If I had said it that way, you wouldn't have tried to tell me that I didn't feel hot. You would have let me and the statement alone. Or, you might have sought the cause of my feeling and attempted to do something ("Here, let me hang your jacket up"; "I'm sure your talk will go well"; "I'll bet you feel warm after just coming in from the cold"; "I didn't mean to embarrass you by asking those questions"; "Let me open the window a bit"), depending on your understanding of the source of my discomfort.

That was a very simple example. But what do we do if a subordinate tells us something like: "My wage rates are too low."? Do we look for the personal referent and try to understand why he feels that way? No, our habitual reaction is to explain carefully the care and expense the organization went to in setting fair and equitable rates, the logics of management employed (whether time study, some job evaluation system, merit rating, etc.), and then assure him that his wage rates are indeed *not* too low after all. What does he say after all of this? Right! "My wage rates are too low." Depending on our habitual ways of responding, we either terminate the interview because of the press of urgent business, or suggest some improbable form of ancestry, or say "gitahelloutahere," or something.

Let's take a look at the following statements. Are they statements of fact or feelings? Or could they be either? Mark each one, and then we will talk about them.

Fact	?	Feeling	Statement
____	____	____	1. This Company is a good place in which to work.
____	____	____	2. Women's place is in the home.
____	____	____	3. The reason for inflation is the administration in Washington.
____	____	____	4. My boss is a nit-picker.
____	____	____	5. The marketing department would give away the store if we didn't watch them.
____	____	____	6. The food in the cafeteria is pretty bad.

114 Communication Chap. 5

Fact	?	Feeling	Statement
____	____	____	7. The production department has no schedule discipline.
____	____	____	8. This tool is dull.
____	____	____	9. I wasn't given enough authority to get the job done properly.
____	____	____	10. Long hair on our male employees will drive away our customers.
____	____	____	11. This new sales territory is too small for me to meet my quota.
____	____	____	12. This exercise is dull and uninteresting.

These are all statements of feelings, probably. Do you agree? I say "probably," because it might be possible to agree on some way to objectively verify statements 7 through 11. For statement 7, we might be able to agree on a definition of "production discipline" and how we would measure it. For item 8, we might be able to agree on an "expert's" opinion. (But don't poor workers tend to blame their tools?) For item 9, we might agree on what authority is, how much authority was given, and whether the lack of authority caused the failure to get the job done properly. For statements 10 and 11, we might be able to agree on definitions and measurement criteria and tools, but this would be difficult. And if you said that item 12 is a fact, you are clearly wrong!

Let's look at some of the characteristics of feelings.

1. They are highly subjective and reflect our needs, emotions, attitudes, values, etc., in the situation.
2. They act for us as a system of absolute truths, and further "proof" to us is unnecessary.
3. They are not "right" or "wrong," but just *are;* they can be agreed with or disagreed with—depending on your own feelings.
4. They are not irrational, but nonrational; they are not illogical, but nonlogical; such terms simply do not apply.
5. They represent a very large portion of our communications, but often cannot be made explicit.
6. They are often disguised as facts.

The point in recognizing feelings as feelings is in this last point. As Roethlisberger says: "Two of the most important and time-consuming pastimes of the human mind are to rationalize sentiments (feelings) and to try to modify sentiments with logic."*

---

* Fritz J. Roethlisberger, *Management and Morale,* Cambridge, Mass.: Harvard University Press, 1941, p. 31.

Awash, as we are, in a communications sea of feelings, how can we operate effectively? Here are some ideas which, if practiced, can be helpful.

1. Be nonjudgmental—accept stated feelings as feelings, even when they are disguised as facts.
2. Listen—which is much more than keeping silent; it is an active skill.
3. Encourage a full expression of feelings by making such statements as: "Could you tell me more about how you feel?" "Tell me more." "Tell me more about how you see it." Use "open-ended" questions.
4. Don't let another person's feelings react on your own. Or when they do, recognize that this is what is happening. (Statements of feelings often make us feel challenged, become defensive, etc.)
5. Look for the personal referent. What is the other person telling me about his needs in the social situation he is in?
6. Above all, don't try to argue with feelings. Make sure that they are facts and stated as facts first. Most of the time, what is being expressed are feelings.
7. Show the other person that you accept his statement of feelings and that you will take them into account, if you can, in deciding what to do.
8. Try to learn to express your feelings as feelings. "I feel that. . . ." "To me, ..." Try this on the 12 items on the "fact or feeling" quiz you took earlier.

These are simple ideas, and you could easily memorize them and repeat them. But to understand them and to apply them in your habitual way of dealing with the world will take experience.

GETTING FEEDBACK

How can we find out if communication, rather than the illusion of it, has really taken place? One way to find out would be to see what response you get in the form of activity by the intended receiver. If the activity looks right, then probably the communication was a success. But you can't watch for action every time, and to await the action each time would be costly and sometimes painful ("I'll hold the spike. You take that sledge hammer there, and when I nod my head, you hit it.").

Another good way is to get some feedback from the receiver to see if the "picture in your head" has been adequately transferred to his head, which is what communication is all about. Getting feedback from the intended receiver is pretty simple when you are talking to one person ("Now tell me your understanding of what I told you." "Tell me what it is you are going to do." "Take a minute and repeat back what I said." etc.). Getting feedback from larger numbers of people or when you are not in a face-to-face situation is more difficult. For example, let's assume that you urgently need to communicate something to your subordinates. Let's list the forms and the channels such a communication downward might take:

Form	Channels
requests	memos
regulations	meetings
policies	conferences
procedures	letters
orders	public address system
commands	newspapers, etc.
rules	
announcements	
bulletins	
directions	
instructions, etc.	

Now list the forms and channels of communication *upward* used in your organization. To make it easy for you, list in the space provided *any* form of upward communication used, not just those used to get feedback to determine whether communication has taken place.

Form	Channels
_____	_____
_____	_____
_____	_____
_____	_____
_____	_____
_____	_____
_____	_____
_____	_____
_____	_____
_____	_____
_____	_____

How many items did you list? As many as two forms and two channels? If so, your organization is exceptional in its upward communication.

The fact is that our forms and channels of upward communication are few. We are oriented primarily toward downward communication. It really is "dark at the top of the stairs." This orientation tends to trap us in the illusion of having had communication take place. You have probably never been called to a meeting by subordinates who want to find out just what the heck you were trying to say. Or, you probably never got a letter from the intended receivers asking the same thing. It takes guts to say, "Boss, I don't know what you are talking about—what is it you expect of me?" or even, "Let's see if I'm reading you right. Here's what I understood you to say."

The responsibility for good communications belongs to the one trying to communicate. Next time, ask yourself questions like these:

How can I get feedback to find out if the "picture in my head" was transmitted correctly?

How urgent is it that the "picture" transmitted be received with accuracy? What will it "cost" if it isn't? (The consequences can range from minor annoyance to catastrophe.)

Is it important that *everyone* understand? Or most? Or some? Or a few?

Can and should several channels be used at the same time? Or should they be spaced over a period of time?

How can questions, doubts, concerns, etc., about the intended communication be reported back without distortion?

Getting "two-way" communication going takes longer, looks inefficient and disorderly, and is noisy. It can be disheartening to see how really badly your "clear-cut" communication was received. But making the effort to get feedback is the only way you can be sure that communication is taking place.

NOW THAT I'VE TOLD YOU . . .

Now that I've given you some of the ideas I have found useful in the area of communication, let's see how well I've communicated. Mark the statements below either true or false. If the statement is partly or mostly false, mark it false. Then compare your answers with mine, and compute your score. Ready?

Test

True	False	Statement
____	____	1. If we make sure we told him, he knows.
____	____	2. You cannot be sure what you have said until you get a response to it.
____	____	3. A communication about something new must be planned with greater care than a communication about routine operations.

118 Communication   **Chap. 5**

True	False	Statement
___	___	4. The illusion in one-way communication may be comfortable, even though it may lead to unfortunate results.
___	___	5. When a person understands something clearly, he can communicate it clearly.
___	___	6. If the receiver of a communication raises no questions and says he understands, he understands.
___	___	7. A word's meaning depends largely on what the receiver associates with the word.
___	___	8. Telling him (them) why you are telling him (them) can help in communicating.
___	___	9. Since nearly everybody in an organization knows the goals to be reached, top-level decisions are largely understood and accepted.
___	___	10. You don't fall into the trap of trying to argue logically with someone's feelings.
___	___	11. The feelings which people have, and state as facts, often "get our goat" and make us less able to cope with them.
___	___	12. There is a free flow of information both upward and downward in your organization.
___	___	13. One-way communication will appear to the observer as being orderly and smooth-running.
___	___	14. Really seeing how poorly you have communicated can be embarrassing.
___	___	15. You really understand the "pictures in my head" that I was attempting to get across in this section, because I have explained them to you.

Answers

1. False
2. True
3. True
4. True
5. False
6. False
7. True
8. True
9. False
10. False
11. True
12. False
13. True
14. True
15. False

Score

How did your answers compare with mine? Check your level of agreement below.

___   14–15   We're on the same wave length. Now can we practice these ideas?
___   12–13   There's a little static in the system.
___   10–11   "Play (read) it again, Sam."
___   6–9   Back to the drawing board.
___   3–5   The greatest problem in communication is the illusion of it.
___   1–2   We both flunked the course. Let's stop trying.

CHAPTER **6**

EFFECTIVE THINKING

Suppose you were to decide to take a few lessons from the local golf pro to try to better your game. When you arrived at the appointed hour, he wouldn't sit you down and give you a lecture on "how to be a good golfer" or some similar topic. Instead, he would ask you to step up to the tee and hit a few. Then, he would take you from *where you are* and would try to help you become aware of what you are doing now which prevents you from being a better golfer.

"Keep your left arm straight," he says to you. "Look," you say, "I'm not paying you your hourly rates to tell me the obvious. Keeping my left arm straight is the first thing I learned about playing golf!" *The fact is, however, that you are not, but you don't know it.* The pro works with you until you finally become aware of your habits. Then and only then can you do something about them.

Your habits of thinking are important in your effectiveness as a manager. But I have little confidence that telling you about your habits here (or giving you a lecture on good golfing) will really make any impact in your life. Your habits are deeply ingrained, they are a consistent part of your outlook, and they are practiced hourly.

CASE STUDY—THE SALES MANAGER

In order to change your habits, you must first be helped to become aware of what you are doing now. Let's begin by looking at a case study of a specific situation and then identifying your thinking about the case. As you read the case over, what do you see "going on" here?

THE SALES MANAGER

Bill Downs, Director of Marketing for the Pierce Products Company, took advantage of the time made available to him by an unexpected cancelled appointment and reflected on his next scheduled appointment—with Joe Fields, one of his section heads in marketing. Joe Fields had been promoted to section head five months ago, but the indications were that Joe was not making it.

After Joe had been selected for the job, Bill Downs had followed a "hands off" policy, in keeping with his belief that a newly appointed manager should be allowed to "sink or swim." Joe was beginning to "sink," Bill thought. Two of Joe's subordinates had complained to Bill that Joe wouldn't delegate authority to them and that the number of reports Joe required of them was excessive and was interfering with their ability to get their work done. Therefore, Bill decided that it was time to have a talk with Joe.

Bill's reflections were interrupted by his secretary's announcement that Joe Fields had arrived. There was a knock at the door, and Joe came in.

BILL: Good afternoon, Joe. Won't you come in and have a chair.

JOE: Thanks, Bill, I'm a few minutes early, but your gal said you were free. What did you want to see me about?

BILL: Well, it has been five months since you took over the new position down there, and I wanted to discuss your progress and some potential problems that I think you are having.

JOE: What problems?

BILL: Well, let me get right to the point, Joe. I'm given to understand that you won't delegate authority to your subordinates and that you are requiring too many reports of them.

JOE: You knew when you promoted me that I had never managed an operation that size. And it has taken some getting used to, believe me. I do require reports and make a lot of the decisions myself. Perhaps too many. But I'm still trying to get a feel for the job.

BILL: That's not the point. In a larger operation you can't afford to do everything yourself. You have got to use your people.

JOE: Look at the sales volume. It has grown every month since I've been on the new job. Or do you have complaints about the results I'm producing?

BILL: No, your sales volume is up to expectations, but it probably won't stay that way if you keep on requiring all those reports of your people.

JOE: If I've been given the job, I think I should be allowed to use my own control systems. Especially if the results being produced are satisfactory. What do you expect after only five months on the job?

BILL: But we can't afford to lose any good men because of unreasonable requirements for reports.

JOE: May I ask where you are getting all the information on the way I operate?

BILL: From two of the people who work for you. I don't think it important to mention their names. But they are two of our best people. You know that we have an open-door policy and that anyone can come in to see me.

JOE: Mr. Downs, you may call it an open-door policy, but I call it by-passing and undercutting my authority. I'm working ten and twelve hours a day to do a good job without any support from up here. Evidently, production of sales isn't enough. If that's the case, maybe you had better get yourself another boy.

BILL: Now take it easy, Joe. I'm just trying to be helpful . . .

SECRETARY: Pardon the interruption, Mr. Downs, but the President's office called, and he'd like to see you right away.

BILL: Joe, I'm sorry that I've got to run now. But think about what we've talked about, and we'll get together again for another chat.

What is "Going On" in the Case?

Now that you have read the interview between Bill Downs and Joe Fields, check *all* the statements below which reflect *your* thinking about this situation. Do this before reading on.

_____   1. Bill Downs, Director of Sales, is a poor and inept manager.
_____   2. Both of these managers are trying to do a good job for the firm.
_____   3. Bill Downs is at fault here. He is to blame for his "sink or swim" and "open-door" policies.
_____   4. Joe Fields' hesitancy to delegate and his requirement for reports are probably caused by his being new on this larger job.
_____   5. This is a problem in communication.
_____   6. Joe probably feels frustrated at the close of the interview.
_____   7. Bill shouldn't have been so blunt in beginning the interview. He should have established rapport first.
_____   8. Bill probably doesn't see how the interview looks to Joe.
_____   9. A good director of marketing wouldn't have let this happen.
_____ 10. Joe Fields probably feels a lack of support from Bill Downs.
_____ 11. The management is the cause of the problem.
_____ 12. Bill Downs is trying to be helpful to Joe Fields.
_____ 13. Bill Downs should "wise up" in his handling of subordinates.
_____ 14. Joe Fields must be puzzled about the lack of appreciation for his sales record in the last five months.

Looking at Your Analysis

One of the limiting factors in effective management is habits of thinking which "get in the way" of effective analysis or diagnosis of the situations being faced. The *even*-numbered items in the case analysis are analytical statements; the *odd*-numbered statements reflect habits of ineffective thinking.

Putting the even-numbered statements together, we get an analysis like this:

> Both of these managers are trying to do a good job for the firm. Joe Fields' hesitancy to delegate and his requirements for reports are probably caused by his being new on the larger job. Bill Downs is trying to be helpful to Joe, but Bill probably doesn't see how the interview looks to Joe. Joe must be puzzled about the lack of appreciation for his sales record over the last five months and probably feels a lack of support from Bill Downs. Joe probably feels frustrated at the close of the interview.

This reflects an attempt to understand "what's going on here" in this specific situation. When this kind of an analysis is made, effective action can then be decided on.

The odd-numbered statements, on the other hand, reflect habits which prevent useful thinking about the situation. Let's look at each of the odd-numbered statements a little more closely.

1. Bill Downs is a poor and inept manager.

Name-calling: This takes the form of putting a label on people in the situation ("He is stupid," "He is a poor supervisor," etc.). A person who does this is classifying people in a way that has meaning only to himself. Let me make up a nonsense word and show you how this works "He is a VIF!" "Why do you call him that?" "Because he behaves that way." "What is a VIF?" "Someone who acts like that." This is a self-contained logic system which has little meaning, and it therefore offers no help in making an analysis of a situation.

3. Bill Downs is at *fault* here. He is to *blame* for his "sink-or-swim" and "open-door" policies.

Judging and blaming: This is the tendency to look for the villian in the case. We somehow feel that if we can just figure out who is at "fault," we have done something useful. Roethlisberger calls this "the search for the spherical S.O.B.—one who is an S.O.B. from every point of view." But being satisfied with doing this prevents effective analysis, since we somehow feel as if something significant has been done. "He is to blame." "That policy is bad." "He is at fault." Such statements are not helpful and get in the way of effective thinking. "Even God doesn't presume to judge a man 'til the end of his days."

5. This is a problem in *communication*.

Generalization: This is to deal only with some general characteristic of a situation rather than to pay attention to details. Practically everything can be said to be a problem in communication—a problem with the boss, an impasse in labor negotiations, the talks at a peace conference, etc. Such a broad statement frequently inhibits further thinking.

7. Bill *shouldn't* have been so blunt in beginning the interview. He *should* have established rapport first.

Should/ought: This is second-guessing people without trying to understand why they are behaving as they are in this specific situation. Doing this prevents our trying to understand why these people *did* behave as they did. Remaking the situation is pointing out that if things hadn't happened as they did in the past, then we wouldn't be faced with the problems we face now. Statements such as "He shouldn't have done that"; "It would have been better if . . ."; "He ought to have done this . . ."; and "The U.S. shouldn't have gone beyond furnishing military advisors" are not really helpful in working with current problems.

9. A *good* director of marketing wouldn't have let this happen.

Unrealism: This is trying to make people or organizations or policies, etc., into some ideal rather than trying to understand them as they are, e.g., "This wouldn't have come up in a well-run company"; "A good policy statement wouldn't have permitted this." To think effectively about a specific situation requires that we drop preconceived ideas.

11. The management is the cause of this problem.

Oversimplification: This is to see events and their causes as being very simple rather than complex. Every day we hear people who can explain all of our complex problems as being caused by "the Communists," "the Democrats," etc. People and events are complex, and an analysis must be made of this complexity. Finding a simple explanation for something which is really complex prevents effective thinking.

13. Bill Downs should "wise up" in his handling of subordinates.

"Magic wand": This limiting approach comes about when we are considering action. We act as if someone could wave a magic wand to change the people and the situation, e.g., "Those employees should snap out of it"; "The company policies should be changed immediately." Effective action can only be taken step by step by someone connected with the situation.

These, then, are examples of habits which frequently prevent effective thinking in administrative situations.* If you checked any of the odd-numbered items, you may wish to think about these habits in your own thinking. Once you become aware of your habits, then you can do something about them. But habits cannot be changed from "outside" yourself.

---

* In the currently popular "transactional analysis" frame of reference, most of these statements would be classed as being in the parental mode.

PRACTICE APPLICATION

You may find it interesting to have some more experience in recognizing the unhelpful ways in which some people look at the world. The more you become familiar with such ways of thinking, the more able you will be to recognize these habits in yourself. In the exercise that follows, try to match the statement with the appropriate limiting habit of thinking.

Commonly made statements about situations. In the space provided, put the letter of the nonuseful habit from the right-hand column that matches each statement.

Limiting habits of thinking

a) Name-calling

b) Judging and blaming

c) Generalization

d) Should/ought (remaking)

e) Unrealism

f) Oversimplification

g) "Magic wand"

_____ 1. "It would have been better if the supervisor hadn't said that to the employee."

_____ 2. "I think that the supervisor was completely at fault. His action was stupid."

_____ 3. "The main problem here is a lack of leadership."

_____ 4. "The foreman should improve his relations with his people."

_____ 5. "A good supervisor wouldn't have let this problem come up in the first place."

_____ 6. "This company policy is a bad one."

_____ 7. "An effort should be made to clear up this situation."

_____ 8. "The supervisor should not have hired Bill in the first place. Had he hired someone else, he wouldn't have this problem."

_____ 9. "This manager is just inept. He is just a poor manager."

_____ 10. "The new head of Quality Control shouldn't have taken on the new job."

_____ 11. "An effectively run department doesn't have problems."

_____ 12. "The drop in sales was due to unscrupulous competitors."

Answers

Here are the ways in which we would categorize the fragments of statements in the practice application:

1. d) Should/ought (remaking)
2. a) Name-calling
   b) Judging and blaming
3. e) Unrealism
   c) Generalization
4. g) "Let there be light" (magic wand)
5. e) Unrealism
6. b) Judging and blaming
7. c) Generalization
   g) "Let there be light" (magic wand)
8. d) Should/ought (remaking)
9. a) Name-calling
   b) Judging and blaming
10. d) Should/ought (remaking)
11. e) Unrealism
12. f) Oversimplification

It really doesn't matter if you didn't agree 100% with these answers, since there is some overlap in the categories. The important thing, however, is that you become more sensitive to these limiting habits.

CASE STUDY—THE MARSTON MANUFACTURING COMPANY

Now that you are at least more familiar with some of the habits which get in the way of effective thinking, let me give you another case for your analysis. This case is about two people in the Marston Manufacturing Company—Bob Ash, the director of sales, and Henry Baker, a young production superintendent. As you read the case, what do you see happening? What is going on in the case? If you were Bob Ash, what specifically would you do now?

MARSTON MANUFACTURING COMPANY

"I'll be damned if I'm going to hold still for your making the shop to blame for next quarter's loss. And there will be a loss, you can bet your sweet life on that," said Henry Baker, Marston's young production superintendent.

"If there is a loss, we'll just have to take it," answered Bob Ash, Marston's director of sales. "Passing a temporary increase on to the wholesalers is no answer."

Bob Ash had been expecting this confrontation with Henry Baker. He had been through the same type of argument many times before, it seemed to him. He had talked to Alice, his wife, about it the night before.

"Henry Baker is another one of those 'young men on the make,'" he had told her. "There seem to be more and more of these young people in the business. They have a plan for themselves all written down. And in headlines the plan says: 'Be identified early as a comer with high potential,' and they are, and they're put into positions of too much responsibility too soon. And then it's up to the old-timers to complete their education."

Alice said, "Well, it hasn't been that many years ago that you were a 'young man on the make.' Somebody had to complete your education, didn't they? Wasn't it Pete Haskins who helped you so much?"

"Yeah, Pete helped me a lot, I've got to admit that. But I think he had a little more to work with."

"He said modestly," Alice teased.

"No, seriously, whatever my experience gave me before I was promoted, it did give me a sense of values. And that's what seems to be missing with so many of the young people today. Their abilities to gather facts and analyze them are good. Better than mine, probably. But they don't seem to have any principles. They will take action that brings them an immediate advantage rather than consider what is right and just over the long haul."

"Well, the young people of today *do* seem to be more pragmatic. But with the world changing so fast these days, perhaps a flexible approach to the world is an advantage," Alice said.

"Flexible is the word, all right. Do what is expedient, be opportunistic, and the devil take the hindmost. Oh well, I guess that's part of my job—to be his teacher. How about another cup of your super, mountain-grown coffee?"

"Coming right up, professor," Alice said, heading for the kitchen.

Bob Ash had grown along with the Marston Company. He had been hired shortly after he got out of the military service. His first position had been in sales, as had most of his experience. But Bob had also worked in many different parts of the company's operations. It wasn't a formal policy or program of the company, but for many years the practice had been followed of transferring people around in order to give them broad experience.

Bob had come back to the home office seven years ago as the assistant director of sales under Pete Haskins. Pete was a much-respected man who had helped found the company in the 'thirties. Pete had retired four years ago, turning the reins over to Bob Ash. At that time Pete had said, "It's time that we turned the old war horse out to pasture. The new young blood should have a chance."

This attitude toward youth seemed to be prevalent within the company, which had initiated a practice of recruiting M.B.A.'s from the top graduate schools of the country and placing them in positions of responsibility early. Too early, Bob felt. And it was up to the "old heads," like himself, at age 49, to teach them the trade, Bob had reflected.

The issue that had brought about Bob's present meeting with Henry Baker was a routine draft of a recommendation to the executive committee that prices to wholesalers be increased by 7 percent, starting with the next quarter. This was necessary, the draft had stated, because of the increase in the price of raw materials. Prices for these raw materials were expected to drop the following quarter, the recommendation noted, at which time the temporary increase to wholesalers would be removed. A cover note to the draft stated that the director of finance had concurred with the recommendation. "Marshaling his forces," Bob had thought. (The director of finance was a young man also.) All that the recommendation needed was Bob's approval to be delivered to the executive committee. And Bob was determined not to let this happen.

Bob's conversation with Henry Baker began with a discussion of production costs generally.

"Aren't there any other ways to get the costs down?" Bob asked.

"Not through any increase in productivity. We are working at top efficiency now. Our rising costs are due only to the increase in cost of raw materials. And, as I have told you before, we could switch to plastics to make the two end-frames and the spindle and save a pot full of money."

"And, as I've told you before, doing that would get us a pot full of complaints from breakage," Bob said.

"Breakage might increase some," Henry responded, "but not very much, if it is used correctly. But you keep saying that's too much to expect."

Bob answered, "Yes, it is too much to expect that the consumers would carefully read and follow our directions to keep from breaking the units. And you should know what a hassle it is when broken units go back to the retailer, and he has to turn them over to the wholesaler for them to be returned to us. Changing materials isn't the answer."

"Well, that's it, then," Henry replied. "You have a clear-cut choice. Either switch to other materials and expect some breakage, or raise our prices to reflect what we have to pay for materials. Take your choice."

"There is another alternative that you haven't included in your 'either-or' positions," Bob pointed out. "That is, to absorb this temporary increase—if we are really sure it is temporary. In the long run, we will keep our good relations with the wholesalers, even if it will mean taking a temporary loss."

"The wholesalers, again. Sometimes, Bob, you make me wonder who we are in business for—for us or the wholesalers," Henry responded with some heat.

"We are in business for both! And throw in the retailers, too. If they don't prosper, we don't! And you had better not forget that," replied Bob, beginning to get annoyed.

"I'll be damned if I'm going to hold still for your making the shop to blame for next quarter's loss. And there will be a loss, you can bet your sweet life on that," Henry said.

"If there is a loss, we'll just have to take it," answered Bob. "Passing a temporary increase on to the wholesalers is no answer."

"Well, that's my recommendation. And it will go up to the executive committee tomorrow morning with or without your concurrence. And if it's without, then I think you have a problem," said Henry.

After Henry had gone, Bob began to wonder if he *did* have a problem. The first quarter's earnings had been quite low, and the executive committee had been quite determined that this not happen again. Still, good relations with the wholesalers was something that *must not be compromised,* Bob felt. Regardless!

Bob wondered what approach he might take with the executive committee the next morning.

What's "Going On" in the Case?

Now that you have read the Marston Manufacturing Company case, jot down some notes about what you saw happening in the case. List everything you feel is important to reach an understanding of the case.

Looking at Your Analysis

Now that you have made some notes on your analysis of the case, let's analyze your analysis. Here are some questions you might raise about your notes:

1. Did you use any of the approaches we discussed earlier (name-calling, judging/blaming, generalization, should/ought, unrealism, oversimplification, or "magic wand") in thinking about action? Look over your notes carefully, since we usually express these habits in very subtle ways. Were some of your statements about the people or the issue *clearly* expressions of these habits? Were some of your statements *probably* expressions of them?

2. Did you see the issue as natural and normal, or did you think that it should not have even arisen? Did you see the issue as symptomatic of something even more important underlying this surface problem? If so, what did you see as the underlying problem?

3. Did you see the habits which limit thinking being employed by Bob Ash and Henry Baker (Bob's generalizations about "young managers" and Henry's either/or approach)? How did these approaches affect their behavior in the case?

4. We saw more of Bob's point of view toward Henry through Bob's discussion with his wife. What was Henry's point of view toward Bob? Did you think about this and guess what it might be, even though it wasn't clearly stated in the case? Would this be helpful in your understanding?

5. Did you identify with either Bob or Henry? Could you say why you were able to "take sides" so easily? If you did identify with one of the people, did it get in the way of your understanding of the other person?

6. In placing yourself in Bob Ash's shoes in considering action, were your plans specific or vague? Do you have a clear idea of what you would probably do in a real situation if faced with such an issue?

7. What other facts would you have liked to have had in making an analysis of this case? In a real situation, how could you get needed but missing facts such as these?

8. What has your analysis of your analysis told you about how you tend to look at the world now? In what ways, if any, would you like to change your approach?

CASE STUDY—THE REGIONAL OFFICERS MEETING

After you have taken a close look at your analysis of the Marston Manufacturing Company, take a look at the case that follows—"The Regional Officers Meeting." As you read through the case, think particularly about the action you would take as Susan Barker, a regional personnel officer for an agency of the United States Government.

THE REGIONAL OFFICERS MEETING

"Susan Barker, how do you vote?" the chairman asked. The eight men around the conference table became quiet and looked at her.

"Well, here is my chance," thought Susan as she returned the gaze of the eight men convened for the quarterly meeting of the regional personnel officers. The vote on the issue was now four to four, and her vote would be the deciding one. "But should I take the chance?"

The issue at hand was the interpretation of an existing regulation. Since many regulations were written in general terms, consistency in application depended on agreements among the regional officers. Susan was personally inclined to vote a particular way on the issue. But of greater concern to her was the handling of such issues.

On the surface, a majority vote settled the question of interpretation, and the decision would be followed by all those concerned. Actually, those voting against the final decision would continue their resistance by making administrative decisions based on what they still felt the interpretation should be. The resulting inconsistencies would cause widely differing practices among the regions. Susan felt that it was sheer chance that these differences had not come to light yet. But when they did, she felt, it would become a scandal of national dimensions.

The pretense that the final vote indicated a real agreement was never discussed openly at the meetings. The group seemed to be uninterested in a full discussion that would really change people's views. There was no real consensus reached and, therefore, no real commitment to act in concert. The votes at this meeting indicated acquiescence only "for the record." Each participant then went his own way. Susan thought that it was more important to put this pretense on the table and talk about it than to go through another meaningless vote.

Susan Barker had been promoted to regional personnel officer about a year ago. She had been working for the government for 11 years as a career employee and was the only woman to hold the post of personnel officer within the agency.

Coming to Washington on the airplane from St. Louis, she had thought about the meeting and what might be an effective role for her. In the four such sessions she had attended since her appointment, she had changed from a passive learner to a more active participant. She felt, however, that she was still not taken seriously by many of the personnel men.

Susan had recently read a remark in the newspaper by a nationally known black woman who felt that she was discriminated against because she was black and a woman and that the most serious instances of discrimination occurred because she was a woman. There were some parallels, thought Susan. She was used to the changes of the subject that occurred when she entered a room; the glances in her direction when an off-color story was told; the many self-conscious slips and allusions to her gender. She would join the group in Washington for a social drink, she decided, but she wouldn't stay on for the most-of-the-night poker sessions.

Being a woman in a man's world presented difficulties, of course, but Susan had come to live with these. She had not "tried to be one of the boys," as some women do with coarse language or other "masculine" behavior. Nor did she seek

Case study—the regional officers meeting 131

or expect different treatment. But sometimes she had the strong impression that she was only partially accepted, as a "token" woman appointee, and that she was not really expected to have ideas of substance or to make a contribution.

But now, here was an opening. Susan wondered if she should refuse to vote and, instead, bring up what a vote at these meetings really means—that it is just a pretense—but that this is more serious in the long run than any vote on a single issue. Or should she "go along" with the pretense, voting as she was inclined? Would time alone change her acceptance in this group? Would it be better to talk to each member singly about the matter rather than bring it up in the group? Should she wait until she knew she would be taken seriously by all? Would her introduction of this new topic cause greater or less acceptance of her as a person and the contribution she could make?

"Susan Barker, how do you vote?" the chairman asked. The eight men around the conference table became quiet and looked at her.

You are Susan Barker. Specifically, what would you do? Why?

Your Analysis of the Case

In the space below, make notes about your analysis of the case. What do you see as the real issues here?

Your Action

In the space below, write down what action you, as Susan Barker, would take. State, as specifically as you can, why you would take the action you have decided to take.

If you really were Susan, with eight pairs of eyes looking at you, would you really take the action you have just described?

This time, I'm *not* going to help you think about the action you have decided on by presenting any content here. You will have to analyse it yourself and decide whether it was "the right action" or not.

How does this make you feel? Does it make you a little mad? Do you feel that you have been "short-changed"? A bit disappointed? Or, do you find that it really doesn't matter a bit to you? Why do you suppose you feel as you do?

In using cases, the instructor wants you to learn to make your own analyses of real situations and decide on effective action, and then to take that action. The instructor will not be with you in your day-to-day activities to help you gather the facts you need for an analysis, or to pose questions for you to think about, or to help you to analyze your own thinking, or to tell you if your action was "good" or "right." To do these things would be to create an unreal dependence on someone who won't be there when you will need him. As one graduate of a school using the case-method of teaching wrote back, " You taught me how to analyze cases, but all I find out here in business is a mess!"

Along with your increasing awareness of your present habits of thought and a greater diagnostic ability, you should also begin to have confidence in your own judgment. If your reacting to the lack of an "answer" is something like "Well, that's okay. It would have been interesting to read, but I really don't need it," you are showing a measure of confidence rather than dependence. And this is to be highly desired.

SUMMARY

Increasing your awareness, that is, seeing what your own approaches in thinking are now, is a difficult thing to do through introspection alone. It is easier to observe yourself (not easy, but easier, mind you) in spontaneous interaction with others. If you are reading this book and discussing it with others, each discussion will provide you with some feedback on your present thinking. If you are reading this book as part of a formal educational program, your instructor will probably use other cases for discussion. Such discussions can give you many opportunities to see yourself.

Perhaps another good way of becoming more sensitive is to begin looking for these habits in others. Ineffective thinking is relatively easy to spot in others. After you have learned to pay attention to habits in others, you may be able to see that you are doing the same things. When you become more aware of what you are now doing, you can then do something about it. Sure, you know the rule: "Keep your left arm straight." But what you don't know is that you aren't.

CHAPTER 7

MANAGING CHANGES

Managing changes is an almost continuous activity of a manager—not the earthshaking kind of changes usually, but the small, day-to-day kind. But how these changes are handled can determine the quality of relationships which exist in a shop or office and can determine how the job gets done. Communication plays a large part in managing change effectively, as it does in every facet of working relationships. Before you can manage changes for others, however, you should first have an understanding of how you react to change.*

HOW DO YOU REACT TO CHANGE?

When nonroutine changes are proposed or announced, each person evaluates what the change will mean to him personally. Initially, and depending on several factors, the relatively healthy, "normal" person may react to change in one or more of the following ways. He may feel that the change is destructive or threatening; he may not know how he feels about the change; he may be uncertain, but generally positive about the change; or he may feel very good about the change.

Assume that you are the assistant branch manager of a bank and that you have been there two months. We'll list five situations. You are to assign a value to each from the following scale:

−5	−4	−3	−2	−1	0	+1	+2	+3	+4	+5
Destructive		Threatening			Don't really know		Uncertain, but positive		Very good	

(*Each of the items on the next page should be considered independently.* In the right-hand column, indicate your initial feelings about each situation.)

---

* The model for this discussion of change was adapted from one suggested in a booklet: F. C. Mann and F. W. Neff, *Managing Major Change in Organizations,* Ann Arbor: Foundation for Research on Human Behavior, 1961.

135

136 Managing changes Chap. 7

Situation	Your assigned value from the scale
a) You are offered a promotion to assistant manager of the trust department in the district office, where there is a sudden opening. You have no experience in this area and would have to be making important decisions without background experience.	_____
b) The district office has approved a morale survey to be made in all local branches. It would be designed, administered, and used as a thesis by a graduate student at the state university. Results will be identified by branches, and the district office will see the results before they come to the branch.	_____
c) Without explanation or warning, the branch manager brings in another assistant manager, "Red" Blake, who is several years younger than you and was a football star and honor student in college. The only thing you know is what the branch manager told you: "Clean out the next desk for him and split your duties with him so he can learn the branch operations."	_____
d) The tellers ask if they can take on more of the decision-making functions within the branch, without your approval. This would include writing and signing their own letters, handling inquiries from customers in person or by telephone, etc. This was tried in the branch you came from, with near-disastrous results. (One lawsuit based its case against you on the argument that the teller was your agent.)	_____
e) The branch manager, who has a good reputation as a "developer," wants you to learn more about his duties. He proposes that you go with him to see important customers, attend important district meetings, take an active role in representing the bank to the community, etc. This will prepare you to take over the management of a branch.	_____

If you have not done so, review each of the five unrelated incidents above and assign a plus or minus value to each, according to the scale devised earlier. Then, let's talk about it.

"People Resist Change"—Or Do They?

The phrase "people resist change" is widely heard. But it represents such an oversimplification, such a generalization, that it is useless for all practical purposes. Sure, under some circumstances people do. But under others, they don't! What affects our feelings toward a change? Our evaluation of a change is influenced by several factors:

1. Extent of information we have about the change
2. Extent of our participation in the change decision
3. Our trust in the initiator of the change

Action maze on managing change   137

4. Our past experience with similar changes
5. The perceived social impact of the change
6. Our individual personalities.

In the five incidents you rated on p. 136, we tried to influence your reaction by emphasizing one or another of these factors. The five incidents were written with the thought that you would assign the values as shown in the scale below.

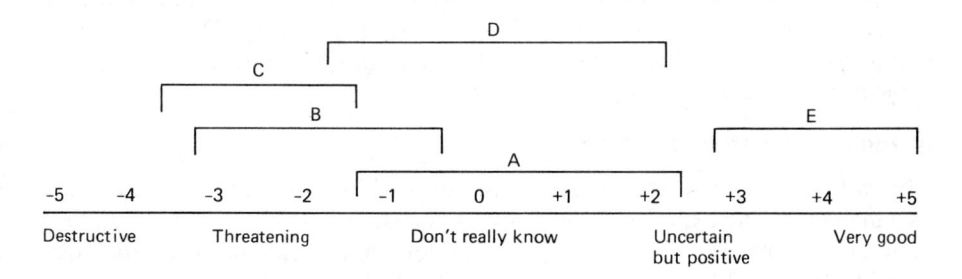

```
                          D
                 C  ┌─────────────┐
              ┌─────┴──┐
           B  │        │                    E
        ┌─────┴──┐     │                 ┌─────┐
        │        │  A  │                 │     │
  -5  -4  -3  -2  -1  0  +1  +2  +3  +4  +5
Destructive   Threatening   Don't really know   Uncertain      Very good
                                              but positive
```

Were the values you assigned for your feelings in this range? If not, why not, do you suppose? If they were in this range, why do you suppose they were? Let's talk about it. In the first situation, we emphasized your lack of experience in this area, which can be scary. On the other hand, the change was a promotion. These two factors operating together would cause you to rate the situation somewhere around the middle of the scale, we felt. In situation (b), having someone asking very pointed questions and with the results to be identified with you and seen by the district office first, can be a threatening experience. We therefore felt that your feelings toward this change would tend to be negative. In situation (c), your lack of information about, and participation in, the decision, as well as the possible reaction by the social group, would probably make this change seem destructive or at least threatening. We brought your negative past experience to bear in situation (d). We felt that this would keep your rating somewhere near the midpoint—from mildly threatening to mildly positive. We expected you to see situation (e) as being a very good change. This activity would help you grow in a protected way so that you didn't get "out of your depth" too soon. But you would be developing for the future.

"People resist change" under *some* conditions. The manager's job is to learn to look at the conditions and make plans to manage the change effectively.

ACTION MAZE ON MANAGING CHANGE

It was Mary Parker Follett who first clarified for me the idea of a circular response. She quotes a factory manager as saying, "I am in control of a situation until I behave; when I act, I have lost control of the situation."* We take an action, and we get a response to that action. Now we must react to the response, and our reaction gets another response, which we must react to, and so on.

Because I know of no teaching tool that can illustrate this circular response and give a person an experience with it in a learning situation, I created what I call the "action maze." In the next few pages one is presented on the subject of managing change. Just begin by following the instructions. When you have completed the action maze, we will talk about your experience with it and the subject of managing change.

Introduction and Instructions

This will be an experiment in a new way of thinking about the action you take as a manager. The experiment begins with the statement of a problem requiring action on your part. The course of action you choose can and will differ from that of others. The path you move down will depend on your attitudes and actions at each point.

There is no single conclusion, nor a single path which you should take. The number of pages you turn to has no relation to the quality of your solution.

This "booklet within a book" will be used differently from most of the books you have seen in the past. Instead of reading the pages consecutively, (pp. 1, 2, 3, etc.), you will decide on p. 2, for example, what action you would take and then *turn to the page indicated* next to your choice. Other action choices will refer you to other pages, back and forth, as you go along.

Page numbers for this section are given in boldface type at the bottom outside corner of each page, such as #1 on p. 140. Follow these numbers instead of the page numbers at the top of the page.

Please *write down* each page you turn to and the choice you select on that page on the "Page and Choice Record Sheet."

The Situation

You are an assistant branch manager of a medium-size branch bank. (During this activity take action as *you* would—don't say "If I were a banker, I would . . ." With slight modification, the situations described could happen in any setting. Be yourself.) You were transferred to this position two months ago, and the move represented a promotion from a much smaller branch. You have been "getting your feet on the ground" during the last two months, but have been taking a more active management role recently.

---

* See *Dynamic Administration: The Collected Papers of Mary Parker Follett*, ed. Henry Metcalf and L. Urwick, New York: Harper & Bros, 1940. This book will be well worth your while if you can find a copy. Try the local libraries.

Some of the older employees are used as informal "lead" people, but every employee technically reports to you. In addition to the branch manager and yourself, there are nine regular tellers, one for loans, and one who handles exchange matters.

The district office of the bank is in the same city as your branch. The home office is several hundred miles away.

Turn to the next page.

140 Managing changes — Chap. 7

PAGE AND CHOICE RECORD SHEET

Keep a record of the pages you turn to and the choices you select on this page. If you feel that turning back to this page each time would be awkward, simply record your pages and choices on a separate sheet of paper.

You will probably not use all of the spaces below.

Some of the pages will not offer you a choice, but will refer you to another page. Then, just leave the choice space blank and indicate the new page.

Now turn to p. 2, where the first incident is presented.

Page	Choice		Page	Choice
2				

(Go to the top of the next column)

Action maze on managing change

As you enter the bank one morning, the branch manager stops you and says:

"I wish you could see what you can do about the dress styles being worn by our women employees. We seem to have a wild assortment of the mod look, the bare look, and the no-undergarment look.

"These styles may be acceptable in an office where there is no contact with the public, but they're not acceptable here!

"We just haven't been specific enough in the handbook of procedures or in new-employee orientation."

Of the responses listed below, select the one which is most like that you would probably make. Then write down your choice and the new page on the "Page and Choice Record Sheet" and turn to the page number indicated. (Please do *not* turn to the other pages.)

A. Tell him that you will handle it right away. *(Turn to p. 6.)*

B. Say, "All right," but do nothing about it because the branch manager will probably get over it. *(Turn to p. 16.)*

C. Explain that these are just new styles and that each person should be allowed a personal preference in dress. Use the bold colors and styles of the men as examples. *(Turn to p. 11.)*

2

You Are Not Following Instructions

Nowhere were you instructed to turn to this page. Remember, we said that this would not be like a regular book, in which you follow the pages in sequence. Instead, here you will skip around, depending on the action you decide to take. Now turn back to p. 2 and select the number of the page you should be on, which depends on the action you decided to take.

3

Action maze on managing change

You have decided to hold a general meeting with the women employees to announce the new dress standards. Select the approach you would most probably use and turn to the page indicated.

A. "I have here a statement of the new dress standards for each of you. I'll pass them out now and give you a chance to read these here.

 (Pause)

 "Do any of you have any questions?" *(Turn to p. 29.)*

B. "You and I both know that to keep any job, a certain amount of conformity is required. It's part of the price we pay for getting paid. Now, I have nothing against the new dress styles. Personally, I think they are great. But if the management feels that our clothes styles are too bold, then we've got to tone them down. I'm sure that each of you understands the importance of following management's orders and will give your fullest cooperation." *(Turn to p. 15.)*

C. "Your concern and ours is with good customer relations. Most important is how you handle each transaction, and you are doing a good job with this. Good relations are what bring people to this bank instead of to the one across the street.

 "Dress styles have changed rapidly in the last few years, and I think that's healthy. However, to keep our good customer relations, it seems important that we not be the leaders in fashions which many of our older and most important customers find it hard to adapt to.

 "These new guidelines for dress styles worn in the office are designed to be helpful. If any problems come up as a result of them, please let me know. I'll talk to each of you in the next few days." *(Turn to p. 8.)*

4

You have fired Peggy. We don't think you would win an "unfair labor practice" charge which she would undoubtedly bring about. This, she would charge, was being fired for union activities. Anyway, Peggy is off the job for now, even though you will probably have to pay back salary when she is reinstated. Do you feel that you chose the best course of action in firing her?

Now turn to p. 27 for the next incident.

5

Action maze on managing change   145

You have told the branch manager that you will handle the situation right away. Of the alternative approaches listed below, select the one you would most likely take, record your choice and the new page, then turn to the page number indicated.

A. Decide on a reasonable dress standard for those in contact with the public, i.e., a more specific interpretation of the existing general rules. *(Turn to p. 19.)*

B. Appoint a small advisory committee to help you set dress standards. *(Turn to p. 13.)*

C. Appoint a committee from among the women employees to draw up a set of specific rules governing dress in the office. The decision of this committee will be final. *(Turn to p. 22.)*

6

146 Managing changes Chap. 7

You have decided to call in several of the senior women employees and discuss your new dress standards with them. After talking to the women, you receive a very positive response from them. They seem to feel that such rules are not only necessary, but long overdue. Rather than using other forms of communication, you ask them to spread the word around about the new dress standards.

Turn to p. 9 for the next events.

7

Action maze on managing change

You have given each employee affected a copy of the draft standards. During the next few days, you make it a point to informally ask for comments from each person. Most of the employees express themselves as being generally favorable; a few make suggestions for minor changes, which you accept as improvements.

All but Peggy, who is active in "women's lib" and whose boyfriend is active as an organizer for white-collar unions. Peggy says, "This is just a bunch of baloney, but it's what could be expected from such a poor management group. If we had a union, you wouldn't be trying such childish things as this."

Select the choice of action you would most probably take and turn to the page indicated.

A. Tell her that the idea of a union among bank employees is ridiculous and that she should keep such feelings to herself. *(Turn to p. 23.)*

B. Tell her that you are sorry she feels this way toward the change in standards and that the other girls have accepted the change as needed. Thank her for expressing herself so openly. Take no other action. *(Turn to p. 14.)*

C. Ask Peggy into the conference room for a discussion. *(Turn to p. 17.)*

Several days later, two of the four return to report that there seems to be resistance to the new standards. One of the women says that she met not only disagreement, but also abuse. The women ask you to take some other action to ensure compliance.

Select the course you would most likely take and turn to the page indicated.

A. Write up the standards and post them on the two bulletin boards in the office. *(Turn to p. 25.)*

B. Discuss the new standards with those who seem to be the offenders. Do this when they are actually wearing the clothes. *(Turn to p. 30.)*

C. Have a general meeting with the women employees and announce the new dress standards. *(Turn to p. 4.)*

D. Do nothing. This "tempest in a teapot" will probably blow over. *(Turn to p. 20.)*

9

Action maze on managing change

You have told Peggy that she has the wrong attitude and that you didn't want to hear any more of this kind of talk. Peggy says, "Well you certainly are going to hear more of it! I'm quitting the bank as of right now. But I'm going to start an organizing campaign like you never saw before in this banking organization. And when I'm talking to you over the bargaining table, you'll listen to me then!"

You tell Peggy that you are sorry she feels this way about the new dress standards. You remind her to follow the stated terminating procedure.

Peggy storms out of the office.

Well, it's a relief to be rid of her. Or are you rid of her?

Now turn to p. 27 for a new incident.

When the branch manager asks you to "see what you can do about the dress styles," you try and show him that these are just new styles and that you believe that each person should be able to express his or her personal preference in dress, provided that modesty and good taste are observed. You point to the change in men's styles in the last few years—bolder patterns and colors in suits, shirts, and ties, and to the change in men's hair styles. This attempt really seems to get him excited. He says, "That's just the point! We have a lot of customers who come to us because of their trust in us to safeguard their money. If they walk in here and the place looks like a gathering of hippies, they'll just walk right out again. Our sales *will* go down; I know it and you know it! Why, suppose the district manager should walk in here on a day when the place looks like a costume party is going on. What do you suppose that would do to our futures? Now get something done about it!"

You say, "all right," and he leaves.

Turn to p. 6 and select the action you would take.

11

Action maze on managing change   151

You have asked Peggy to tell you more of her feelings about working at the bank. After mentioning a few more quite negative things, Peggy goes on to describe her frustration about not being able to get an acting job on the stage. The latest blow was being turned down for the lead by an amateur group. This was quite a shock to her, and it made her hopes for a career on the stage pretty dim.

She began to cry toward the end of her comments. You just let her finish. After a few minutes, she says, "Well, I'd better be getting back to work. The rush period is about to begin."

You decide to take no further action at this point. Turn to p. 14.

12

You have decided to appoint a small committee to help you determine the dress standards to be followed. You select two of the senior women, one who is widely respected in the Branch and has six years of service, and a young newcomer.

Five hour-long meetings over the next five weeks bring forth no clear consensus. The senior women think that the idea of standards is a good one, and one of the women keeps pushing for the adoption of standard uniforms, such as a few banks have. A good deal of time is spent on questions of costs, design, suppliers, etc., before the idea is finally dropped.

The woman with six years of service seems to try honestly to reflect the feelings of the rest in the office, which is a very liberal viewpoint and which amounts to having no standards at all. The young newcomer doesn't feel that the dress styles being worn in the office present any problem at all.

After the five meetings, you develop a reasonable set of standards. They are perhaps more liberal than they might have been without the group's advice.

What would your next step most probably be?

A. Discuss the new standards with the small advisory group and, with their acceptance, ask them to spread the word around. *(Turn to p. 9.)*

B. Give each of the employees affected a copy of the draft standards and ask for their comments. *(Turn to p. 8.)*

C. Thank the group for their help and advice. Then post your finished list of dress standards on the bulletin boards. *(Turn to p. 25.)*

D. Discuss the new set of standards at a general meeting of all the employees. *(Turn to p. 4.)*

13

Action maze on managing change

You have decided to take no action at this time.

In a few days, things have settled down again. As you might have hoped, Peggy's militant attitude turned people away from the various causes she was pushing for.

Now turn to p. 27 for the next incident.

14

By taking this attitude in your meeting with all of the women employees, you are really saying, "Don't get me wrong! I'm a good guy. But the managers up there have ordered this, so we will have to obey."

Is this a responsible attitude for a manager to take? We don't think so. Turn back to p. 4 and select a different action.

15

Action maze on managing change

You have said "all right" to the branch manager's request that you "see what you can do about dress standards" in the office. But you have done nothing, thinking that the branch manager would get over his feelings.

A week later, the branch manager approaches you at the end of the work day and says, "I thought you were going to take care of the dress styles in the office! But it seems to be getting worse! Miss Gibson," (one of the black women employees), "had the nerve to wear that African dress today. A dashiki, or whatever you call it. Mrs. Charles Howard, who is an important customer, was in my office today and mentioned it. This has got to stop! And I expect you to see that it does."

Well, doing nothing didn't seem to work. So it is time to take some action.

Turn to p. 6 and select the action you would take.

16

156 Managing changes Chap. 7

You have asked Peggy to come into the conference room. She continues her tirade against the bank management. In her view, the whole management group is old-fashioned, ultraconservative, "stuffed-shirts," anti-union, and chauvinistic, keeping women from being promoted.

Select the response you would probably make and turn to the page indicated.

A. "Peggy, you musn't show feelings like this even if you have them. You have the wrong attitude if you have any hopes of getting ahead in the bank. Now I expect you to show more loyalty and be a cooperative employee. I don't want to hear any more of this kind of talk." *(Turn to p. 10.)*

B. "Peggy, I'm going to have to let you go. You have become a source of dissension with your continual fighting with the bank management and trying to stir up the other employees. I see no other course than to let you go as of right now. I'll arrange for you to turn over your keys and go through the termination procedures at once." *(Turn to p. 5.)*

C. "Go on, tell me more about your feelings about working at the bank, Peggy." *(Turn to p. 12.)*

17

Action maze on managing change

You have delayed the start of the construction of a new drive-in window until the second weekend from now. This will enable you to talk to the employees. How would you go about this?

Select an approach from the choices below and turn to the page indicated.

A. Hold a brief meeting to describe the reason for the changes. Pass out copies of the new floor plan and a brief description of how the new window will be staffed. Then tell the employees that you will be talking with them individually and in small groups over the next few days to get their ideas and find out their feelings toward the changes. *(Turn to p. 41.)*

B. Hold a brief meeting to describe the reason for the changes. Pass out copies of the new floor plan and a brief description of how the new window will be staffed. Then tell the employees that another meeting will be held next Monday to get their feelings and ideas. Set the two ground rules: (1) there can be no costly changes in the structure of the building, and (2) there will be a drive-in window. *(Turn to p. 31.)*

C. Call a meeting and inform the employees of the changes. Show them the blueprints and describe how the new system will function. Ask for their questions and comments. *(Turn to p. 44.)*

18

You have chosen to make the decision yourself about a reasonable dress standard for those women employees who are in contact with the public. This would seem to be a pretty big undertaking. For instance, would you ban all dress styles not in fashion some years ago? Or, would you go the measurement route—specifying how long or short clothing must be? Or, would you specify only general standards, e.g., "acceptable day-time business wear."

Almost any decision you might make would seem to risk future problems. But let's assume that you have drawn on "the wisdom of Solomon" and have reached a decision on proper standards. How would you go about introducing your decision?

Select the course you would probably take and turn to the page indicated.

A. Write up the new standards and post them on the two bulletin boards in the office. *(Turn to p. 25.)*

B. Call in the senior employees and discuss the new standards with them. Ask them to spread the word. *(Turn to p. 7.)*

C. Discuss the new standards with those who seem to be the offenders. Do this when they are actually wearing the clothes. *(Turn to p. 30.)*

D. Have a general meeting with the women employees and announce the new dress standards. *(Turn to p. 4.)*

19

When you ask your senior women employees to spread the word around about the new dress standards, two of the three report resistance and ask you to take some other action to ensure compliance. You decide to do nothing and let it blow over. Several days later, the two women again ask that you take some action. They report that they are being subject to more abuse over the new standards. You decide that you should take action of some sort.

Turn to p. 9 and select the course of action you would most likely take.

160 Managing changes

This page was not supposed to be used in this action maze. By turning to this page, therefore, you have indicated that you are not on the right track.

Turn back to your previous page and see what page you should be on.

21

Action maze on managing change 161

You have appointed a committee from among the women employees to draw up the new list of dress standards. The results from their informal meetings are disappointing. In effect, every dress style one could imagine as "accepted street daytime wear" would be acceptable within the bank. You know that the branch manager would not accept this broad standard, so you decide to take another course of action. You thank the committee for their "recommendations" and say that they will be taken into account in the final standards decided upon.

Turn back to p. 6 and decide what other course you would take.

162 Managing changes Chap. 7

All seems quiet for the next several days, and you are relieved to be able to spend less time on the dress standards situation. Then one of your senior women employees says that Peggy is stirring up the other employees about the new standards and is using this as an issue to try to get a "white-collar" union effort going. A check with one of the other girls shows that this is the case. You must decide what, if anything, should be done.

Select the course you would probably take and turn to the page indicated.

A. Do nothing other than inform your branch manager and, if he wishes, the district office. *(Turn to p. 14.)*

B. Issue instructions to have a "pink slip" included with Peggy's paycheck, telling her that her services will no longer be needed after that day. Make arrangements for a cash audit, key clearance, and other termination procedures. *(Turn to p. 5.)*

C. Call Peggy in for a talk. *(Turn to p. 17.)*

23

Action maze on managing change

You ask Mrs. Grimes (loans) and Miss Tarbok (exchange teller) to come into the conference room for a talk. Both are visibly upset, with Mrs. Grimes still fighting back tears. They point out that both of them need desks to work on in order to handle customers properly. They show you a place on the blueprint between the conference room and the storeroom where their desks could be placed. (See the place marked "X" on p. 28.)

You feel that they really don't need desks, especially Miss Tarbok. And the place they point out is really too small. After all, they were at teller windows before they were moved to make room for some new tellers.

Of the responses listed below, choose the one you would probably make and turn to the page indicated.

A. Tell them that there really isn't enough space to fit two desks in there comfortably and that there isn't a pressing need for them to have desks. Ask them to give the new arrangement a try. *(Turn to p. 37.)*

B. Ask them to go on and tell you more about their feelings about the change in office layout. *(Turn to p. 26.)*

C. Tell them that they are both acting very unbusinesslike, but that you are willing to overlook it, provided they go back to work and try harder to be more cooperative. *(Turn to p. 46.)*

24

Managing changes

You have decided on reasonable dress standards and have posted a notice describing them on the two bulletin boards in the office. When the notices first went up, there was a flurry of activity around them, but this quickly died down.

Two employees have come to you to ask if this meant that they would be required to buy a new wardrobe. You tell them that this isn't expected, that you are sure that they have clothes which are well within the standards, and that hereafter their new clothes might be bought with these standards in mind.

One situation you have noticed following the change is that the women employees are calling in to report illness more often—so often, in fact, that this is creating a problem in staffing the teller windows, even with temporary on-call help. This creates long lines during rush periods and more complaints from customers than usual.

One week after the notice was posted, you are approached by four of the women employees. Their spokesman seems to be a girl named "Peggy," who you have heard is active in "women's lib" and who has a boyfriend who is active in "white collar" union organizing activities.

Peggy says, "We have been asked to speak for all the women about the arbitrary, new standards you stuck up on the board without any warning or explanation or consideration of our views. We would like to ask that you reconsider your decision and accept the decision of a committee made up of the people affected."

Select the course you would probably take and turn to the page indicated.

A. Tell the girls that this was a management decision made with the best interests of the employees and customers in mind and that the decision will stand. *(Turn to p. 23.)*

B. Tell the girls that you will reconsider the decision and will be glad to have a group of those affected advise you. You will select the group and will make the final decision, however. *(Turn to p. 13.)*

C. Tell the girls that you will reconsider the decision and will be happy to have a group of them make the decision. *(Turn to p. 22.)*

25

Action maze on managing change 165

You have asked Mrs. Grimes and Miss Tarbok to tell you more about their feelings about the change. For a few minutes they continue talking about their need for desks, how customers would be inconvenienced, and that sales would fall off because of the poor service, etc.

After a few moments' pause, Mrs. Grimes says, "I guess another big problem with the change is that we feel that we have been demoted by going back to the teller windows. At the desks we were just a bit better than the others. And sometimes we let them know it. Now we have to go back and 'eat our words.' But I guess we are big enough to handle ourselves under these conditions. What do you think, Mary?" Mary (Miss Tarbok) agrees. You suggest that a desk be moved to the area they suggested, for use by either of them when the need arises, but that normally they will work at the teller window. They both seem very grateful for the offer and go back to work in much better spirits. You make arrangements for one of the vacated desks to be moved to the area.

Now turn to p. 39.

26

Ever since you arrived at this larger branch, it has been obvious to you that one way to increase service (and sales) is by having a drive-in window for customers. Your formal proposal for one was approved by the branch manager and has just been approved by the district office. The blueprints were drawn up, and the contractor was selected by the district office. The contractor has assured you that the work can be done in one weekend, and he is free both this weekend and the next. (There is to be little structural change, since an existing window will be used.)

This new plan will require that the line of teller windows be repositioned and that the loan teller and the exchange teller be moved to teller windows. (They had been moved to desks several years ago to make room for more regular tellers.) See the diagram on p. 28.

As you have reflected on the new arrangement, you have decided that the fairest course would be to have the drive-in window staffed through rotation by the regular tellers, with a new one going to the window each time the signal bell rings. This would spread the extra walking and extra work fairly.

The teller staffing the drive-in window would carry the slips and cash back to her regularly assigned window, go through the necessary accounting procedures, and return to the drive-in window to complete the transaction. The loan and exchange tellers would not take their turn at the drive-in window, since their jobs are specialized. (They both had been regular tellers before "graduating" to the more complicated jobs, so they could take over if really needed.)

Please turn to the next page (p. 28).

27

Action maze on managing change   167

You have spent many night and weekend hours in designing the new office layout. The diagram below shows what the final product will look like.

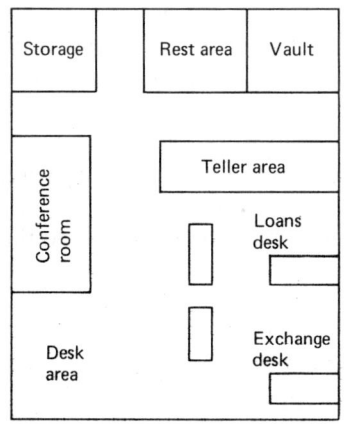

```
┌─────────┬──────────┬──────┐   ┌─────────┬──────────┬──────┐
│ Storage │ Rest area│Vault │   │ Storage │ Rest area│Vault │
├─────────┼──────────┴──────┤   ├─────────┤ X               │
│         │                 │   │         │                 │
│ Conf.   │    Teller area  │   │ Conf.   │    ┌────────┐   │
│ room    │    ┌─────┐      │   │ room    │    │ Teller │   │
│         │    │Loans│      │   │         │    │  area  │   │
│         │    │ desk│      │   │         │    │        │   │
│         │    └─────┘      │   │         │    └────────┘   │
│         │    ┌─────┐      │   │         │                 │
│ Desk    │    │Exch.│      │   │ Desk    │                 │
│ area    │    │ desk│      │   │ area    │                 │
└─────────┴────┴─────┴──────┘   └─────────┴─────────────────┘
      Old arrangement                  New arrangement
```

It looks as if everything is ready to go. Look over the various actions listed below and decide which one you would most probably take. Then turn to the page indicated.

A. Call the contractor and arrange for completion of the work this weekend. Arrange for security guards to be present. Mention to the employees that you will have a surprise for them on Monday.   *(Turn to p. 38.)*

B. Call the contractor and tell him to go ahead this weekend. Make security arrangements. Call a meeting and inform the employees of the changes. Show them the blueprints and describe how the new system will function.   *(Turn to p. 33.)*

C. Call the contractor and ask him to schedule the work for the weekend after next so that you can talk to the employees and make the arrangements beforehand.   *(Turn to p. 18.)*

28

You have called a meeting about the new dress standards. You have passed out a listing of them and have given the people a chance to read the new standards. When you ask whether anyone has any questions, no one says anything for about 30 seconds, and then a girl named Peggy speaks up. (Peggy is active in "woman's lib" and has a boyfriend who is active in organizing white-collar unions.) Peggy says, "Yes, I have a question. How do you expect us to hold still for such a childish list of rules? We are adults, after all, although I think that this has been overlooked. The people we come to work with, have lunch with, and ride home with all can wear modern dress. But in your arbitrary way, you say we can't. This just isn't fair!"

Select the response below which you would probably make and turn to the page indicated.

A. Explain the importance of presenting a good public "image," because a bank's relationships are built on trust. Otherwise, ignore the comment. Ask if there are any other questions. When all questions have been answered, you dismiss the meeting. (*Turn to p.* 23.)

B. Ask Peggy to come into the conference room as soon as the meeting is over. State the necessity for such guidelines in a banking office. (*Turn to p.* 17.)

29

Action maze on managing change

Rather than making a general announcement of the new dress standards, you have decided to discuss them privately with those individuals who present problems in their dress. In the next few days, you talk to three such people. The first, a new young girl, says that she didn't know anything about any policy in this regard and that she patterned her dress styles after those of the other women in the office. She agrees to "see if she can dress a little more conservatively" in the future if this is what is required to keep her job. (You meant no threats and were a little surprised to have her take your remarks this way.)

The second woman began crying as soon as you brought the matter up. She said that she was a widow and was trying to put her only son through college on the limited bank salary she earned. She made most of her own clothes, but had purchased three new outfits with her savings. All three outfits were supposed to be "in the latest style," and she had thought they would be appreciated at the bank. Because she had been quite tearful throughout the interview, you ended the discussion by saying, "Let's talk about it later."

The third interview was something else; it was with Peggy, who was active in "women's lib" and whose boyfriend was active as an organizer for "white-collar" unions. From the beginning of your conversation, she was aggressive, accusing the bank management of having a double standard, allowing the new styles with the male employees (bright clothes, sideburns, face hair, etc.), but picking on the women. She heatedly accused the bank management of being "male chauvinists."

Peggy didn't listen to your explanations or arguments, but kept repeating how unfair the new policy was. As you were getting nowhere with the discussion, you ended it. Peggy's last remark was, "You haven't heard the last of this."

Turn to p. 23 for the next installment.

30

You arrange to discuss the feelings and ideas about the change at a meeting of all employees. When they really accept the fact that their ideas and wishes are wanted and needed to make the change work, the discussion becomes quite lively. The suggestion on staffing the drive-in window for a whole week by one girl is quickly accepted, as is the idea of a contest for the best way to publicize the new drive-in window service.

One idea, for having a "courtesy queue" (to prevent long lines at any one window), gets a lot of discussion, since several of the girls say that they have certain customers who always go to them. With the further suggestion that a sign "If you would like to see a particular teller, wait at the head of the line until she is free" be added to the posted instructions, this idea is adopted.

At your suggestion, the proposal to have everyone learn to handle loans and exchange is tabled for further study.

One idea that came up was to have a permanent committee with rotating members for "customer service improvement." This idea is accepted by acclaim.

Mrs. Grimes and Miss Tarbok ask that a desk be made available for their use when talking with customers. The group agreed that this was reasonable, since the nature of the service they provided was different. You had said that you would see if this couldn't be arranged.

You felt that the meeting was a success and that all would support the change and make it work. You tell the contractor to begin work on the coming weekend.

Please turn to p. 39.

31

Action maze on managing change

After telling Mrs. Grimes and Miss Tarbok how indispensable they are and how you are counting on them, Mrs. Grimes says, "What you *say* sounds good, but it doesn't match the way we are treated! After all of these years of good service, we were rewarded by being demoted. We both need desks to give proper service to customers."

Of the responses listed, select the one you would most probably take and turn to the page indicated.

A. Tell them that there isn't enough space to install the desks where they want them. Ask the two women to give the new arrangement a try. *(Turn to p. 37.)*

B. Ask them to go on and tell you more about their feelings about the changed arrangements. *(Turn to p. 26.)*

C. Tell them that they are acting very, very unbusinesslike, but that you will overlook it if they go back to their jobs and try harder. *(Turn to p. 46.)*

172 Managing changes   Chap. 7

You have made arrangements to have the contractor go ahead this coming weekend. You have called a meeting to describe the changes in the branch office.

Of the approaches listed below, which one represents the one you would most probably take during the meeting? After making your selection, turn to the page indicated.

- A. You describe the changes and indicate by pointing and moving to the area exactly where the new teller windows, drive-in window, etc., will be. Stress that the change will take a little getting used to, but that it will increase service (and sales over a period of time). *(Turn to p. 42.)*

- B. State that you know there is always a resistance to change and that this is to be expected, but that this move will increase job security in the long run. Ask for an expression of feelings and ideas about the change. *(Turn to p. 36.)*

- C. First describe the importance of keeping the leadership with the increased competition from other banks. Next, describe the convenience of having a drive-in window. Then show them the blueprints and stress that these are tentative plans which can be changed if better ideas are submitted. *(Turn to p. 44.)*

33

Action maze on managing change

The contractor completed the work in one weekend, as he had promised. On Monday morning, the employees' reaction to the new arrangements seemed to be mixed. Some were quiet about the change; others voiced their opinions that the new arrangements were unworkable. Some of these comments were subtle ("I was just getting used to the old way."), and some were quite open ("It will never work!").

The most visibly upset employees were Mrs. Grimes and Miss Tarbok, who handle the loans and exchanges, respectively. You had told them to leave their desks in the open area so that they could switch the materials to their new teller windows. Miss Tarbok (who is in her early fifties) showed signs of weeping, and frequently went to the rest area while making the change-over. Mrs. Grimes reacted to the good-natured banter of the others with some hostility. You infer that those who were quiet about the change are either in favor of it or indifferent. Since these people were in the majority, you decide to ignore the other few.

Miss Tarbok and Mrs. Grimes may present another case, however. What, if anything, would you do about them?

Select the choice below which you would probably take and turn to the page indicated.

A. Ask the two women to come into the conference room for a talk. *(Turn to p. 24.)*

B. Tell them that they should give the new arrangement a try to see if it isn't workable. *(Turn to p. 37.)*

C. Ignore their feelings toward the change. They will get over it. *(Turn to p. 43.)*

Both Mrs. Grimes and Miss Tarbok react to your comments in the same way. They announce that they are quitting as of this moment. They say that they will arrange to balance their work and turn in their keys, but that is *all!*

You try to persuade them to change their minds, saying that you didn't mean your comments the way they have taken them. Mrs. Grimes says, "There was only one way to take your statements, and you ought to be ashamed to reward long service and hard work in this way. Life is too short to work in a place like this. But you may be sure that the district office and the home office will be informed about the way you treat people."

With that, they both leave.

This leaves you with a problem. You have got to find someone who can take over loans and exchange in a hurry. But you did the best you could. After all, everyone knows that "people resist change."

Now turn to p. 188.

35

Action maze on managing change

At your meeting the employees seem reluctant to express their feelings and ideas about the change in office layout. You stress the fact that management wants their ideas, but they are not forthcoming. What would you do now?

Select a course of action from the alternatives below and turn to the page indicated.

A. Give each employee a copy of the new layout and say that you will be talking with them individually and in small groups. *(Turn to p. 41.)*

B. Encourage them to give their ideas for the success of the new arrangement and better service for customers. *(Turn to p. 44.)*

C. Say, "Don't you have any ideas? If so, speak out. Now is your chance to be heard." *(Turn to p. 42.)*

176   Managing changes Chap. 7

You have suggested that Mrs. Grimes and Miss Tarbok give the new arrangement a try. Mrs. Grimes says, "All right, but it isn't going to work." They then return to the job of changing from their desks to teller windows.

Two weeks after your talk with them, Mrs. Grimes asks the branch manager for a transfer to another branch within the system. Miss Tarbok begins to be absent from work frequently. A month later she resigns.

Well, you have handled the problem with the two women, haven't you? Now turn to p. 47.

37

Action maze on managing change

The contractor completed the work in one weekend, as he had promised. On Monday morning, the reaction by the employees to the new office layout was mixed, but generally unfavorable. Not a great deal was said to you openly, but you overheard comments such as "I was just getting used to the old arrangement" and "It will never work."

Particularly confusing was the plan for staffing the new window. On the few occasions when a car did appear at the drive-in window, there seemed to be arguments about "whose turn it was." The tellers pointed out that when the new window was busy, so were the teller windows inside. This system had to be changed somehow.

Friction seemed to be arising with Mrs. Grimes (loans) and Miss Tarbok (exchange teller), who had rejoined the teller window line. Mrs. Grimes seemed to be taking a lot of time off, and Miss Tarbok seemed to be showing quite a bit of hostility toward the tellers. This hostility was mutual.

In short, the change has resulted in much resistance. You notice that the error rate is up, and there are greater numbers of complaints from customers than usual. Each night several of the tellers are staying late in order to reach a balance of their accounting transactions made during the day. This is unusual. You hope that the resistance by most will go away with the passage of time. But something probably should be done about Mrs. Grimes and Miss Tarbok.

Select the action choice below which you would probably take and turn to the page indicated.

A. Ignore their feelings toward the change. They will get over them as time passes. *(Turn to p. 43.)*

B. Ask the two women to come into the conference room for a talk. *(Turn to p. 24.)*

C. Tell them that they should give the new arrangement a try to see if it isn't workable. *(Turn to p. 37.)*

178   Managing changes   Chap. 7

When the employees came to work on Monday, the change of the office layout had been completed. There was a good spirit in the air as the tellers arranged their new workplaces. Mrs. Grimes and Miss Tarbok adjusted well to the new arrangement and were mixing in well with the other tellers. You overheard two of the tellers explaining the changes to customers and stressing how the customers would be better served by the new arrangement. Your impression is that this explanation was common whenever a customer commented on the change. As the week progressed, more and more customers were using the drive-in teller window, and the arrangement was working well.

Turn to p. 48.

39

Please turn to p. 38.

180 Managing changes   Chap. 7

During the next few days, you talk with the employees individually and in small groups. With two exceptions, the feelings about the change in the office lay-out are favorable and seem to be accepted as necessary. The two exceptions are Mrs. Grimes (loans) and Miss Tarbok (exchange teller). Both pointed out that they needed desks in order to handle customers properly. But after all, they were both at teller windows before they were moved to desks to make room for additional tellers. Therefore, you don't pay too much attention to their views.

The other employees advanced a number of good ideas, such as:

1. Have the teller windows roped off and "fed" by use of a courtesy queue away from the teller windows where a person would stand until a window was free. He would then go to the free window. This would get away from making customers pick a line at the windows without their knowing how long the transaction ahead of them would take.
2. Have everyone trained to handle loans and exchange.
3. Have a contest for the best way to publicize the new drive-in window.
4. Assign the new window to one girl for a whole week; this would avoid continual decision-making about whose turn it is. The person assigned to the window would make her own arrangements for coverage at breaks, etc.

What will you do with these ideas? Select the course of action you would most probably take and turn to the page indicated.

A. Adopt those that seem feasible and make them a part of the planned changes.   *(Turn to p. 38.)*

B. Present the suggestions to a meeting of all the employees.   *(Turn to p. 31.)*

C. Do nothing about these suggestions for changes at this time, because they don't involve the contractor.   *(Turn to p. 40.)*

Action maze on managing change 181

In a meeting, you have described the changes to be made with the installation of a drive-in window. The questions and comments from the group deal almost entirely with the staffing of the new window. You explain your system of taking turns in staffing the window, but this doesn't seem to be accepted too well.

Anyway, you have had the meeting to head off any potential opposition. So now the contractor may proceed.

Turn to p. 38.

42

The friction between Mrs. Grimes and Miss Tarbok on one side and the tellers on the other seems to be growing worse instead of better. It has reached the point where it is beginning to be noticed by a few customers. It is clearly time to have a talk with them. You ask Mrs. Grimes and Miss Tarbok into the conference room for a talk.

Of the approaches listed below, which one would you probably take? Then turn to the page indicated.

A. Tell them that they are behaving in a very unbusinesslike way and that you expect more from them because of their greater experience and maturity. Tell them that you simply will not have them acting as they are and that you will take further action if they don't stop it at once. *(Turn to p. 35.)*

B. Ask them to describe their feelings with the new change in office layout. *(Turn to p. 26.)*

C. Encourage them to try and do better. Tell them that you are counting on their cooperation to make the new change work, because they are both indispensable to the smooth working of the office. *(Turn to p. 32.)*

43

Action maze on managing change

You have called a meeting to discuss the new changes with the addition of a drive-in window. You have shown them the new blueprints and have stressed that these plans are tentative—they can be changed if there are better ideas. Well, the new ideas start coming thick and fast! One proposes expansion of the rest area; another proposes an expansion of the building itself. Another proposes a change in location altogether! These suggestions are not feasible.

There is some discussion about the staffing of the drive-in window, but you point out that this isn't a structural change, so this should be put off for a later decision.

None of the proposed changes was better than the plan you came up with, but since you let them in on the decision, you must provide some kind of response.

Of the choices listed below, select the one you would probably take; then turn to the page indicated.

A. Explain that, if the branch manager approves, you will send the suggestions to the district office. *(Turn to p. 45.)*

B. Explain that the suggestions made are not feasible and that, unless there are strong feelings on any of them, you will go ahead on the original plan. *(Turn to p. 38.)*

C. Tell them that their ideas will be considered in the final plan. Then tell the contractor to go ahead with the original plans. *(Turn to p. 40.)*

You have told the group that if the branch manager approves, you will send their suggestions to the district office. When you take them in, the branch manager says, "I see nothing here that beats your original plan. Most of the ideas would call for getting capital assets approval, and this would be next to impossible right now, even if the ideas were good. Go ahead with your original plans."

You explain informally to the employees that the ideas are not feasible at this time and that you have told the contractor to proceed.

Turn to p. 38.

45

Action maze on managing change 185

You have told Mrs. Grimes and Miss Tarbok that they were acting very unbusinesslike, but that you would overlook their behavior if they went back to work and tried harder. They leave.

Later in the day you notice that Mrs. Grimes is not at work. Miss Tarbok tells you that Mrs. Grimes had a sick headache and had to go home. Several days later, Mrs. Grimes asks the branch manager to arrange for a transfer "for personal reasons" to another branch within the system.

Miss Tarbok, too, begins to have a problem—frequent absences. A month later, she resigns.

Well, you have handled the problem with the two women, haven't you?
Now turn to p. 188.

46

You have decided to let the passage of time heal the wounds caused by the change in office layout. And I guess that the wounds are healed, in a way.

Three weeks after the change, Miss Tarbok and a teller have resigned, and Mrs. Grimes has transferred to another branch. The numbers of complaints from customers are declining somewhat. But there are still a high number of errors in the accounting procedures.

But after all, everyone knows that "people resist change."

Now turn to p. 188.

47

Over the next few days and weeks, things settle down within the office. The change in office layout is working well, and many customers have spoken favorably of the new drive-in service. The "customer service committee" has been functioning well, and many suggestions have been passed on to you. Most were very good ideas and have been adopted.

Mrs. Grimes and Miss Tarbok feel very positive about the new arrangement. They do make occasional use of the desk reserved for them and seem to feel that this is a real mark of status, but that it is also based on a real need. They have even suggested that they begin teaching the tellers about loans and exchange!

Now turn to the following page.

48

188   Managing changes   Chap. 7

ANALYSIS OF YOUR ACTION MAZE ACTIVITY

In the exercise at the beginning of the chapter, in which you reacted to changes that might be imposed on *you*, we tried to structure your responses on the basis of the several factors that influence a person's feelings toward change. These factors are:

1. The extent of information one has about the change
2. The extent of one's participation in the change decision
3. One's trust in the initiator of the change
4. One's past experience with change
5. The perceived social impact of the change
6. Individual personality

The first three of these factors are controlled largely by your actions; the last three may be outside of your control, but must be taken into account when you manage change.

Each of the numbered statements that follow is one of the six factors that influence the way in which a person reacts to change, as we have discussed. Below them, in two columns, I have listed the pages and choices you might have selected. Refer back to the "Page and Choice Record Sheet," on which you recorded the pages you turned to and the choices you made, and circle those you selected below. This will help you to analyze whether you were providing complete or limited information, getting full or limited participation, and acting in ways which produced or limited trust. (You had no direct control over the last three factors, but their positive and negative influences built into the maze are indicated for each.)

1. *Extent of information about the change* (real two-way communication, the need for the change, the benefits, effects on duties and working relationships, concern with how subordinates feel about the change, what to do if and when problems arise, etc.).

Complete information		*Limited information*	
Page	Choice	Page	Choice
4	C	4	A, B
9	C	9	A, B, D
13	B, D	13	A, C
18	A, B, C	19	A, B, C
19	D	28	A
28	B, C		
33	A, C		

2. *Participation in the change decision* (desire to get real participation—not lip service, i.e., not a "feeling of participation" without the substance, the level of contributions by the group, what was done with their suggestions, etc.; this may be done through representatives).

Full participation		*Limited participation*	
Page	Choice	Page	Choice
6	B, C	6	A
25	B, C	22	
31		25	A
36	A, B	36	C
41	B	41	A, C
		44	A, B, C

3. *Trust in initiator* (behavior tells others that he has their best interests in mind—not looking out for his own needs only—he won't "put you down," he perceives conditions which will have an impact on other people, is concerned with how change will affect others, deals with feelings as feelings—not with logic, etc.).

Trust-producing behavior				*Trust-limiting behavior*	
Page	Choice	Page	Choice	Page	Choice
4	C	28	C	8	A, B
6	B, C	32	B	17	A, B, C
9	C	33	B	23	B
13	D	36	A, B	24	A, C
17	C	41	B	29	A
18	B, C	43	B	32	A, C
19	D			34	B, C
24	B			38	A, C
25	B, C			43	A, C

4. *Past experience with change* (good or bad memories of changes of this sort, what impact the change had on them and their objectives, etc.).

Positive

Only the assistant manager's experience with change is given as a positive experience (drive-in window issue).

Negative

None are explicitly given, but we should know that they are present. A change from the normal routine brings ambiguity and causes extra energy to be expended until the change becomes routine.

5. *Perceived impact on social group or on the social role one fulfills* (change in formal or informal organization of the group and roles performed, gain or loss seen in status by the persons affected by the change, etc.).

Positive   *Negative*

Page   Page
31   26
39   32
48   41

6. *Individual personalities* (early learned assumptions about what one or another type of treatment by the world "out there" means to one's self, status, progress, etc.). A change may "trigger" behavior which might not otherwise arise.

Positive

As far as we can tell, the Bank personnel are well adjusted.

Negative

Peggy's natural aggressive behavior becomes a problem when the change in dress standards is announced. In part, her aggression is caused by her frustrations over not getting the career she wants (p. 12).

Mrs. Grimes and Miss Tarbok seem to need a great amount of support and reassurance about their status. Their previous actions toward the other tellers may play a large part in their feelings toward the change (p. 26).

Now that you have circled the pages you turned to and the choices you made, look over the resulting "profile." Were some of the first three factors (information given, participation, trust) handled particularly well? Were there some that weren't? This analysis should give you some insight into how you handle a change now.

Responses to Change in the Action Maze

After a person has evaluated the meaning a change has for him, the change is reacted to. (This reaction may occur in an instant, may come about after the person has thought about it, or may quietly build up to a large problem caused by many small reactions.) These reactions may be pictured on a scale, with acceptance at one end and resistance at the other end. (See scale on p. 191.)

Analysis of your action maze activity

Acceptance   *Resistance*

Join in	Support	Accept	Tolerate	Resist	Oppose

I have tried to have the reaction of the people involved in the bank changes reflect the degrees on this scale when (and if) you turned to these pages:

Join in—p. 48
Support—pp. 31, 39
Accept (most)—pp. 8, 41
Tolerate—pp. 34, 41, 47
Resist—pp. 9, 20, 25, 34, 37, 39, 43
Oppose (Peggy)—pp. 10, 17, 23, 29, 30, 35

In this way, you were supposed to meet with different reactions to your plans, depending on the path you took.

The manager's job in managing change is to make an analysis of the factors that will influence the evaluation of the change made by those affected. The plans made and action selected will play a large part in the reaction received. Therefore, it seems likely that the change will be most successful if people react to the change by wholeheartedly joining in, supporting, or at least accepting it.

A Note on the Action Maze

Earlier, we noted that the *total number* of pages you turned to had little to do with a satisfactory solution to the problems faced. You might have turned to as few as 12 pages (2, 6, 13, 8, 17, 12, 14, 27–28, 38, 31, 39) to have handled both issues satisfactorily. On the other hand, the selection of a particular set of 11 pages (2, 6, 19, 25, 23, 5, 27–28, 38, 43, and 35) would not have resolved either situation very well. Many other paths could have been taken, also.

There were quite a few alternative endings built into the maze. In the first situation (dress standards), for example, the alternative endings were:

Peggy is fired (p. 5)
Peggy quits with threat (p. 10)
Peggy settles down (p. 14)
Group tolerates change (p. 14)

The alternatives for the second situation (office layout) were:

Mrs. Grimes and Miss Tarbok quit (p. 46)
Mrs. Grimes transfers; Miss Tarbok and another teller quit; complaints and errors high (p. 47)
Change resisted (p. 38)
Change tolerated with exceptions (p. 34)
Good adjustment, high spirits (p. 39)
Change well accepted (p. 48)

Thus, as in "real life," the ending depended in large part on your actions.

192 Managing changes Chap. 7

Now let's apply these ideas to real changes in which you are involved.

PLANNING FOR YOUR CHANGES

Every manager has to spend a great deal of time in planning and carrying out changes. These may be large changes, but usually they are small ones. Select a change that you are thinking about making. Then analyze its impact on people by using the checklist that follows. (If some of the items don't apply, disregard them. If you think of more items, add them.) Above all, be honest with yourself in your evaluations.

1. The change selected for analysis: _____

   _____

   (This can be a change in product, the allocations of resources, organizations or locations, routines, methods, or systems, machinery or equipment, etc.)

2. *Who will be affected by the change?* (Employees, customers, suppliers, upper levels, interfacing groups, the public, etc. How much will each group be affected? What is the best that could happen? What is the worst? Etc.)

   _____

   _____

   _____

   _____

   _____

3. *Extent of information about the change?* (Can we give full information? Do we want to? Why or why not? What will limit the information we can give? What do they know or suspect now? What background is needed to understand the change? Can we face up to the disadvantages, or do we have to gloss over them? If we don't communicate, what will that in itself communicate? Etc.)

   _____

   _____

   _____

   _____

   _____

4. *Participation in the change decision?* (Do we really want participation in the change decision? If so, why? If not, why not? What do we stand to lose? To gain? Could we get participation in the basic decision? In the implementing decisions? Are we skilled enough to get participation? Are we trying to make it look like their decision when it really isn't? Etc.)

___

5. *Trust in the initiator?* (Who will be seen as the initiator? What is his "internal credit rating," or trust level? Would our channels be believed? What is our track record for being honest? For giving *all* the facts? Etc.)

___

6. *What past experience have they had with change?* (How have similar or related events impacted them? What memories will we be bringing back? Will we be stirring up good feelings or bad feelings? Etc.)

___

7. *How will the change affect the social groups involved in the change?* (What will be the favorable impacts? The unfavorable? How will it affect existing social groupings? How will new people be introduced, or new associations change the existing social arrangements? Etc.)

8. *How will the change affect individual personalities?* (How will most of the people affected react to the change? Who is likely to quit over the change? Who is likely to take this up as a "cause"? Who won't care? Why? Etc.)

9. *How can we test the assumptions we have made above?* (What is our "confidence level" about them? Which are key assumptions which if wrong will make us *very* wrong? Etc.)

10. What do your answers to the questions above tell you about your attitudes? (Consider your attitudes toward sharing information, getting participation, building a climate of trust, perceiving other's points of view, etc. Do you want to make any changes here?)

What we wish to avoid are unexpected reactions to a change we make. If this occurs, our analysis wasn't good enough.

CHAPTER 8

GROUPS AT WORK

A manager forms or is given a group through which to accomplish certain goals. Other groups to which he belongs also take a lot of time and are an important part of his organizational life. Because of their own needs and personalities, people bring to the work group different preferred ways of behaving. Each group will be different, depending on the "mix" of the people. This is true for long-term groups, such as work groups, and for short-term groups, such as ones formed for a special purpose.

The interactions of the people in the work group will help determine how and often how much work gets done. Some of the people will help the group come together as a group. Others will tell a joke at the right time in order to relieve tensions. Still others will help the group become involved in the task and come up with a better product. These interactions can be better understood if the manager has a greater awareness of the makeup of groups and their functioning.

First, let's look at groups and their functioning. To do so, let's talk primarily about meetings, since here individuals come together to perform some specific task. This will enable us to more clearly see groups at work. This same type of behavior takes place in any work group.

ALL I NEED IS ANOTHER MEETING

Sound familiar? This is how many of us feel. But today's organizations depend on meetings for many, many purposes—reaching a consensus, solving problems, making decisions, coordinating activities, and getting and giving information, to name a few.

Here is how a meeting might go:

> Harry Booth decides to call a meeting of people in the organization who will be affected by an unexpected announcement that a competitor is lowering prices "across the board" on his products. Harry asks his secretary to phone "the guys from accounting, advertising, cost control, and some-

one from the manager of manufacturing's office, and stress the importance of their being there or being represented at this meeting. And, oh yes, better have someone from the general manager's staff. And someone from market research.''

The next day, 20 minutes after the announced starting time, Harry says, ''Well, we might as well get started. I had expected a few more people, but perhaps they will join us when they can. I guess you all know why we are calling this meeting.'' Harry goes on to stress the importance of the decisions to be made in the meeting. At this point, Pete Yeager from the manufacturing manager's office says, ''Now wait a minute. I don't have any power to commit manufacturing to a course of action decided on here.'' Bill Young says that he doesn't either.

''Well,'' Harry says, ''we can at least air the implications to our organization of this price change and see what needs to be decided. Then we can ask for a firm decision at a later meeting.''

The meeting gets under way and lasts two hours. This was a half hour longer than Harry had told people it would be. Almost no decisions are made, although a few interim assignments were given.

Afterwards, Harry said, ''It was a good meeting. Sure, there was a lot of joking and laughing, but I think a relaxed atmosphere is best. No, we didn't get a lot accomplished, but first meetings are often like that. After all, you've got to start somewhere.''

One member of the group attending the meeting seemed to sum up the feelings of the others when he said, ''What a waste of time!''

I know you have never run a meeting like this, but have you ever attended one? Let's look at another example.

Jim Farrell prides himself on running a ''no-nonsense'' meeting. He gives participants plenty of advance notice and expects those invited to be there. He begins promptly on time. He follows his agenda strictly, and everybody has a copy of it. In an effort to be fair when differences arise, and to ''nail down'' the decisions agreed to, he uses *Roberts Rules of Order*. He publishes minutes of the meeting to announce decisions made by the group and to follow up on assignments.

Jim admits that sometimes he ''pushes'' the group to make a decision by the stated time of adjournment, but feels that this is necessary. He takes pride in using his leadership skills to keep the meeting ''on the track.'' ''If I didn't,'' Jim says, ''the group would be all over the place, talking about things that have nothing to do with the topic. People have to 'check their emotions at the door' when they come to my meetings.''

Let's follow two participants down the hall after one of Jim's meetings. One says to the other, ''Jim's crazy if he thinks most of those decisions will work. I suppose everyone voted for the same reason I did—just to get the meeting over." "Yeah," says the other, "just wait until Charlie Burns hears about the one on new billings. Then you'll really see the stuff hit the fan. What a waste of time."

I know you have never run a meeting like this one, either. But have you ever attended one?

LET'S LOOK AT YOUR BEHAVIOR IN MEETINGS

In beginning to talk about meetings, let's do something unusual—let's begin by looking at your behavior as a member of a group meeting. Let's do this by first having you fill out a questionnaire. Then, we will discuss just what we are up to in asking that you answer it.

QUESTIONNAIRE

How Would You Respond?

Introduction

In the typical meeting within an organization, the power and authority relationships among those present may inhibit the feelings expressed by members of the group and obscure clues to behavior we might otherwise notice. Yet, feelings and behavior need to be understood if you are to better understand the group's functioning.

Let's make this meeting one of a problem-solving, decision-making task force made up of people from many parts of the organization. Let's say that the group has a nominal leader who sets and convenes the meetings and gets out minutes (of sorts), which record agreements reached at the last meeting and note interim work to be done. But the expectations are that the group will govern itself. Here, you will consider yourself as a *member* of the group.

The 20 response situations given below use 20 names of people, and a group this large might not really work too effectively. But the different names are used to lessen the influences which might arise when we use names of real people you might know.

Instructions

In each situation given below, check the *two* responses of the five given which you would most likely make as a group *member*. Just place a check mark by the two. There are no "right" or "wrong" responses, so select whichever two appeal to you most "off the top of your head." Your honest responses may give you some insights into your activity in working with groups.

Work rapidly in making and marking the two responses you choose. Do not go back and change your first answer. This is "forced choice," so you *must* select *two* of the five responses.

1. When Bill started to "clown around" in the meeting, I
    _____a) wished the leader would stop him
    _____b) encouraged him
    _____c) tried to get on with the topic
    _____d) expressed my annoyance
    _____e) felt like being a clown myself

2. When Alice said, "I don't see that we are getting anywhere in this meeting," I
    _____a) summarized what I thought we were accomplishing
    _____b) thought the leader should respond to her
    _____c) told a joke her remark reminded me of
    _____d) said that she hadn't been paying attention
    _____e) told her I felt the same way

3. When Dick started to criticize Mary's remark, I
    _____a) said, "Let's give her a chance to explain it"
    _____b) said, "At least *she* is trying to be helpful"
    _____c) said that I like her idea
    _____d) suggested a break to "cool off" the discussion
    _____e) wished that the leader would say something

4. When Charlie said that he liked my idea very much I
    _____a) said, "Let's examine it to see if it will work"
    _____b) felt very warm toward him
    _____c) made a "flip" remark
    _____d) asked the leader how he liked it
    _____e) told him that he seemed to like everything that was said

5. When Pete said, "The leader should keep us on the track," I
    _____a) said that I could see why he would feel that way
    _____b) told Pete that he would help us if he would share some of the responsibility for this
    _____c) suggested that we stop for coffee
    _____d) felt the same way
    _____e) told him that this wasn't necessary

6. When Alan asked the leader what his ideas were, I
    _____a) was glad he did
    _____b) told him to stand on his own feet
    _____c) listened to see what the leader had to add
    _____d) said, "That's a good idea, Alan"
    _____e) changed the subject

Let's look at your behavior in meetings

7. When Howard told a funny story, I
   - ____a) told one, too
   - ____b) said, "Let's get back to work"
   - ____c) laughed and encouraged him
   - ____d) told him to be quiet
   - ____e) wished that the leader would stop him

8. When Paul agreed with Fred, I
   - ____a) agreed with him, too
   - ____b) said his remark was out of order
   - ____c) asked Fred to repeat his idea
   - ____d) told them to break up the mutual admiration society
   - ____e) began to think of other work I was supposed to be doing

9. When Betty called Peg's idea stupid, I
   - ____a) agreed with Betty
   - ____b) told Betty to act like an adult
   - ____c) hoped that the leader would say something
   - ____d) said, "Let's talk about the idea further"
   - ____e) started to have a quiet conversation with Bill about another matter

10. When Ed proposed a new tack, I
    - ____a) said, "Let's try it"
    - ____b) asked the leader if he thought this was a good idea
    - ____c) told Ed that he was making a real contribution
    - ____d) said, "You're changing the subject again!"
    - ____e) said that I was thirsty and asked whether I could bring anybody anything

11. When Tom said that we could be finished in another hour, I
    - ____a) said that I was too tired to continue
    - ____b) asked the leader if we could just as well meet at another time
    - ____c) said, "Well, let's get it finished now"
    - ____d) said, "Tom, don't you have anything else to do?"
    - ____e) tried to get the group to support Tom

12. When Peg asked the leader to keep better order, I
    - ____a) remarked, "That's the best idea I've heard in a long time"
    - ____b) said that it would certainly help
    - ____c) told the group about something funny that happened to me
    - ____d) told Peg to stop being so dependent
    - ____e) said that everyone should help to keep us "on the track"

13. When Ben began a side conversation with Paul, I
    - ____a) said, "Now cut it out and work on the problem with the group"
    - ____b) wanted to get in on their conversation, too
    - ____c) thought that the leader should break it up
    - ____d) continued to work on the problem
    - ____e) started to describe a personal experience to Ralph

14. When the group disparaged my idea, I
    _____a) became silent
    _____b) asked the leader what he thought of it
    _____c) said that they wouldn't recognize a good idea if it jumped out and bit them
    _____d) said, "Let's see what better ideas we can come up with"
    _____e) turned to John to discuss it further

15. When I realized that I was mad at Henry, I
    _____a) told him so in no uncertain terms
    _____b) wished that the leader would change the subject
    _____c) tried to better understand his point of view
    _____d) said, "Let's take a break"
    _____e) turned to Lucille, who I thought felt the same way

16. When David made a proposal, I
    _____a) turned to see what the leader's reaction was
    _____b) nodded and smiled at him
    _____c) changed the subject to a lighter topic
    _____d) resisted it
    _____e) said, "Let's see how this might solve the problem

17. When several members dropped out of the discussion, I
    _____a) ignored them
    _____b) suggested that the leader list on the blackboard the points made so far
    _____c) became silent, too
    _____d) tried to get them involved again by asking for their ideas
    _____e) said that everyone had a responsibility to help

18. When the leader offered to help, I
    _____a) felt warm toward him
    _____b) said that I didn't need any help
    _____c) felt that I was being rescued in the nick of time
    _____d) thought that this might move us toward our goal
    _____e) made a joke out of it

19. When George turned toward me, I
    _____a) looked away
    _____b) asked him if he saw any solution
    _____c) smiled at him
    _____d) said that I didn't think that the group was even close to a solution
    _____e) asked him what he thought he was looking at

20. When Joe got up and left the meeting, I
    _____a) said that the group shouldn't allow this
    _____b) kept on working
    _____c) asked, "Where do you think you're going?"
    _____d) got up and left with him
    _____e) said, "Hurry back, we need your ideas"

What the Questionnaire Was All About

In looking at the behavior of group members, I thought it would be useful to first look at the emotions underlying the operations of the group. In this, I draw heavily on the observations and theories of W.R. Bion of the Tavistock Institute in England, which were developed further by Herbert A. Thelen and his associates at the Human Dynamics Laboratory at the University of Chicago.*

Bion points out that the usual working group moves back and forth among a mixture of emotional states or modes. We have all observed that groups which aren't too heavily restrained seem to be working hard at times, then take time out to joke or relax, then seem to want the leader to do all the work, etc. We all have seen group members who seem to be changing the subject a lot, others who want to fight over everything, and others who are warm and friendly toward everyone. Groups, too, seem to take on a certain character. Some are always ready to fight, others seem to get very little work done, or quite a lot of work done, etc.

The work mode and the emotional states can be pictured like this:

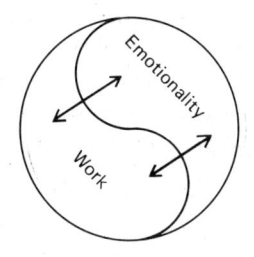

The emotional states coexist with the work mode. So it isn't a case of work *versus* emotionality, but of work *and* emotionality. One doesn't exist without the other.

Bion classified the emotional states as being in one of three categories: pairing (warm emotions and support toward an individual or the group), fight/flight (escape from the task at hand through aggression or forms of withdrawal), and dependency (reliance on others for support and direction). Other researchers have separated fight from flight and have identified other cate-

---

* I have drawn on the ideas of people associated with the Human Dynamics Laboratory, at the University of Chicago in this discussion. My major published source is Dorothy Stock and Herbert A. Thelen, *Emotional Dynamics and Group Culture,* New York: New York University Press, 1958. This book, published as Number 2 of the Research Training Series for the National Training Laboratories, describes research associated with Bion's theories.

My questionnaire is similar to their "Reaction to Group Situations Test," but has the advantage (in my use here) of being self-scored.

gories, such as counterdependency. For my purposes here, I have used the following categories and definitions:

Flight: the need of the individual to avoid any of the other modes through physical withdrawal, disinterest, daydreaming, excessive laughter or joking, etc.

Fight: the need of the individual to resist any of the other modes through verbal attack or other hostile action, through the subtle resistance to an idea, by manipulating the group, etc.

Support: the need to establish warm, positive, personal relationships with individuals or the total group through expressions of friendship, support, or partiality for another member or his ideas (often nonverbal—nodding, smiling, etc.).

Dependency: the need of the individual to achieve security through something external to himself. Expressed through appealing for support from the leader or the group, desiring direction and control, feeling that the group or oneself is inadequate to cope with the problem, etc.

Work: the need of the individual to engage in and master problem-solving activity. It is activity effectively directed toward some goal. The goal may be directed toward the solution of a shared work task or toward problems within the group which are hindering movement toward solution of a work task.

A group doesn't move step by step through the emotional modes to the work mode, but moves back and forth among them and work. The stages are not always clearly seen, but the leader can sense them through the overt and covert acts of members as the group functions.

In the usual management group meeting the authority structure will tend to mask the feelings of the members—except for dependency, which is usually encouraged by the designated leader. But the other feelings are there, and their expression may become very subtle.

Each individual has a preferred mode or modes of operating in a group, these modes arising from the behaviors which best satisfy the individual's own emotional needs. These modes are his habitual responses as a group member. But the individual doesn't use one or another mode exclusively; each person has a "profile."

The questionnaire "How Would You Respond?" was an attempt to help you see what your "profile" might be in group operations. As you have probably seen by now, each situation in the questionnaire establishes one of the modes of flight, fight, support, dependency, or work, and each of your choices of responses represents one of the modes. In the first question, for example,

Bill's activity (clowning around) could be responded to in five ways:
   a) wished the leader would stop him (dependency)
   b) encouraged him (support)
   c) tried to get on with the topic (work)
   d) expressed my annoyance (fight)
   e) felt like being a clown myself (flight)

But I asked you for two choices. Why? Because I thought your first choice would probably reflect the usual stereotype of the "good" group member who is warm and friendly and work-oriented. (I also thought you might be trying to "guess what response would make you look good.") But I really wanted you to gain some insight into your preferred modes of operating in a group. Therefore, forcing you to include your second choice may more accurately show your own "profile."

Determining Your Profile

You can determine your profile by tabulating both of your two choices on the form that follows. The alternative choices are grouped by the mode they were supposed to reflect. Go back through your questionnaire and circle on this summary sheet the two choices you selected. Then make a count for the "Summary totals" at the bottom of the form. We will then talk about "what it might mean."

(Following the "question number" on the tabulating sheet, the modes of each cue statement are given. "When Bill started to clown around in the meeting, . . ." is an example of a cue statement. The mode in this first instance is "flight.")

Sheet for Tabulating Your Choices on the Questionnaire

Question number	Flight	Fight	Support	Dependency	Work
1 (Flight)	1e	1d	1b	1a	1c
2 (Work)	2c	2d	2e	2b	2a
3 (Fight)	3d	3b	3c	3e	3a
4 (Support)	4c	4e	4b	4d	4a
5 (Dependency)	5c	5e	5a	5d	5b
6 (Dependency)	6e	6b	6d	6a	6c
7 (Flight)	7a	7d	7c	7e	7b
8 (Support)	8e	8d	8a	8b	8c
9 (Fight)	9e	9b	9a	9c	9d
10 (Work)	10e	10d	10c	10b	10a
11 (Work)	11a	11d	11e	11b	11c
12 (Dependency)	12c	12d	12a	12b	12e
13 (Support)	13e	13a	13b	13c	13d
14 (Fight)	14a	14c	14e	14b	14d
15 (Fight)	15d	15a	15e	15b	15c
16 (Work)	16c	16d	16b	16a	16e
17 (Flight)	17c	17a	17d	17b	17e
18 (Dependency)	18e	18b	18a	18c	18d
19 (Support)	19a	19e	19c	19d	19b
20 (Flight)	20d	20c	20e	20a	20b

Totals

Summary totals

Flight: _____
Fight: _____
Support: _____
Dependency: _____
Work: _____

Let's look at your behavior in meetings   205

Now that you have made a count of your responses, you should get some clue as to your preferred emotional mode or modes underlying your stated interest in work. Now, if you ignore your "work" choices, what do you get? Here are some examples of profiles:

1. Flight: _____ 2
   Fight: _____ 3
   Support: _____ 8
   Dependency: _____ 3
2. Flight: 0
   Fight: 0
   Support: _____ 8
   Dependency: _____ 7
3. Flight: _____ 7
   Fight: _____ 7
   Support: _____ 2
   Dependency: __ 1
4. Flight: _____ 2
   Fight: 0
   Support: _____ 12
   Dependency: _____ 6

Each individual may be characterized as having one or two preferred modes of operation, and this questionnaire may indicate some possible clues as to what yours are. Note well that we talk about "possible clues" to your behavior. All we can say for certain is that given a questionnaire, you answered it as you did. We can't really be sure that you would answer it the same way if you took it over again (before seeing the reasons behind it, that is.) But the questionnaire may get you to start thinking about how you may act in groups.

Sure, there were a lot of things "wrong" with the questionnaire itself. Some people react to a "forced choice" instrument of any kind. And some of your choices fall into two modes. For example, the response to item 11 (When Tom said that we could be finished in another hour, I. . .) might have been (b) (asked the leader if we could meet just as well at another time). Although choice (b) was classed as dependency, flight was certainly implied also. In such cases, I've used the overt, surface nature of the response in classifying the response. In other cases, you may have chosen the lesser of the evils—none of the responses seemed to be good choices for you. Such are the limitations of any questionnaire. Now let's get back to talking about your profile.

The Modes in Operation

People are complex, of course. We can't "write them off" with a simple generalization or short-hand label, and it would be a mistake to try to do so. There is no "goodness" or "badness" implied in any given profile—it just *is*.

All of the emotional modes are helpful in a group's operation. Excluding the "fight" people might bring harmony, but little work might get done. Sometimes the group needs to "flight" in order to renew the vigor of attack on the problem.

Each mode can be helpful in expressing the emotional needs of the group at a given point in time. Depending on what the group is doing, we may act to prolong the mode the group is in, or to change the mode to one with which we are more comfortable. We may feel more friendliness toward those who share our preferences as to one or another mode. (An exception, however, seems to be the dependency mode. Those who prefer this mode seem to resist describing their own role as such and reject dependent behavior in others.)

If one or another of the emotional modes is not present in members of a group, the group will deal differently with the tasks faced, and the outcomes may well differ, also. In one study, the problem-solving and decision-making efforts of groups of 468 Air Force officers were scored along scales of 16 variable qualities. The groups which contained a high *fight* mode tended to dig into the problem, raise many issues, and use the widest range of ideas. In addition, members of these groups showed a high level of emotional involvement and commitment to act on the proposed solutions.

The groups with high *dependency,* by contrast, tended to confine themselves to what they believed to be the ideas approved by the "authority" figures. Their products showed a narrow range of ideas and little emotional involvement in or commitment to act on the proposed solutions.

Groups with high *flight* characteristics, as you would imagine, tended to avoid digging into the problems. Their products showed a narrow range of ideas and little emotional involvement to act on their proposed solutions.

There was only one group out of those studied which had a high tendency toward *support* (pairing); therefore no generalizations were drawn.* (And don't *you* generalize, either, about Air Force officers!)

I think a special word should be said about the help provided to groups by people with a "fight" preference. In the study of the Air Force officers, the groups with high "fight" characteristics tended to dig deeper into the problem, raise more issues, and employ the greatest range of ideas. Often, such characteristics emerge when there is dissent or conflict present in a group discussion. (However, the dissent must be directed toward the issues being discussed, not personalities, and should not be so severe as to block any attempt toward resolution.) This beneficial aspect of the "fight" mode can easily be demonstrated in a group teaching setting. In my own work, for example, I give small groups a situation to discuss and a course of action to be selected. In half the groups, however, I place an associate (a "plant") who has been directed to

---

* From a study made by John C. Glidewell and reported in Stock and Thelen's book, cited earlier (pp. 122–126).

Let's look at your behavior in meetings   207

take a view in opposition to the group's choice. Productivity, as measured by the number of reasons listed for the group's choice of action, is much higher in the groups where there is dissent. The groups where there is no conflict reach a decision in a very few minutes. They do not dig very deeply into the issue and can report only a very few reasons for their choice.

As another example, one industrialist is said to take up an item on the agenda for discussion and, if there is no dissent to the general view, reschedule it to a later time, when dissent may appear. He feels that without a conflict, the issue won't get complete consideration. How many group decisions have you been a party to which might have been changed completely if there had been full exploration of a dissenting view?

It takes more emotional energy to cope with dissent, for the accent is frequently on harmony and "sweetness and light" as the standard of behavior by group members. But the need for dissent should be appreciated and encouraged for greater productivity. If conflict doesn't arise naturally, you may have to employ means to ensure it, such as appointing a "devil's advocate" or opposing views for debate on the issue. But if the role of dissent is understood and appreciated by the group, and if there is a climate of trust, dissent will usually arise naturally.

The relationship between the work and emotional components of group activity may be shown as a grid or matrix in which work is represented by one axis and emotionality on the other, as shown in the diagram.*

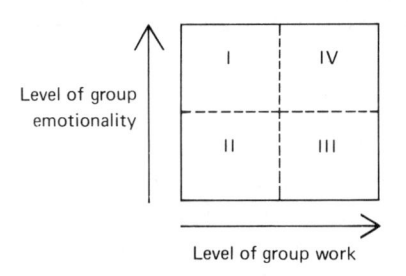

Level of group emotionality

I	IV
II	III

Level of group work

When the group is operating within area I, there is a high level of emotionality and a low work output. We would expect that the group members would express their feelings and that there would be a high degree of involvement and excitement. In area II, there would be little work and little emotionality. We would expect a lack of involvement in the meeting and a "flatness" to the group's efforts. In area III, the group would be working hard and expressing few emotions. The meeting would be sober, deliberate, and function on a

---

* Adapted from the discussion of a "field graph" in a study by Dorothy Stock and Saul Ben-Zeev, reported in Stock and Thelen, pp. 196–198.

highly intellectual plane. In area IV, both work and emotionality would be high. We could expect the members of such a group to be excited, eager, and involved.

OTHER WAYS OF LOOKING AT GROUPS

Bion's frame of reference about the operations of people in groups is not the only one available, of course. But I have found it to be helpful as an introduction to the better understanding of groups at work. To the extent that it makes the behavior of people in groups more meaningful and understandable to you, it will be a useful beginning.

Another way of looking at work groups is to make an analysis to identify the informal leader, isolates, subgroups, communication networks, etc. In watching a group in a meeting, you can record who talks to whom; activities being performed by individuals which help the group work, maintain itself as a group, or activities which are nonfunctional for the group; the feelings of members toward one another, the group, or the task, etc. If your interests lie in these directions, there is a wealth of information and training experiences available through such organizations as the National Training Laboratories and associated organizations such as Leadership Resources, Inc.* But since there are a few inexperienced people writing and training in this area, exercise some care in your selection of material.

Here, I'm going to introduce two more notions which I think you will find helpful in working with groups. Then, a checklist in working with groups will be presented.

Hidden Agenda

One simple but meaningful idea coming from the study of groups is that of a "hidden agenda." As the term implies, the hidden agenda is something a participant brings to talk about, but doesn't wish to state directly. Or, it may be a point of view which he is reluctant to express openly, but which guides his actions during the meeting. Two examples follow.

1. One manager has a pressing space problem and has assured his people that he "will get some answers today." The agenda of the meeting, however, does not include any discussion on space and takes up other important matters. Probably, space considerations will creep into his discussion of other items.

---

* Full addresses for the two organizations are:
National Training Laboratories Institute   Leadership Resources, Inc.
1815 N. Ft. Myer Drive   1750 Pennsylvania Ave. N.W.
Arlington, Virginia 22209   Washington, D.C. 20006

2. The representative from manufacturing feels that the sales people are "starry-eyed drummers" who are completely impractical. When a new sales plan is enthusiastically adopted by the sales people, he is reluctant to express his real feelings toward the plan at the meeting.

A hidden agenda brought to a meeting may or may not be uncovered. Sometimes you will get enough clues to ask that it be expressed and dealt with openly by the group. Other times the hidden agenda remains hidden, and the meeting ends with you wondering "what was going on."

Invisible Committee

This is another simple but useful idea. It helps us to realize that people don't come into a meeting feeling neutral. They bring the points of view and expectations of the other groups to which they belong and identify with, and these other factors influence their behavior in the meeting. An engineer who is working on a task force to create new personnel selection procedures, for instance, might bring with him the following invisible forces:

- A conflict within the family group—his son, of high school age, seems to be in some kind of trouble. His grades are slipping, and he is hanging out more and more with the "long-hair crowd." His mother comes to the boy's support in any attempt to discuss the situation. If the kid doesn't snap out of it pretty soon, he'll give up any chance for college.
- An expressed feeling on the part of many of his fellow engineers, which he shares, that the state of the art is changing so rapidly that they are in real danger of becoming obsolete. The shared feeling is that the company should spend more effort in up-dating the present staff.
- Along with other alums, he shares the belief that only the "ivy league" schools have teaching staffs of first-rate quality. In this view, the state-supported schools are second-rate, at best.
- Typically, the other engineers at his level look on the personnel people as well-intentioned, but not very smart, "do-gooders."
- He occasionally sees a small group of other management people who took a course along with him on "Effective Selection Interviewing" and who have been on recruiting trips for the company since the program began. They consider themselves to be seasoned veterans in recruiting and feel that the present system is a fine one.
- Etc.

Some of these "invisible" groups are formal, and others are informal. But as he sits in a meeting to discuss the formation of new procedures, he brings with him certain pressures and attitudes from these groups. Some of them may be in conflict. But each part of his "invisible committee" plays a role in the meeting, and he may be thinking about the expectations of these reference groups. This, in part, explains why it is necessary for the new group to meet until new ties are formed among its members and the new group becomes an important reference group for each member.

CHECKLIST ON WORKING WITH GROUPS

As a manager, you are the designated leader of some groups, as well as a member of many groups within your organization. An increase in your awareness and skills in working with groups can make a notable difference in the performance of these groups.

Some of the items on this checklist involve a greater awareness of the "group dynamics" level of groups at work. Other items are concerned with attitudes toward groups and your own feelings; others deal with skills of membership/leadership.

For each of the following items, place a check in the appropriate column: "I do this now," "I need to develop this," or "Does not apply to my groups."

	I do this now	I need to develop this	Does not apply to my groups
1. I am able to practice "observant participation" in that I can be fully involved on the content/work level of the group's activity, but at the same time be aware of the underlying dynamics affecting the activity.			
2. I am able to be spontaneous in my participation, but at the same time be aware of what I am doing and its impact on the group.			
3. I am able to change my own behavior when I recognize that I am not helping the group.			
4. I am able to look for roles and functions missing, but needed, by the group and supply them.			
5. I am able to create a climate of acceptance of and appreciation for the contribution of everyone —emotional as well as work.			
6. I do not needlessly inhibit emotion-based behavior which is helping the group.			
7. I am able to feel comfortable when the group is temporarily doing something other than "sticking to work."			

Checklist on working with groups

	I do this now	I need to develop this	Does not apply to my groups

8. As a leader, I am able to recognize the dependency trap which would seduce me into doing all the work.
9. As a leader, I am able to play a less active role, at times, in order to develop the group's capabilities.
10. I am able to recognize the important function of conflict and dissent in discussion so as to ensure the thorough exploration of the topic.
11. I am able to see "problem behavior" in a different light, and I try to understand why I am, or the group is, being threatened by the behavior.
12. I am able to express my own feelings naturally in the group (as a leader: "Look, I'm under the gun to come up with a solution by three o'clock. At this rate, I'll never make it, and I'm beginning to get nervous!"; as a member: "I think we're off on a tangent with this discussion. I don't feel we are getting anywhere at all.").
13. In my designated role as leader, I am able to minimize imposing my own structure and control on the group and maximize structure and control *by* the group.
14. I am able to share responsibility with the group for progress—or the lack of it.
15. I am able to create a "trust climate" in which I am trusted by the group, I show my trust in the group, and the members trust one another.
16. I am able to regard people's feelings as a natural part of group operations, and I realize the futility of trying to have real people "check their emotions at the door."
17. I am able to appreciate the importance of involvement in getting commitment to the decision made or the plan of action undertaken.

Now look over your answers. Were your checkmarks in the last column ("Does not apply to my groups") really valid? How can and will you get increased skills for the items marked "I need to develop this"? A greater awareness of the many dimensions of a group at work is the first step. Once you have developed this capability, your range of choices from which your own behavior may be selected is increased, and your work with groups becomes more effective.

CHAPTER 9

PARTICIPATION IN DECISION-MAKING

Nearly every manager today would acknowledge, in general, the usefulness of getting participation by his group in the decisions he is called upon to make which affect the group. The reason for this acknowledgment is usually the vague feeling that to do so improves morale among subordinates by providing recognition, a feeling of respect, a feeling of belonging, and so forth. Also, there is a vague hope that to get participation will decrease resistance and increase the productivity of the group.

Many books and courses discuss "styles of leadership" as if one style may be freely chosen and used by a manager regardless of the situation faced. To suggest that this can be done is to greatly oversimplify the world of the manager.

Increasing participation in appropriate decision-making events can be important in getting better decisions and having them effectively carried out. This is making good use of the human resources available to you. But the phrase "appropriate decision-making events" is a key one. In some situations it would be completely inappropriate for the group to be "in on" the decision; for other situations, it would be completely inappropriate for the group *not* to be "in on" the decision-making.

THE RANGE OF PARTICIPATION IN DECISION-MAKING

Let's look first at the range of participation possible in a decision-making event. For now, let's consider only two factors—the manager's control over the decision and the group's influence on the decision. The mixture of these two factors is shown on the scale at the top of the next page.*

---

* Similar scales are in fairly wide use in management education. The description of points along this scale was adapted from Robert Tannenbaum and Warren H. Schmidt, "How to Choose a Leadership Pattern," *Harvard Business Review,* March-April 1958: pp. 95–101.

214 Participation in decision-making — Chap. 9

Manager's control over the decision →				Group's influence on the decision →		
↑ Manager makes decision and announces it.	↑ Manager "sells" decision.	↑ Manager presents decision and invites questions and discussion.	↑ Manager presents tentative decision subject to change.	↑ Manager presents problem, gets suggestions, makes decision.	↑ Manager defines limits; asks group to make decision.	↑ Manager permits subordinates to funciton within limits defined by his own assigned duties.
1	2	3	4	5	6	7

On the left-hand side of the scale (degree #1), the manager pretty much maintains control over all elements of the decision. I say "pretty much" because the group has some influence in any decision—even if only in the decision maker's thoughts. On the far right-hand side of the scale (degree #7), the group pretty much has complete influence over the decision. I say "pretty much" here because the manager is still held responsible for his operations and cannot completely separate himself from the consequences of the decision. In other words, as one moves from the left- to the right-hand side of the scale, there is an increasing influence by the group on the decision. Read each of the degree definitions with some care.

Practice Application

Now let me describe a situation and ask that you put yourself in it. Then I'll present a few events which call for a decision and ask that you indicate what "degree of participation" you would tend to choose.

First, the situation. Assume that you have a very supportive boss who gives you free rein in handling your subordinates. You notice that he tends to get participation whenever possible from those who report to him.

The group reporting to you is experienced, and you enjoy good relationships with each person. You have confidence in them. The members of the group have good relations with one another. Assume, too, that you have confidence in yourself and have no strong need to maintain control over everything.

Okay, that's the situation which I will ask you to place yourself in. On pp. 215–216 are a number of events which require a decision. Indicate in the blank the number (from the scale shown above) which represents the degree of participation you would use in making the decision. (Consider each event as independent and not related to the others.)

Events requiring a decision	Your selection

1. Due to outside factors, there is a sudden requirement for you to reduce manpower in your unit because of a reduction in the budget for personnel. One-fourth of your group must be laid off. Records of performance, etc., are available for each person. (Indicate the number on the scale which corresponds to the approach you would take.) _____

2. A change decision must be made. It will be quite unpopular, you predict, because it will go against established ways of doing things. Some people may even quit, but the majority of the group will probably go along with the change. _____

3. An emergency has arisen which requires an immediate decision. The outcome of the decision will personally affect each member of the group, but the decision must be made immediately. _____

4. You have been asked whether you will commit your group to an available contract. It would call for working 110% of the normal workload, with erratic overtime and personal hardships for the group members. Successful completion of the task would provide an important gain for a new customer. But to commit and fail would be a serious loss. _____

5. An organizational change is needed which would combine five units reporting to you into three. A great deal would be at stake for the people now heading the units. They have been very competitive as "friendly rivals." _____

6. A highly technical decision is required which needs the expertise of specialized outsiders, which you have obtained. Although the decision will directly affect your group, its members do not have the training and background to contribute to the decision—even though they may think they do. _____

7. A new course of action needs to be decided on. The commitment of individuals in your group is basic to the success of the change, which involves the day-to-day behavior of each. Each individual must "supervise himself" if the change is to work. _____

8. One recurring problem in administration is minor, but annoying to everyone. Several solutions have been tried in the past but without success. You think you have a solution which will work, but unknown problems may arise, depending on the new decision made. _____

9. You have told your boss and others at your level about a new idea you want to try out in your group to reduce costs. They have all been enthusiastic and urged you to try it. You have worked out the plans in detail, but the decision to proceed has not been made. _____

Events requiring a decision   Your selection

10. The decision called for by one situation is obvious to all parties. The delay in making the decision has left the situation ambiguous, which is a big problem in itself.   _____

11. One series of problems has arisen and needs to be resolved. You have some ideas on the subject, but the group is intimately familiar with the problems, the advantages and disadvantages of possible solutions, pitfalls, etc.   _____

12. In one planned innovation, the need for secrecy is essential. If any word of the change is made public, it will drastically change conditions and adversely affect the final outcome. Yet decisions must now be made which will directly affect the group.   _____

13. A decision must be made about the starting and ending times for work. The organization wishes to stagger the times in order to relieve traffic congestion, and each unit can make its own decision. It doesn't really matter what the times *are*, as long as everyone in your group conforms to the decision.   _____

14. You need a creative, innovative solution to a problem. Although there are several very creative people in the group, most do not seem to be very imaginative.   _____

15. Even though they are experienced, members in the group don't seem to want to take on responsibility for decisions. The attitude seems to be: "You are paid to manage, we are paid to do the work, so you make the decisions." Now an issue has come up for a decision which will personally affect every person in the group.   _____

Practice Application—Answers and Discussion

After you have selected your "degree of participation" for each decision-making event, read over these "answers" and the discussion of each situation.

Our
selection   Discussion

1. __1__   This may seem like a "hard-nosed" approach, but in our experience, a layoff is understandably a very trying emotional event for the people it affects directly or indirectly. There can be little calm, rational participation by those affected as to who will "walk the plank." If you *did* get participation or discussion, you might well find that Susie is planning to quit to get married in two weeks; that Hal is going into business with his brother and is planning to leave the organization; and that Pete is about to apply for early retirement. These plans could affect your final decision. But the best course, we

The range of participation in decision-making   217

feel, is to develop the kind of relationship with your people so that you would know these personal plans.

When a layoff must take place, use the available records and your own knowledge, and then make the lonely decision. But also recognize that you probably won't feel right in your stomach for a while.

2. __3__ Presenting the decision as having been made and inviting questions and discussion seems like the best course to us. Degrees 4 and 5 on the scale would be to open the floodgates of dissent over a decision which *must* be made. We would predict that in degrees 6 and 7, the decision would rarely get made, and you would have to take it back and make it after all. Degrees 1 and 2 would not permit exceptions to be aired or support elicited in discussion. In short, a manager can't usually "cover up" his role in an unpopular decision by giving it to the group to be decided.

3. __1__ Decision events may arise—often or seldom—when there is no time to talk to *anyone*. Action is required *now!* When this does occur, and when the decision does "personally affect each member of the group," the situation should be fully explained after the fact, of course. The reception your explanation gets will be a measure of your "internal credit rating."

4. __6__ The kind of commitment required as described in the event can best come from those affected taking full part in the decision-making process. If the organization goal becomes their goal, there will be an all-out effort to meet or beat the challenge faced. This can be quite in contrast to half-hearted responses to a "sales job" when there has been no knowledge about or participation in the decision-making process.

5. __3,4,5__ Making an organizational change is usually an emotional experience for those affected. A change usually suggests an evaluation of people, not merely an evaluation of functions. The change described means that two of the five will be "demoted" and will report to one of the other three. This can be hard to take. It seems unfair, as well as difficult, to ask those involved to make the decision.

It would seem to be better to use degree 1 and 2 rather than 6 and 7. In any case, those changing their reporting relationships will need help to relate to their new positions without a "loss of face."

6. __2,3__ Although it is true that there is often more know-how in the group than we think, sometimes we must call on the outside expert. When the decision is based on his advice, the manager's job then becomes one of making sure that the group members fully understand the decision—including the advice that led to the decision.

7. <u>5,6,7</u> Here again, as in item 4, the commitment of the group members is basic to success. Getting the participation of the members in making the decision can not only create a better decision, but can also ensure support rather than something that will be "lived with" or resisted.

8. <u>3,4,5</u> If it is a minor problem which annoys everyone, and you think you have a "fix" for it, put your ideas on the table and see what the group thinks. It probably isn't important enough to spend a lot of time on it, but it might be useful to get the group's ideas on potential problems before the decision is made.
   Degree 6 or 7 might have been chosen, but the issue probably isn't that important.

9. <u>2,3,4</u> I haven't been able to get much agreement among those I have tried this on. According to the event described, you have really already made a commitment. If you think it is a good idea, and so do your boss and your peers, try it! Even though the "formal decision hasn't been made," for all practical purposes *it has*. So do not try to pretend to the group that it really hasn't. Whether you would use degree 2, 3, or 4 would probably depend on how closely the group members would be affected by the decision.

10. <u>1</u> Go ahead, make the decision and announce it.

11. <u>5 or 6</u> Here, you can share your ideas, get additional inputs from the group, and then decide, or ask the group to make the decision. If the second choice is selected, you become a member of the group (which you are, anyway) and add your ideas to the pot. Remember one main reason for getting the group involved is to get *better* decisions, not merely to give group members a "feeling of participation."

12. <u>1</u> There are some decisions which do involve the need for secrecy, e.g., a land purchase. But these events are really few and far between. Some organizations and some people treat most decisions as if they were state secrets, when it really isn't necessary. But when it is necessary, the decision (and the need for secrecy) should be fully explained after the fact.

13. <u>6 or 7</u> As described here, this is an ideal event for the group to be fully involved in making the decision. Each individual can put forth his own situation, and the decision which best satisfies all will usually be adopted. Those not fully satisfied have had a chance to be heard and will usually go along with the majority. Groups will abide by their own decisions.

14. <u>5</u> There are probably more innovative and creative people in your group than you think there are! But to bring out their best ideas, a

nonjudgmental climate must be created, one in which a person is not punished for expressing new ideas. (As far as I can see, all the programs in "applied imagination," "imagineering," etc., primarily reduce the inhibitors now preventing people from using their imagination and being creative. What happens when a person so "trained" goes back to the job is sometimes another story.)

Getting the group involved in such a decision event can help nurture creative ideas.

15. <u>4 or 5</u> Good decision-making depends on having both information on which to base the decision and confidence, which comes from experience with making them. But to insist that the group make a decision when they don't want to is inappropriate. However, you can start slowly, as in degrees 4 and 5, and increase their influence in decisions as their confidence grows. But some people don't want to have any part in decision-making.

PARTICIPATION IN YOUR OWN SITUATION

Now that you have applied these decision events to the scale and have compared your thinking and experience with mine, let's talk about it. Sometimes we don't try to get more involvement and participation from our subordinates in decision-making because we are afraid the group might "give away the store." And if they don't have complete information, they might! But usually, groups are pretty realistic and conservative in making decisions.

The total situation you are in will have great influence over if and how much participation you will get in decision-making. Let me repeat the situation I outlined for you before I asked you to look at the 15 events:

- Assume that you have a very supportive boss who gives you free rein in handling your subordinates. You notice that he tends to get participation whenever possible from those who report to him.
- The group reporting to you is experienced, and you enjoy good relationships with each person. You have confidence in them. And the members of the group have good relations with one another.
- Assume that you have confidence in yourself and have no strong need to maintain control over everything.

These were important conditions, and they dealt with (1) your boss, (2) your group, and (3) yourself. To have changed any of the described conditions would have been to greatly change your ranking of the events on the scale. (If you *didn't* assume the stated conditions, but thought of your *own* situation, your answers may have differed from ours.) Let's look at the three conditions.

1. *Your boss.* If you have a boss who expects *you* to make all of the decisions and who looks upon getting participation by the group as a sign of your

weakness, your answers would shift to the left on the scale. How do you view *your* subordinates when they get participation in their decisions?

2. *Your group.* The relations described in the stated conditions were very favorable. The group members were experienced. How would your answers have changed if they were all quite new on their jobs? If half of them were? You enjoyed good relations with them. What if there were a great deal of hostility toward "management" because of something like a hard-fought union organizing campaign? Or, what if their previous boss, who just left the group, made all the decisions himself, and made them stick? They had good relations with one another. But what if there were two factions (say, a young group and an older group) who were vying with each other? How would your answers have changed then? You should also note that people who tend to have "authoritarian personalities" and no strong need for independence do not seem to be favorably affected by participation. Such people might see the attempt as a sign of weakness in the manager.*

3. *Yourself.* You had confidence in yourself and no strong need to maintain control over everything. But what if you were recently appointed to manage this group and they were all older and more experienced than you? What if you tried to get participation once and it was a terrible failure? What if you really don't trust the group? What if your personal needs are such that you can't stand much ambiguity or loss of control? How would your answers have changed under these conditions?

The total situation in which you find yourself will have a great bearing on whether and how much participation you will try to get in decisions. So let's take a look at your situation now. Answer these questions:

1. What are the main factors limiting or preventing you from getting more participation now? Consider your boss, your group, and yourself. Number each item. List as many as you can think of.

_____
_____
_____
_____
_____
_____

---

* V. H. Vroom, *Some Personality Determinants of the Effects of Participation,* Englewood Cliffs, N.J.: Prentice-Hall, 1960.

2. Taking each of the items listed above in turn, what, if anything, can be done to overcome it? What specific activity could be planned?

3. What decision-making events are you now, or will be in the near future, faced with in which you could get a greater degree of participation by the people affected? What specific plans and strategy for each?

Many of the decisions in your organizational life are not made by you, but by someone "upstairs." Yet you may frequently be expected to get cooperation (or at least compliance) with such decisions. When the basic decision is made by someone else, the way in which the decision is to be carried out often becomes *your* decision. Timing, procedures to be followed, personnel to be involved, and the like, are left up to you. You can frequently get participation in these decisions by those affected. The basic decision already made becomes one of the limits, or "ground rules." "This decision has been made for these reasons. Now let's decide how we can best carry it out." (The temptation when a decision—particularly an unpopular one—comes down from the organization is to be the "good guy" and have the attitude: "Don't get me wrong—I wouldn't have made that decision. But *they* did, and we will just have to live with it.") If you don't know the reasons behind the decision, you can frequently find them out, and they will be helpful in your explanation to the group.

Increasing participation in appropriate decision-making events can be important in getting better decisions and having them carried out effectively. The appropriate degree of participation will depend on the nature of the decision, on you, and on the situation you are in.

CHAPTER **10**

ORGANIZATIONAL CONFLICT

Organizational conflict is inevitable within most organizations. This is because the various parts within the organization have different points of view; indeed, they should—if the organization is to prosper. Thus the goals of each part can frequently be expected to be in conflict. For example, the manufacturing department would like to have plenty of raw materials available in order to make sure that they never run into a stock-out condition, which would shut down production. But the finance department would like to keep inventories at an absolute minimum in order to avoid the tie-up of large amounts of cash, as well as the costs of storing, guarding, and insuring inventories (said to be from 17 to 24 percent of the dollar amount of the inventory). The purchasing group has yet another point of view, namely, that stocks should be kept at a level dictated by the most economical lot-size order.

The salesmen want to promise early delivery, since this can help them make sales. But promises of early delivery drive production planners wild. The production foreman wants to meet his schedule above all else, and the safety director is more concerned with the accident and injury rate.

The director of the bureau is given an overall charter and a budget. But each department within the bureau has different ideas on how that budget should be divided. Each sees its own service as paramount to meet the stated charter. And so it goes.

The resulting conflict of these different points of view is healthy for the organization *if*—and this is a very big if—the final decision in the conflict takes all these points of view into account. Since conflict is a natural, normal, and expected part of an organization's life, two things become important: reducing anxiety about its occurrence and settling it constructively.

Conflict is approached in many ways, depending in large part on how we were brought up. Which methods you or I use "naturally" in settling conflict depends on our personalities, which is the sum of all our experiences and how we have reacted to those experiences. However, new and more fruitful methods of dealing with conflict can be learned. By the same token, no one method of dealing with conflict is the best or only way for every situation. The effective manager uses the most appropriate method for the particular situation faced. Thus, when the inevitability of conflict is understood, and the reasons for it appreciated, anxiety about conflict is reduced.

Let's see if we can take a closer look at the ways people deal with organizational conflict. In the practice applications that follow, you will be asked to look at four normal conflict situations. You are to rank the alternative actions given, *in the order of their desirability to you,* with "1" being the most desirable and "5" the least desirable. Do this ranking now, and then we'll talk about it.

PRACTICE APPLICATION—WHAT SHOULD HE DO?

Read each of the situations below. Then rank the choices of answers from 1 (most desirable response) to 5 (least desirable response).

Conflict Situation I

Industrial Relations has instituted two new forms to control visits to the plant dispensary. One is a special trip pass to be signed by the supervisor; the other is a "disposition" form to be filled in by the nurse and signed and returned by the supervisor. These forms would put the first-line supervisor back "in control" of his people.

The factory supervisors, however, are not holding still for the new forms. They have refused to fill them out. The Factory Manager is reported to have said, "That's all we need! More forms designed by staff groups to give us more paperwork!"

The Industrial Relations Manager should: (Rank)

_____a) Ask the Factory Manager to at least have his supervisors fill out the special trip pass. You will not require the other form.

_____b) Ask the Manufacturing Manager to order the Factory Manager to comply with your request.

_____c) Go ask the Factory Manager why the supervisors are resisting using the form.

_____d) Cancel the requirement to use the two forms.

_____e) Find another way to record dispensary visits, to keep the supervisors happy.

Conflict Situation II

The Purchasing Manager says that he has found material for the division's main product which he can buy at less cost than that currently being used. The Manufacturing Manager says that the cheaper material would not produce as good results and that he prefers to keep the material currently in use. Quality

Control reports that each will pass inspection equally well. The General Manager should: (Rank)
- ____a) Decide who is right and ask the other to comply.
- ____b) Let the two men settle the conflict as they see fit.
- ____c) Try to smooth over the difficulty. It is important that these two men work together.
- ____d) Suggest that the Purchasing Manager continue his hunt for a cheaper material, but to try to find one which would satisfy the Manufacturing Manager.
- ____e) Ask each of the men to compromise.

Conflict Situation III

The engineering organization is turning new designs over to their own developmental manufacturing unit instead of the factory manufacturing unit. They do this, they say, because they can get test models faster and cheaper for testing, the drawings do not have to be in finished form, and there is a minimum of quality and configuration control. The Factory Manager knows that this is wrong, against company policy, and duplicates effort. The Factory Manager should:
- ____a) Sit down with engineering and ask them how he can better serve their needs for test models.
- ____b) Ask developmental manufacturing to at least share the test models with the factory, since they should *all* be built there.
- ____c) Do nothing about this situation and see what develops.
- ____d) Ask his boss, the Manufacturing Manager, to require that all production orders (except for specified exceptions) be turned over to the factory as the company procedures specify.
- ____e) Go along with the present arrangement so as not to stir up trouble.

Conflict Situation IV

Some months ago a "pool" of draftsmen was created in engineering to be of service to all engineering units. This pool is under the direction of Engineering Administration and has been of use in handling peak loads without the transfer of this skill between organizations. Now, however, the Electronics Design Manager has heard that Preliminary Design has asked for the permanent assignment of the group to *them*, since they are the greatest users of the pool. The Electronics Design Manager should: (Rank)
- ____a) Do nothing. The Engineering Manager will surely see through this "power grab" and will turn it down.
- ____b) Find another way to get his peak loads met. He shouldn't start a fight over something this small.
- ____c) Try to get Preliminary Design to leave at least half of the pool there for the others to use.

_____ d) Go to see the manager of Preliminary Design to discuss the needs of both groups.
_____ e) Ask the Engineering Manager not to permit the move. After all, the pool was created in the first place so that all would get service equally without the need to hire and borrow for peak loads.

DEALING WITH CONFLICT

Before we explain what your rankings in the practice applications might mean, let's talk more about ways of handling conflict. The first writer on this subject I know of was Mary Parker Follett, who was born in Boston in 1868 and died in 1933. She attended Radcliffe College and Newnham in Cambridge, England. In 1900 she founded the Roxbury Debating Club in Boston. She was also active in the Women's Municipal League. Miss Follett never married.

How is that for an opener? Why should a modern manager spend any time with the quaint ideas of an old-fashioned lady? Because I think that Mary Parker Follett is one of the deepest thinkers about management that the world has yet produced. She was and still is respected worldwide for her ideas about the processes of management.

Mary Parker Follett saw five potential ways of dealing with the natural conflicts which arise:

1. *Evasion.* There is nothing "wrong" with this withdrawing from the conflict, but habitually pretending that conflict does not exist is not very productive. Yet we all know people who deal with conflict in this way.
2. *Suppression.* In this mode of dealing with conflict, the individual plays down the differences which exist or gives in to "keep everybody happy."
3. *Domination.* This is handling conflicts through the use of organizational power—either your own "authority" or that of a higher level. But might doesn't necessarily make right. When conflicts are settled this way, resistance doesn't go away; it is just covered up, only to arise again, perhaps over another issue.
4. *Compromise.* Each side gives up (loses) a little or a lot in order to gain peace. But when compromise is used often in settling conflicts, it turns into bargaining—both parties learn to come to the table with exaggerated positions in the hope of gaining more.
5. *Integration.* This method of dealing with conflict is not often used, but seems to offer great promise. Here, the issue is redefined, and a solution is sought whereby both sides can have their desires satisfied, with neither side having to sacrifice anything.*

---

* From Henry C. Metcalf and L. Urwick, *Dynamic Administration, The Collected Papers of Mary Parker Follett,* New York: Harper, 1940. See Chapter I, "Constructive Conflict." See also Robert R. Blake and Jane S. Mouton, *The Managerial Grid,* Houston: Gulf, 1964, and their adaptation, "Denial, Smoothing, Power, Compromise and Confronting."

Miss Follett uses the simple example of two people in a room to illustrate integration. One person wants the window open; the other wants the window shut. "I say that the window should be open!" "No, I say that the window should be shut!" "Open!" "Shut!" The two could evade or suppress the conflict. Or, one might use power: "Look, I'm in charge here. I say the window stays shut, so that settles it." Or, they might compromise by opening it half way, or have it up for 20 minutes and down for 20 minutes. But seeking the integrating solution requires that they bring the real differences into the open; redefine the problem by breaking the whole into its parts and finding the significant—rather than the dramatic—issues in the conflict; resist either/or thinking, in which one's choices must stay within the boundaries of two mutually exclusive alternatives; and re-evaluate and restate the point at issue so that the desires of both sides can be satisfied. Thus, a redefinition of the window conflict might show that one of the people can't work in a stuffy room, and the other feels that the draft blowing on him would not help his cold. With this redefinition the two people can seek the integrative solution, e.g., having a window open in another room, switching places, etc.

Analysis of "Practice Application—What Should He Do?"

As you have probably guessed by now, the alternatives given you to rank in the four conflict situations tried to reflect the five alternative methods of dealing with conflicts. Turn back to your rankings in the four situations given you and list your ranking for each here:

Situation I (new form)
Your
ranking
_____ a) Compromise
_____ b) Domination
_____ c) Integration
_____ d) Evasion
_____ e) Suppression

Situation II (new material)
Your
ranking
_____ a) Domination
_____ b) Evasion
_____ c) Suppression
_____ d) Integration
_____ e) Compromise

Situation III (new designs)
Your
ranking
_____ a) Integration
_____ b) Compromise
_____ c) Evasion
_____ d) Domination
_____ e) Suppression

Situation IV (drafting pool)
Your
ranking
_____ a) Evasion
_____ b) Suppression
_____ c) Compromise
_____ d) Integration
_____ e) Domination

Now you can see the ranking you gave to the five methods, or modes, of dealing with conflict. In the space provided, write down your answers to the following questions about your rankings.

1. Which method or methods of handling conflict did you tend to select as your first choice?

2. Which method did you select as your second choice? (If your first didn't work, would you turn to this method?)

3. Which method or methods did you tend to use the least? (Rank of "4" or "5")

The way a manager settles conflicts depends, in large part, on his total life experiences—particularly those that occurred when he was very young. But if we are aware of different choices available, we can try different methods. And remember, there is *no one best* approach to every situation. If a "steamroller" is coming, for example, you had better get the heck out of the way—don't stop to integrate, or it might integrate you! The effective manager uses the choice most appropriate to the situation.

Now, let's give you an opportunity to see some conflicts occurring in a work setting and to decide what action should be taken.

IN-BASKET ON HANDLING ORGANIZATIONAL CONFLICT*

Introduction

This in-basket will be the same as the "In-basket on Management Practices" which you completed in Chapter 2, except that the items here deal with methods of solving organizational conflict. You are to decide what issue each item of correspondence presents and decide what action you would take (if any) as a result of receiving the item. You will get the most out of this exercise if you think through the item and make notes at the bottom of each in-basket item. Only *after* you have finished the entire exercise should you turn to the commentaries and compare your answers with those given.

Your Situation

As in the earlier in-basket exercise, you are to assume that you are Bob Black, Manager of United States Sales Division of Consumer Products, Incorporated. Your staff and sales zones reporting to you are shown on the partial organization chart on the next page. You report to Bill Nelson, the Director of Market-

---

* Most of this material is taken from my book *The In-Basket Kit,* Reading, Mass.: Addison-Wesley, 1971. Reproduced by permission.

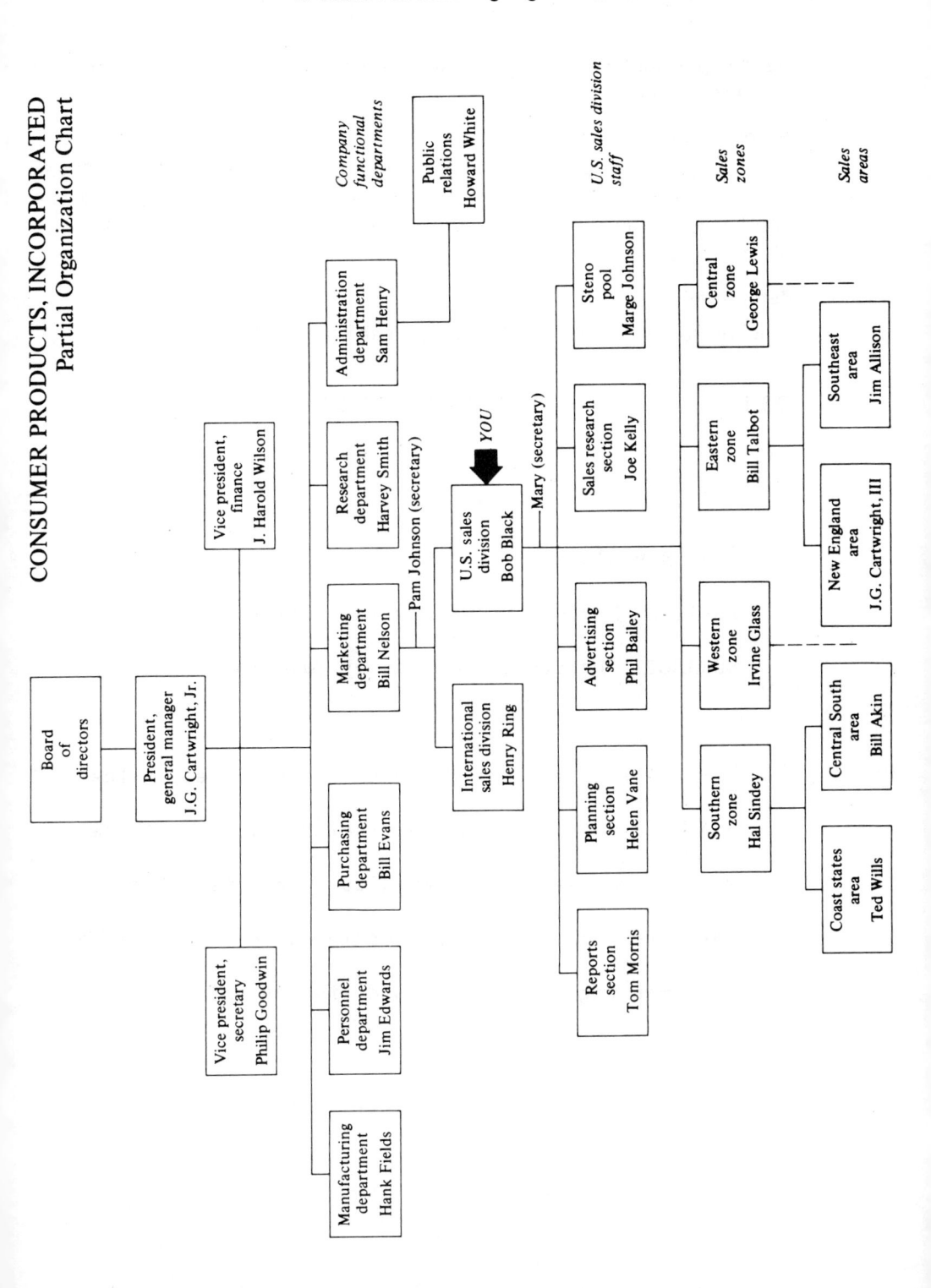

CONSUMER PRODUCTS, INCORPORATED
Partial Organization Chart

In-basket on handling organizational conflict   229

- Board of directors
  - President, general manager — J.G. Cartwright, Jr.
    - Vice president, secretary — Philip Goodwin
    - Vice president, finance — J. Harold Wilson
    - Manufacturing department — Hank Fields
    - Personnel department — Jim Edwards
    - Purchasing department — Bill Evans
    - Marketing department — Bill Nelson
      - Pam Johnson (secretary)
    - Research department — Harvey Smith
    - Administration department — Sam Henry
      - *Company functional departments*
      - Public relations — Howard White
    - U.S. sales division — Bob Black (**YOU**)
      - Mary (secretary)
      - International sales division — Henry Ring
      - Reports section — Tom Morris
      - Planning section — Helen Vane
      - Advertising section — Phil Bailey
      - Sales research section — Joe Kelly
      - Steno pool — Marge Johnson
        - *U.S. sales division staff*
      - Southern zone — Hal Sindey
      - Western zone — Irvine Glass
      - Eastern zone — Bill Talbot
      - Central zone — George Lewis
        - *Sales zones*
        - Coast states area — Ted Wills
        - Central South area — Bill Akin
        - New England area — J.G. Cartwright, III
        - Southeast area — Jim Allison
          - *Sales areas*

230 Organizational conflict Chap. 10

ing. His position and the other functional departments are also shown on the organization chart.

Instructions

Go through the items of correspondence and make notes about the issues you see (how the writers are handling organizational conflict) and the action you would take as a result of receiving the letter. Then turn to the commentaries and compare your answer to those given.

Remember

You are Bob Black, Manager of the United States Sales Division.

OC 1 **INTEROFFICE MEMO**

TO: Bob Black

FROM: H. Fields, Manufacturing Department

SUBJECT: Delivery Promises by Salesmen

I am well aware that promises of early deliveries can help your salesmen make sales. You should be well aware that these unrealistic promises play hell with our orderly production planning. Please do something about this condition at once!

H. Fields

ISSUE(S)

ACTION

OC 2   **INTEROFFICE MEMO**

TO: Bob Black

FROM: Tom Morris

SUBJECT: Manufacturing Department request

It has now been two months since Manufacturing asked us to do a consumer survey on our products. Since these are so very expensive to conduct, and since the results are so doubtful, thus far we have been able to resist.

Since we haven't heard anything more from Manufacturing, it looks like we are in the clear. But it might be a good idea to "lay low" for a while longer, until we are sure this consumer survey idea is a dead issue.

TM:ga

Tom

ISSUE(S)

ACTION

OC 3

Personal

Bob,

Sorry that we couldn't continue our discussion in the dining room the other day. Since you expressed interest in knowing more, and I haven't been able to reach you, I thought I would drop you this personal note, since I am leaving town, to be gone for several weeks.

It seems that the "bad blood" I mentioned has been developing between your advertising man Phil Bailey and Howard White of Public Relations for some time now. I understand that it has now reached the point where they aren't speaking and avoid any contact.

You indicated the importance of these two groups working closely together because of related activities. Well, if they aren't speaking, this can't be working.

I'll plan to see you on my return.

Jim Edwards

ISSUE(S)

ACTION

OC 4A   **INTEROFFICE MEMO**

To: Bob Black

From: Marge Johnson

Subject: Steno-Typing Pool

    I believe that the formation of the Steno-Typing Pool is going to work out very well. During this current shortage of qualified people, it at least ends the practice of having some girls swamped and others idle.

    I have been trying to hire a replacement for June, but no luck so far. Personnel says that finding a replacement might take some time. Because of the lack of one typist, I have had to assign priorities to the work coming in.

    I'm using my best judgment on this. I'm sure that we shall hear about this from some—such as Advertising, who are always late and then demand that everything else stop while they get immediate service.

Marge Johnson

ISSUE(S)

ACTION

OC 4B   **INTEROFFICE MEMO**

TO: Bob Black

FROM: Phil Bailey, Advertising Section

SUBJECT: Delays in Typing Pool

I have noted with increasing concern that delays are growing since the formation of the typing pool. As you very well know, delays in the typing of copy for the ads holds up all subsequent steps.

Since Marge Johnson has been placed in charge of the pool, we evidently hold a low priority in her mind.

Please inform her of the urgent nature of the work we bring to the typing pool, or better still, assign the typists back to each unit so that we can set our own priorities and get our work done.

PB/js   *Phil*

ISSUE(S)

ACTION

OC 5   **INTEROFFICE MEMO**

TO: Bob Black

FROM: Joe Kelly, Sales Research Section

SUBJECT: Compromise on Model 200

We have just completed a series of discussions with the Research department and the Manufacturing department about the new model. Manufacturing held out for the 220 model because it is the least expensive to manufacture. But our consumer research clearly showed that this model lacks "sex appeal." The consumers preferred the 190 design.

We held out as long as we could, but finally compromised to keep the peace. I guess that we can sell the result, which we labeled model 200. I don't think that Manufacturing is pleased with the result either. But you can't win them all.

JK/LM

ISSUE(S)

ACTION

OC 6

> Bob: This is for your signature. This will "jack him up" on getting his reports in on time.
>
> Tom
> Tom Morris
>
> TM:ga

TO: Irvine Glass

FROM: Bob Black

SUBJECT: Timely Reporting

I'm sure that you realize the importance of timely reporting to the Central Office.

Yet for some reason your reports are consistently late in getting to the Reports section.

Please look into this matter and take immediate action to prevent further tardiness of your reports.

Bob Black, Manager
U.S. Sales Division

ISSUE(S)

ACTION

OC 7

TO: Bob Black, Manager, U. S. Sales Division

FROM: Bill Nelson, Director of Marketing

SUBJECT: Meeting with Finance on Credit Policy Change

I have been thinking about our preparation for the meeting with Finance to liberalize our credit policies. I know that we have agreed that this would boost sales and make a dramatic increase in our share of the market.

It seems to me that we should try to anticipate what the point of view of Finance will be, even though we know at the start that we can't do this completely. We should expect a conflict in points of view, since we represent two very different functions within the company. And if we can find the solution which integrates both viewpoints, this conflict is healthy for the organization.

We should, it seems to me, begin with a well-prepared, but not fixed, position. If our position were fixed, we couldn't help but take on a "fight-set." We must not take the attitude that this will be a win-or-lose conflict. Instead, we should expect exploration and open resolution of the conflict. We should be willing to look frankly at all the issues, even--or perhaps especially-- at those which are against our stand.

We must appreciate the expertness of Finance, and work through to a new definition of the problem, and expect a new solution to be reached together.

Please do the preliminary groundwork, and let's plan to meet, with whoever of your staff is appropriate, next Wednesday at 10:00 A. M.

(Pam J.)

ISSUE(S)

ACTION

OC 8

INTEROFFICE MEMO

TO: Bob Black

FROM: Phil Bailey, Advertising Section

SUBJECT: Public Relations Advertising

I hear from the grapevine that the Public Relations section of the Administration department is planning a big institutional advertising campaign. Supposedly, it is to feature the company and its brand names. However, I feel strongly that all advertising should be placed by this office, even though our main concern is working with distributors in placing joint ads. But we are the ones who have the contacts with ad agencies.

I propose that we should wait until their advertising campaign has begun, then take the whole matter to Mr. Cartwright, the president. I'm sure that we can prove that there would have been substantial savings if we had added their volume to ours (if <u>we</u> had handled the ads). I'm sure that the volume of wasted money will get Mr. Cartwright's attention.

PB/js

Phil

ISSUE(S)

ACTION

OC 9

TO: Bob Black

FROM: Bill Talbot, Eastern Zone Manager

SUBJECT: Reports Requested by Finance

Bob, I have put up with most of the riduculous requests from the Central Office, but this latest one from the Director of Finance is the last straw! What on earth could they want with the profit margin on each sale to distributors over $5,000?

I think that those guys at the Central Office are living in an ivory tower. They rarely visit us, they don't know our problems or point of view. The only thing they are interested in is return on investment.

I'm going to have to be a lot more convinced than I am now before we will spend time on reports such as this one.

bt:ovq

ISSUE(S)

ACTION

COMMENTARIES ON THE IN-BASKET ITEMS

Here are my commentaries on the in-basket items. I'll tell you what I had in mind when I included the item, but this is not to be taken as "the school solution." You may very well have seen other issues and planned on other action which might be even more appropriate than those I had in mind. But it might be interesting to you to compare your notes with mine.

Please do not look at these commentaries until you have gone through the in-basket items and have made your own notes on each item.

Commentary on Item OC 1

Issues

This is a classic conflict as discussed earlier. The goal of Manufacturing is an orderly, low-cost production flow. The goal of the Sales Department is to make sales. However, salesmen's promises can wreck production planning. At this point, at least, Manufacturing (H. Fields) is just pointing to the conflict. If it is allowed to go on without any action, he may turn to domination (power) to settle the issue. If his next letter says something like: "From now on we are going to enforce the rules to the letter and not accept orders with less than x months lead time . . . ," we will really have a problem.

Action

The important action here is to meet this conflict head-on. We need many facts first, such as: is any one or two salesmen causing the difficulty, or is the condition general? How much lead time is needed by Manufacturing, and how much is given by the salesmen? What happens when the lead time given is not long enough? How do varying lead times affect manufacturing, sales, and the customer?

We would look for a determination by you as Bob Black to hold an early meeting with Hank Fields or his representative in order to get facts and set guidelines for the salesmen to follow in promising deliveries. This would seem to be an opportunity for an integrative solution.

Commentary on Item OC 2

Issues

To be productive, organizational conflict must be resolved. Here, Tom Morris deals with the conflict by evading it. "Laying low" is a frequent way of dealing with potential conflict; if in this case the request was casual and later forgotten, the evasion worked. But if it was not a casual request, Manufacturing is probably doing *something* about it. Perhaps they will get budget approval for their making the survey, citing your inaction as support. If this occurs, you will lose control of what should be your function.

Action

Manufacturing should be approached directly. Tom Morris might be able to put together a convincing presentation against the consumer survey. At the very least, asking Tom to prepare such a presentation would marshal the facts needed to make a "go/no-go" decision, which could then be reviewed with the Manufacturing Department.

Conflict is most productive when resolved.

Commentary on Item OC 3

Issues

Evasion is frequently seen when organizational conflicts arise. Some people can go for years avoiding each other—to the detriment of the organizational goals. Evasion is not at all uncommon with separate organizations having similar functions, such as advertising and public relations in this case. It's not true that "time heals all wounds"; often, the opposite is true.

Action

Meet with Phil Bailey, the advertising man on your staff. Have him spell out all his feelings about the Public Relations Department and Howard White. Then discuss ways in which he might work to resolve the conflict. Make this resolution a specific objective for Bailey to work on, with weekly reports to you of his progress.

If appropriate and agreed to in your meeting with Bailey, plan to meet with Sam Henry or Howard White.

Commentary on Items OC 4A and OC 4B

Issues

Whenever resources (in this case typists) are in short supply and the demand for these resources is high, there is bound to be conflict. It is therefore inevitable that whoever rations the resources is going to take a lot of static. From Marge's note, we see that she predicts the conflict with Advertising. This may be a self-fulfilling prophecy; she expects it to happen, so it does. Phil Bailey wants to "undo" the pool and get his typists back. But this really wouldn't change the pressure much. Whenever an organization works to a deadline, the "downstream" activities, such as typing, layout, art work, printing, etc., get the pressure.

Action

Reaffirm the need for the typing pool and for the joint setting of priorities. Tell Marge and Phil that they must work out the priorities between them. In case of complete lack of agreement in a critical situation, the matter should be referred to you. However, point out that you expect these cases to be *very* rare.

How can the two be helped to seek the integrative solution together without turning to you to try to settle the issue through domination (power)?

Commentary on Item OC 5

Issues

Compromise is hailed in our culture as a virtue, but it has some very real limitations in the settlement of conflict. When both sides give up part of what they want, neither is fully committed to the compromised outcome, and both may feel that they have "lost." Here, Joe Kelly has smoothed over the conflict through compromise and indicates that he really isn't committed to the result. Nor is Manufacturing. With this settlement by compromise, the final decision has suffered, and both the company and the consumer will lose.

The views of Manufacturing and Sales Research are quite legitimate points of view, and both must be worked into the settlement in order for the best solution to emerge.

Action

Instruct Joe Kelly to reopen the discussion with the Manufacturing Department. Conflict is expected and useful in productive decision-making. Both parties should expect to work together to arrive at a new understanding, a new definition, and a new solution. Before the decision can be considered the "right" one, both parties should be satisfied and committed.

Commentary on Item OC 6

Issues

Tom Morris is trying to use domination, or the power of your organizational authority, to handle a conflict he is having with the Western Zone. The issue is probably a minor annoyance, but the tone of the draft Tom has written for you to sign is cold and formal—almost a rebuke.

It wouldn't help your relationship with Glass to send such a stern letter, because Glass would know good and well that it came from the Reports Section. Thus, this relationship wouldn't be helped either.

When domination is used to settle conflict, resistance doesn't go away—it just gets covered up.

Action

Ask Tom Morris to try to handle this matter himself by working with the people who prepare the reports in the Western Zone. Ask him to explore the problem from their point of view. Do they see the report as being necessary? What is the report used for? Do they know this? What happens when it is late? Do they know this?

If the problem continues and is general, it should be discussed at a routine meeting of the zone managers. If it continues only with this one zone and is serious, this should be discussed by you with the Zone Manager.

Commentary on Item OC 7

Issues

Rather than put in items which demonstrate only the less useful ways of handling conflict, I tried to design this situation to demonstrate the attitudes necessary in settling conflicts through "integration."

Action

Review the letter with the members of your sales division staff who will be preparing your case. Try to make it a guide for you and them in making the preparation. Also, it might make a good discussion item for the staff generally, in learning to apply "integration."

Commentary on Item OC 8

Issues

Bailey wants the Public Relations group to crawl out on a limb, and then he will saw it off. But meanwhile, the company is the loser. If substantial savings are possible, now is the time to get this out on the table and resolve it.

Action

Telephone Sam Henry, Director of Administration, and ask if he is planning an advertising campaign. If he is, arrange for a meeting with him to explore the possibilities of the company saving money by having the two groups work together. Then ask Phil Bailey to prepare facts and figures on the potential savings he sees. Explain why you want them, namely, because it is in the best interest of the company. If his report shows potential savings, meet with Henry and decide on the best course to follow.

This letter from Bailey, along with Item 3, shows that you have some training to do with him. What is the best way to help him see better approaches?

Commentary on Item OC 9

Issues

This is one of the normal creaks and groans in the operation of a large organization. In part, it is caused by the fact that each level of the organization deals with a different level of abstraction. Another cause is that Central Office people often don't have any idea of the total impact of their requests on outlying offices. It takes only three minutes to dictate a request for data. But down at the outlying office, it takes hours, days, and sometimes weeks to prepare a response to each request in the flood of requests.

Action

Find out from Finance what the purpose of this request is; then pass the word down. Usually, the request will turn out to be logical and the information really needed.

If you can arrange to have requests for information of the field channeled through someone in your office, you can make sure that they are really necessary. And if so, you can make them better accepted by making sure that they are well explained. But expect some of this conflict to be inevitable.

HOW DO YOU DEAL WITH CONFLICT?

Now that you have thought through the way conflicts are, and might be, handled, take a minute to think about you and your organization. Here are some questions which might be of help.

1. What are your inner feelings toward conflicts which arise?
    a) Do you consider conflicts to be natural and expected?
    b) Do you feel up-tight? Challenged? A bit frightened or nervous? Dared? Comfortable? Wish they would go away? Welcome them? It all depends . . .? (On what?)
    c) Why do you suppose you feel as you do?

2. As you perceive your own methods of operating, how do you tend to settle conflicts now?
   a) Which of the five described methods (evasion, suppression, domination, compromise, and integration) do you tend to use the most often?
   b) If the first attempt doesn't work, what do you use then?
   c) What do you tend to use the least?
   d) Do you stick to one method even when it isn't appropriate to the situation faced?
   e) Why do you suppose you use the methods you do?
   f) What other methods of handling conflict do you think you would like to try? Why?

_____
_____
_____
_____
_____
_____
_____
_____
_____
_____

3. How would you characterize the climate in your organization for handling conflicts?
   a) What are the usual, expected methods?
   b) Do some people or groups avoid each other when they should be working together?
   c) Are there a lot of "power plays"?
   d) Is the emphasis on "sweetness and light"?
   e) How is compromise looked upon? As a virtue?
   f) If you tried a new method, how would it be received?

_____
_____

4. How would other organizations which interface with yours describe your organization's efforts when conflicts arise?
   a) Have you any way of finding out how they view your group?
   b) Do members of your group avoid others in the organization?
   c) Do you frequently/sometimes/seldom call on higher authority to settle arguments in your favor?
   d) Do you send carbon copies of "fight" correspondence to a higher boss (or pretend to)?
   e) Is your group known as "hardnosed"? Always ready for a hassle? Great compromisers? Or how?
   f) Do you want to change the image people have of your group? How can you go about this?

5. How are arguments settled among the people in your group?
   a) Do some tend to avoid others in the group? Why?
   b) Do you stress being "just one big happy family"?
   c) Do you find yourself being the arbiter or mediator very often?
   d) Do you stress compromise as a good method for settling disputes?
   e) Do you feel that integration would work more often?
   f) Do you often/sometimes/never discuss how arguments and conflicts are being handled by your people?

6. How would you summarize what you are doing and what you would like to be doing in handling conflicts?

CHAPTER **11**

MOTIVATION

The subject of motivation is getting its share of attention these days—in books (How to Motivate Your Salesmen); in articles ("Developing the Will to Work in Anybody!"); and in courses ("This course will show your supervisors how to instill enthusiasm in workers" and "Motivation for success!"). Certainly, we need to understand the subject better. By the same token, many of the ads and slogans strongly suggest that motivation is something we "do" *to* people—that motivation comes from outside the person. But I wonder if this is so.

The rapidly changing make-up and outlook of working people suggest that motivation is something that we need to look into carefully. The mature manager of today and yesterday has had his outlook, values, and attitudes shaped or influenced greatly by the economic depression of the 1930s. These influences have been great, but they would be difficult for him to describe, because they are so much a part of him.

In the same way, today's affluence is shaping young people in ways that they take for granted. They, too, would find it difficult to describe these influences. Or, if they do try, we don't know what *they* are talking about. And even when we try to "talk some sense into them" by explaining about hard times and how important it is to get a good, steady job, they don't seem to listen. This is one of the major features of the "generation gap" (or chasm). The pictures in our heads don't seem to have the same meaning for the young people, in their world. In the future, we are going to have more and more young people with us in our organizations. Whether they are working "with us" will depend, in part, on our understanding of their work aspirations and what motivates them.

ABOUT "THEORIES"

In this section we are going to look at some "theories," so let's spend a few minutes talking about the word. Why should a practical manager spend any

time with "theories"? *Webster's Dictionary* gives three definitions of the term:
1. "a coherent group of general propositions used as principles for the explanation of a class of phenomena";
2. "a proposed explanation the status of which is still conjectural, in contrast to well-established propositions that are regarded as reporting matters of actual fact";
3. "a particular conception or view of something to be done and the method of doing it; a system of rules or principles."

Under which of these three definitions would you place the following ideas? (indicate 1, 2, or 3)

_____a) "Staff" people should not have authority over "line" people.
_____b) According to Einstein, mass and energy are equivalent, and one can be converted into the other in accordance with the relationship: $E = MC^2$. (C is the speed of light.)
_____c) Fear of unemployment is the real key to employee productivity.
_____d) The many rival theories about how people learn.
_____e) An employee should have only one boss.

Einstein's theory of relativity (item b) is the only one that belongs in the first category. Items (a) and (e) are part of a large body of organizational theory, ideas about organization which may or may not be currently useful. With regard to item (e), for example, F. W. Taylor (the "father of scientific management") proposed some years ago that every worker have "functional foremen"—seven in number, as I recall—each of whom would perform one of the aspects of the foreman's job (planning, discipline, etc.). The popular idea that each worker should have just one boss is a notion backed up by biblical authority. But now many organizations have turned to "project" management, in which many in the organization have several bosses.

The second classification, to which items (c) and (d) belong, comprises the kinds of theories we are concerned with here, namely, *proposed* explanations. Generally, such theories oversimplify complex causes, but they can be useful in helping us think about the world. Every person has a whole set of theories which guide his daily actions. These assumptions about the world may or may not be "common sense."

APPLYING THEORIES TO BEHAVIOR

To move into the area of applying theories to behavior, let's take a look at two studies made by behavioral scientists. One of these studies took place many years ago; the other, more recently.

In the first study, managers of the Western Electric Company's Hawthorne plant, together with the faculty and staff of the Harvard Business School, undertook to study the relationship between fatigue and productivity. The

Applying theories to behavior 261

study, which took a total of 114 weeks, was divided into 13 periods. During the first three periods, productivity was measured in the workers' regular department; they were then moved to the test room, and a special group bonus was established. During the next eight periods, variations were introduced —allowing "break" periods (rest pauses) of different lengths and at different times, shortening the work day, eliminating Saturday morning work for one period, and providing lunch in five of the periods. Production was carefully recorded to determine if fatigue was being relieved by the changes. Then, in the twelfth period, the original conditions were reinstated—regular working day, no breaks, no lunches provided.

Put on a researcher's hat for a minute. What would you expect to find as you introduced these changes to reduce fatigue? How do you think they would probably affect the workers' productivity? (In scientific terms, this question would be stated as: "What is your working hypothesis?") Then, based on your expectations in the other test periods, what would you expect to happen when there was a return to the original conditions for more than two months in the twelfth period? State your reasoning in the space below before you read further.

_____
_____
_____
_____

To summarize (briefly) the results of a very detailed study, productivity went up in almost every case—even when a return was made *to the original conditions!* The relay-assembly workers expressed their greater satisfaction with the test-room situation, including the changed relations with supervision, increased attention, etc. Absences for illness and personal reasons decreased. The workers involved in the study became a group which had loyalty, a leader, and whose members helped one another.

If it weren't for the return to the original conditions (the twelfth period), a close relationship between productivity and monotony and fatigue might have been assumed to have been proved. But the results from this period made it impossible to draw conclusions as to this close relationship. How do you account for what happened? (What is your "theory" to explain what happened?) State your theory before you read further.

_____
_____
_____

Before we see what the researchers thought about what happened, let's look at a second study. But let's approach this one a little differently. Here are the attitudes of two supervisors in a work setting. Read the two statements and then answer the questions.

1. "My job is to keep my people busy in doing what they are supposed to, how they are supposed to. I spend a lot of time with them about their jobs, giving them specific directions and showing them just how to do it well. They expect me to be critical when they do a poor job, but I'm impartial about this. 'Be firm, but fair,' that's my motto. And I put the pressure on for good performance. This is what I'm paid to do. It would be nice to get involved with these people and their personal problems, but that's a luxury in my book. Let's get the production out first."
2. "I let my people do the job the way they want to, as long as they accomplish the objectives. Let them make the decisions about their jobs; they know them better than I do, anyway. Mistakes? Oh, I generally ignore them. They have learned something by making a mistake. Of course, sometimes I do step in and show them how to do it right, if that's the problem. I take an interest in each one of them. If they have a personal problem, I generally know about it. After all, that's my job."*

In your view, which of these two supervisors is doing the better job? Which attitude comes closest to your own? Which attitude would be rated the best by your boss? Which supervisor would tend to have the greater productivity, would you guess? Write down your ideas about these two attitudes and your prediction as to the production of both before reading on.

---

* I have tried to cast some research findings as the attitudes expressed by these two supervisors. The research is reported in Rensis Likert's book, which will be discussed later. Other aspects affecting productivity, but not considered here, are group processes, communication, and influence.

The Researchers' Findings and Conclusions

The study by Elton Mayo and others at the Hawthorne plant is something of a classic today. In attempting to isolate the effects of fatigue and monotony on productivity, the researchers took great care to create stable conditions and then to change one variable at a time to measure its impact. This is one approved method of research.

After 114 weeks of study and the keeping of elaborate and exact records, the researchers began to realize that:

> The experiment they had planned to conduct was quite different from the experiment they had actually performed. They had not studied the relation between output and fatigue, monotony, etc., so much as they had performed a most interesting psychological and sociological experiment. In the process of setting the conditions for the test, they had altered completely the social situation of the operators and their customary attitudes and interpersonal relations.*

Thus, the notion of looking at the social situation was begun. In trying to carefully introduce single variables and measure them, they had introduced a whole range of variables much more important than the planned changes. When you ask the workers about the rest periods before and after trying them, you change the situation. Other things were changed, also, but this expression of interest in the workers was so important to the results of the study that this factor is today known as the "Hawthorne effect."

With the insights and generalizations (theories) in use today, we may look back at this study from the late 1920s and feel that the researchers were incredibly naive—*in the same way that researchers and managers in the future will undoubtedly look at our attempts at research and the notions we hold today!* The Hawthorne studies are valuable to us even if (or perhaps because) they didn't find what they set out to find. But neither did Columbus.

Now, let's look at the second and more recent study. Rensis Likert and his associates, at the University of Michigan studied high- and low-producing groups to try to discover the reasons for this condition. Interviews determined that the supervisors of the high-producing groups were "employee-centered" (supervisor 2) rather than strictly "production-centered" (supervisor 1). Employee-centered supervisors tended to give their people a general outline of the work to be done, leaving the details up to the workers. There was no close checking on the workers; the supervisors assumed that the workers were responsible. The workers handled problems which arose, largely by themselves. Production-centered supervisors, on the other hand, tended to emphasize their authority role, giving detailed instructions on what to do and how to do it. If things were not going right, they might step in and do it themselves.

---

* F. J. Roethlisberger and W. J. Dickson, *Management and the Worker,* Cambridge, Mass.: Harvard University Press, 1947, p. 183.

The production-centered supervisors pushed hard for production. When they met with opposition, they pushed harder. They ignored the social and personal needs of employees. They were driving, defensive, and authoritarian. The employee-centered supervisors, on the other hand, were sensitive to the social and personal needs of the employees and dealt with them rather than ruling them out of order. When employees were given responsibility and controls were relaxed, the employees tended to have higher productivity. In both cases, the employees tended to react to the two different styles of management through varying rates of production.*

We must be careful about what we *think we know* after seeing the results of this study. As the researchers were careful to point out, these findings may not always be true, particularly in the short run. Other studies have shown that different people on different jobs in different settings may operate best under a different management style. We all like to generalize, to find a simple answer to "what makes people tick." But we really can't, and we do so only at our peril.

QUESTIONNAIRES

What we have done so far in this section is to establish (we hope) that theories are not necessarily the ideas held only by impractical people in ivory towers, but that we all have them and use them continually; that every "practical" manager draws on theories (or makes them up) to explain his observations; and that generalizations from research findings must be made with some care. Now let's get more into ideas on motivation. Answer the two questionnaires that follow. Your answers will be used a little later to test some ideas advanced about motivation.

JOB PREFERENCE QUESTIONNAIRE

In answering this questionnaire, you will be asked to rank groups of five statements. There are no "right" or "wrong" rankings. The best responses are those which reflect your real feelings. The more open you are, the more possible it will be for you to gain insights into your real preferences.

In ranking, it is often easier to pick your top choice first, then your last choice, then your choice next to the top, then the one next to the lowest. The remaining choice becomes your middle choice. By each statement below, place a number that indicates its importance to you within the group of five statements. Use "5" to indicate your

---

* It is always a problem to quickly summarize research, particularly when the research has been conducted in a complex area such as human motivation. The exact findings, the care with which the research conditions are described, and the qualified statements of conclusions are all too easily glossed over, and this is a disservice. I would urge that you read the book *New Patterns of Management* by Rensis Likert, New York: McGraw-Hill, 1961. This book describes quite a few related research efforts into motivation and draws some important implications about authoritative vs. participative styles of management.

highest ranking, then, "4," "3," "2," and "1" to indicate your lowest ranking. (For now, disregard the letters by each question.)

1. Rank these factors as to their importance to you in a job ("5" is high, "1" is low).
   - L. _____ Being given recognition and attention for achievement
   - V. _____ Working for a strong, stable organization
   - Q. _____ Opportunity to belong to a good group
   - D. _____ Developing your abilities to their full potential
   - G. _____ Opportunity for independent thought and action

2. Rank these factors as to how concerned you would be with them on a job ("5" is high, "1" is low).
   - H. _____ Able to accomplish the job on your own
   - R. _____ Development of close friendships on the job
   - W. _____ Good benefits and job security
   - M. _____ A source of pride when you accomplish something
   - E. _____ Real achievement and personal growth required

3. Rank the most important factors to you in going to a new job ("5" is high, "1" is low).
   - A. _____ The learning and growth you would obtain from the experience
   - K. _____ Prestige and respect from others because of the job
   - F. _____ Freedom to operate on your own
   - P. _____ Friendliness of co-workers
   - U. _____ Assurance that you would maintain job security

4. Rank these factors in the order you would like them most in a job ("5" is high, "1" is low).
   - T. _____ Congenial working relations
   - I. _____ Able to set own directions and make own decisions
   - B. _____ Interesting and meaningful work
   - X. _____ Few changes so that you knew where you stood
   - N. _____ The job being seen by others as important

5. Rank these factors as to the need for them to be present for you to work your hardest ("5" is high, "1" is low).
   - Y. _____ Stable and orderly job to be done
   - C. _____ Meaningful work and growth opportunities
   - O. _____ Full credit for accomplishments
   - J. _____ Freedom and independence to get the job done
   - S. _____ A real feeling of belonging to a team

Now list and total the point ranking assigned to these letters:

I	II	III	IV	V
A. _____	F. _____	K. _____	P. _____	U. _____
B. _____	G. _____	L. _____	Q. _____	V. _____
C. _____	H. _____	M. _____	R. _____	W. _____
D. _____	I. _____	N. _____	S. _____	X. _____
E. _____	J. _____	O. _____	T. _____	Y. _____

Totals: _____   _____   _____   _____   _____

LIKED MOST/LIKED LEAST QUESTIONNAIRE

In every job there are things about it that we like and dislike. That is true for the jobs we have liked very much and true for those we haven't liked very much.

1. Think back to a job that you liked very much. Then list as many things as you can that you liked the most about it, and those things which you liked the least about it.

    Liked most   Liked least

    _____   _____
    _____   _____
    _____   _____
    _____   _____
    _____   _____
    _____   _____
    _____   _____
    _____   _____
    _____   _____
    _____   _____

2. Now think back to a job that you didn't like very much at all. List as many things about it that you did like, and the things about it which you disliked.

    Did like   Didn't like

    _____   _____
    _____   _____
    _____   _____
    _____   _____
    _____   _____
    _____   _____
    _____   _____
    _____   _____
    _____   _____
    _____   _____

SOME THEORIES OF MOTIVATION

Before we take a look at what your responses on the questionnaires might mean, let's talk about some background. (In discussing the background, it will be useful to keep in mind that in working with people as *individuals,* we must remember that they are striving to maintain and enhance their own self-image, as they perceive it. Thus, we are moving up the abstraction ladder from a specific individual, to "people in our organization," to "people we pass in the halls," to "workers in our type of industry," to "workers," to "the labor force in this country." As we move up the ladder, we are getting farther removed from our referent individual and in the process, glossing over many, many unique differences among individuals.)

In this discussion about motivation, I will use the word "need" to mean the individual's internal push (as in "drive"), which seeks an outlet. "Need" will also be used to mean some condition which the individual wants. We all have multiple needs which move us toward goals, but naming these needs presents a bit of a problem. Psychologists have defined as many as 50 needs, but too many become meaningless, just as too few would not describe differences in goal-seeking behaviors which it might be useful to note. Any such list is a compromise for the sake of convenience, and the terms used should be viewed as approximate, with overlaps expected.

Now let's look at two theories about motivation and a description of two different sets of assumptions about people and their motivation.

Maslow's Hierachy of Needs

The late Abraham Maslow, of Brandeis University, postulated that all men share certain needs which can be arranged in a hierarchy of levels, from the most fundamental body needs to that of self-fulfillment. As adapted from Maslow,* needs can be identified at six levels. From lowest to highest, they are:

1. *Basic:* primarily physiological survival needs of food, water, air, protection against extreme temperatures, rest, etc.

2. *Security (safety):* safeguarding against danger, threat, or deprivation. This could be shown as a desire to maintain benefits, have a strong, secure company, or a lack of change or instability.

3. *Social:* wanting to be a part of something larger than oneself, belonging, for sharing and association, for giving and receiving help, friendship and love, etc.

---

* In his original concept, Maslow listed these needs: physiological, safety, love, esteem, and self-actualization. (*Motivation and Personality,* New York: Harper & Brothers, 1954.) Later researchers have identified "independence" as a separate category of need.

4. *Esteem:* self-confidence, achievement, competence, status, recognition, appreciation, deserved respect, etc.

5. *Independence:* setting and working toward own objectives, having authority to get the job done, freedom, etc.

6. *Self-fulfillment:* to be able to attain one's own limits—"what one can be, one must be," growth, learning, development, self-actualization, etc.

The reason it is important to understand these needs, according to Maslow, is that our unsatisfied needs serve as both a stimulus for action and a pilot for the direction that action takes. Unmet needs define both the values we seek and our value-seeking behavior.

Maslow suggests that we must satisfy our basic needs first, for if these needs are not satisfied, nothing else is very important to us. If our basic needs are reasonably well satisfied, then our security needs become important. Once these needs are relatively well satisfied, we move up the ladder to the social needs, etc. But note that once our needs at a particular level are satisfied, they *cease to be motivators*. If I am not hungry, food doesn't provide much motivation for me. We can all think of exceptions, of course. The person who has been deprived for a long period has the desires associated with that unsatisfied need pretty deeply implanted. We all know people who, even though they are financially well-to-do, act as if they were still quite poor. We know other people who must have continual group contact and approval, despite their piled-up rewards for accomplishment. And, as Maslow points out, the need for self-fulfillment seems to be unsatiable.

As you have guessed by now, the "Job Preference Questionnaire" which you filled out earlier was an attempt to see if your preferences about conditions on the job could be ranked to provide some clues about the needs that are most important to you. The assumption here is that you would assign a higher rank to the statements showing your unsatisfied needs; in other words, that these are the factors which really motivate you. Now turn back to your summary following the questionnaire. The five columns summarize your rankings of these needs:

Column I (A,B,C,D,E): self-fulfillment
Column II (F,G,H,I,J): independence
Column III (K,L,M,N,O): esteem
Column IV (P,Q,R,S,T): social
Column V (U,V,W,X,Y): security

(The "basic" needs were not included in this questionnaire; I thought that anyone who might take this questionnaire would have these needs relatively well satisfied.)

Since you ranked the items with a value of "5" for high and "1" for low, the factors are already weighted, and you should be able to readily see what your profile might be. There may be one or two needs which have higher point totals than others, or there may be a balance of all need classes in your stated preferences. We might speculate that if your "self-fulfillment" total was high, you tend to seek out and enjoy work in which learning, growth, personal challenge, etc., are involved. If you don't find these through your work, we might expect them to be reflected in your hobbies and leisure pursuits; if in neither situation, we might expect a measure of frustration. If your score for "independence" was high, we could expect you to enjoy activities and work which allow a high degree of self-direction and control. If "esteem" is important, we would expect you to seek out and enjoy activities in which group recognition and approval are forthcoming. If being a member of a team, sharing, and association are important to you, we would expect this to be reflected in a high point total for the "social" category. Similarly, if your security needs are high, we would expect you to prefer jobs which are stable and secure and in which there are no threats to your benefits.

I have "hedged" in the discussion of interpretations of what your scores "mean." That's because I'm not certain that this simple ranking of preferences stated is either valid or reliable. But your expressed preferences may be interesting for you to think about.

Now answer these questions about your "profile":

1. Would you have answered the questionnaire the same way a year ago? Why or why not?

2. Would you have answered the same way if you took the questionnaire over again right now? Why or why not?

3. Would you have answered it the same way if you had just lost your job? Why or why not?

4. Would you have answered it the same way if you had taken it in, say, 1936? Why or why not?

5. Would you have answered it the same way if you were black (white) and living in the South (North)? Why or why not?

6. Would you have answered it the same way if you were a member of the poorer classes in, say, India? Why or why not?

7. How would your subordinates have answered the questionnaire? If differently from you, how so? Why? If about the same, why?

The idea of a hierarchy of needs may encourage us *not* to think of people as complex, different, and changing, and this would be a mistake. Let's assume that several people are riding in the first-class section of a train. Two of the men are talking (social needs). One woman is about to assume a new position, and she is reading in her field and thinking about what her future will bring (esteem). Another man is designing a new racing boat, one of his important hobbies (self-actualization). Another is planning to open his own business (independence). Suddenly, there is an accident, and the parlor car is overturned. Now what needs are paramount to these people?

Take another situation. A man is hungry, and since it is almost the customary time for luncheon, he stops by a friend's office and persuades her to go to lunch with him. He takes her to a very expensive restaurant, orders without letting her see the menu, and insists on a wine of a particular year. He then begins telling her of a recent successful accomplishment. What needs are motivating him in this case?

There is nothing very simple about our needs, how we express our needs, or how we attempt to satisfy them. If we are hungry, from a nutritional standpoint there is not much difference between a hamburger, french fries, and a salad at the diner and a $19 luncheon at El Swanko, but a lot of other needs are involved in the two experiences.

The nature of a person's complaints can be analyzed to determine what needs are unsatisfied. For example, no one likes to stand in lines or queues to get something. But what's at the other end of the line? Food? A business permit? Opera tickets? A dance?

All of us have all of the needs Maslow identified, but they may differ in intensity with each of us.* But many people tell me, "Yeah, but salesmen are a different breed of cat, man. The only thing that motivates them is the good old green dollar." Well, I don't believe that, and neither do you! But I do believe this: if money is the only way you have to pay a person, you can never pay him enough! Money may be important to salesmen, but to satisfy what needs? To satisfy the basic or security needs only? Or to give them a place in their group?

---

* Maslow advanced another idea that is interesting to ponder, namely, that these few identified needs are perhaps but the lowest in a hierarchy of hundreds of classes of needs which will come into view as the future unfolds.

Or for the esteem to belong to the million-dollar round table? Or to make them independent? Or as a sign of accomplishment? Money may be stressed by managers of salesmen, but it may be satisfying needs at various levels.

Now that you have taken a look at what your profile might be in Maslow's suggested hierarchy, what about your subordinates' profiles? Are they a different "breed of cat"? Or are they motivated by the same needs of self-fulfillment, independence, and esteem as you found you were? Do your policies and practices assume that these needs are important? What about the idea that a satisfied need ceases to be a motivator? Do the policies and practices of your organization seem to reflect this idea? Or are they based on the idea that the basic and security needs are the only ones which ever need be considered, and that once a policy or practice handles these, you can forget about motivation?

McGregor's Summary of Assumptions (Theory X and Theory Y)

The late Douglas McGregor was head of the School of Industrial Relations at the Massachusetts Institute of Technology when his book *The Human Side of Enterprise* was published.* In this book, McGregor examined the assumptions that seem to underlie the policies, procedures, work rules, and management customs in organizations. These assumptions are not often made explicit, but if you keep asking "but, why?" to rules, procedures, etc., they will finally come to light. (I'll demonstrate this later.)

One set of assumptions McGregor identified are:

1. The average human being has an inherent dislike for work and will avoid it if he can.
2. Because of this inherent dislike for work, most people must be coerced, controlled, directed, and threatened with punishment to get them to put forth adequate effort toward the achievement of organizational objectives.
3. The average human being prefers to be directed, wishes to avoid responsibility, has relatively little ambition, and wants security above all else.

McGregor calls these assumptions about people "Theory X" as a shorthand label. What do you think about those assumptions? Some people are like that, no question about it. But how many, that's the point. All but a few? Almost all? Some? Most? A few? If we believe that these assumptions about people are true, it would be natural for us to attempt to "motivate" people from outside, by using a carrot or a stick. It would be logical for us to exercise tight direction and close control and not to expect people to want to know about things that will affect them or to want any "say" in decisions that affect them. Conversely, if we act in these ways, then we do feel the way about people which the assumptions identify.

---

* Douglas McGregor, *The Human Side of Enterprise,* New York: McGraw-Hill, 1960.

272 Motivation Chap. 11

McGregor identified another set of assumptions about people which seem to be emerging from behavioral science research. These are:

1. The expenditure of physical and mental effort in work is as natural as play or rest.
2. External control and threat of punishment are not the only means for bringing about effort toward organizational objectives. Man will exercise self-control in the service of objectives to which he is committed.
3. Commitment to objectives is dependent on rewards associated with their achievement. The most important rewards are those that satisfy needs for self-respect and personal improvement.
4. The average human being learns, under proper conditions, not only to accept but to seek responsibility.
5. The capacity to exercise a relatively high degree of imagination, ingenuity, and creativity in the solution of organizational problems is widely, not narrowly, distributed in the population.
6. Under the conditions of modern industrial life, the intellectual potentialities of the average human being are only partially utilized.

McGregor called these assumptions "Theory Y" to distinguish them from the more traditional, Theory X assumptions. What do you think about *these* assumptions? Some people are like that, too. No question about it. But how many? All but a few? Almost all? Some? Most? A few?

Which set of assumptions seems to underlie the practices in your organization? Why? Are the expectations of the people—particularly newcomers—changing? What would you have to do to change from one list of assumptions to the other? Here is a list of familiar practices in many organizations. How would you classify each? Under "theory X" assumptions? Under "theory Y" assumptions? Or could they be either? (Check the appropriate column for each.)

Typical practices	"Theory X"	"Theory Y"	Either
time clocks	____	____	____
management by objectives	____	____	____
restriction to work area	____	____	____
method studies	____	____	____
incentive pay	____	____	____
employee ratings	____	____	____
suggestion system	____	____	____
guards at the gate	____	____	____
close quality inspections	____	____	____
small span of control	____	____	____

Some theories of motivation

Typical practices	"Theory X"	"Theory Y"	Either
detailed work plans	___	___	___
specialization of work	___	___	___
conformity in dress required	___	___	___
strict compliance with rules	___	___	___
10-minute (enforced) breaks	___	___	___

Do not read any further until you have placed a checkmark for each item.

As you may have discovered, the mere existence of these practices does not make them representative of either "Theory X" or "Theory Y." There may be good, practical reasons for each of the practices. However, these practices may also reflect underlying assumptions about people. Sometimes, the difference lies in the administration of the practice. For example, one organization may have a production contract that requires close quality inspections by another organization. Or, close inspection may reflect management's belief that the workers just do sloppy work. Why? Because they don't care. Why don't they care? Because that's just the way they are. And since they are that way, there's no reason to give them any feedback on the quality of work they are producing because it won't make any difference in their behavior. So, naturally, management has to have an outside agency make the inspections. Right?

You may restrict people to specified work areas for reasons of safety, security, and so on. Or, you may do it to keep people from "goofing off" and wandering around. Why would they? Because they just don't like to work and will "goof off" whenever they can get away with it. But, why? Because that's just the way they are. And since they are that way, we have to provide restrictions on their movements while at work.

Your organization may follow the practice of having a small span of control—having each manager supervise only a small number of subordinates—because of the nature of the product or service you provide. Or, you may follow this practice to make sure that subordinates keep busy. Why is such close supervision necessary? Because subordinates will slow down if you don't keep after them. Why will they do that? Because they are lazy and don't like to work. And because they are this way, we must provide close supervision, which means a small span of control.

Even a practice such as "management by objectives" may reflect the two sets of assumptions described by McGregor. If the boss says, "We are going to have a management-by-objectives program, and here are yours!" this would seem to reflect one set of assumptions. On the other hand, the boss might say, "As you know, the organization is interested in beginning a management-by-objectives program. Here are the objectives I have tried to set based on my part of the bosses' job. Look them over and think about what you would propose as your objectives. Then, let's get together and talk them over." This approach would seem to reflect a different set of assumptions.

Some of the practices required by organizations seem restrictive, and indeed they are. But they are often quite legitimate and necessary, and subordinates can be helped to see the reason for these requirements. All of us must work under restraints of one degree or another. But it's often how these restraints are applied and administered that makes the difference. "Theory X" assumptions shouldn't be seen as only causing a condition of "toughness," nor "theory Y" assumptions as creating a condition of "freedom and happiness."

Take a close look at your own practices and those of your organization. Keep asking "why?" to each of them. In this way, your real assumptions about people and what they are like may come into view. And what you see may surprise you.

Herzberg—Motivators and Hygienic Factors

Frederick Herzberg and his associates conducted an extensive series of interviews in an attempt to determine what motivates people.* They found that when the people talked about the things they really liked about their jobs, these factors were related to:

1. achievement
2. recognition for achievement
3. the work itself
4. responsibility
5. advancement
6. possibility of growth

Herzberg calls these factors *motivators*.

On the other hand, when the people identified the items about which they were dissatisfied, these factors were related to:

1. supervision
2. company policy and administration
3. working conditions
4. interpersonal relations with peers, subordinates, and superiors
5. status
6. job security
7. personal factors

These factors, which Herzberg calls *hygienic* factors, are seen to have no power to motivate, but they become sources of dissatisfaction if the minimum conditions expected are not met. Restated, the hygiene factors have no power

---

* F. Herzberg, B. Mausner, and F. M. Andrews, *The Motivation to Work*, New York: Wiley, 1959.

to motivate, but their lack can cause dissatisfaction. In this view, positive motivation can come only from real accomplishment on a meaningful job.

Now let's take a look at the second questionnaire you filled out earlier, "Liked Most/Liked Least." What did you say you liked about the job you liked? Did you identify the "motivators" Herzberg suggests? (You wouldn't use his words, necessarily. His factor of "achievement," for instance, might have been stated as: "Really felt I was getting somewhere on that job.") On the job you liked, what *didn't* you like about it? Do the "hygiene factors" begin to appear?

What did you list about the job you thought of which you didn't care for? Could you list some things which you did like? Were they "motivators" or "hygiene factors"? What didn't you like about that job? Does this list show the absence of motivators"? In general, have you "proved" Herzberg's ideas by showing that they represent your feelings about your jobs? If not, why not, do you suppose?

If you have shown the validity of Herzberg's ideas through your own experiences and your own expectations toward your job, that raises some interesting questions. For instance:

1. Are your subordinates motivated by the same things you are? Or, are they motivated by different things?
2. When you make changes to "motivate" people better, do you look at their jobs? Working conditions? Elsewhere?
3. What do your external advertisements for people feature? How about internal advertisements?
4. What are the selling points you use in recruitment? Benefits? Accomplishments possible? Something else?
5. When changes are made to increase the satisfactions of subordinates, what things are changed? Their jobs? The hygiene factors? Something else?
6. What do you suppose are the real reasons why people quit your organization?
7. If you were trying to talk someone out of leaving, what arguments would you use to try to get him to stay?
8. What should you be giving your attention to when you want to "motivate" people?

Other researchers have attempted to replicate Herzberg's findings and the resultant "theory," with mixed results. Some feel that the ideas do hold true for well-educated professional and semiprofessional workers, but not for blue-collar workers. Others have reported successful application with all types of people. But Herzberg's distinction is a useful one and helps to remind us that we should look beyond working conditions for motivation—into the jobs themselves. But what about all of the dull, dreary, monotonous, unchallenging jobs in this world? Is it true, as some people suggest, that we can only make the pay and working conditions as attractive as possible, and then try to get people to fill them in quiet desperation? Or, do some "types" of people really like these jobs? Research findings are limited, so we have to use our own assumptions.

WHAT ARE YOUR ASSUMPTIONS ABOUT MOTIVATION?

Now that we have looked at some theories of motivation, it's time we took a look at *yours*. It's not what the "experts" say about motivation that's important; it's what *you* really believe. To see what you really believe, fill in this questionnaire just as far as you can go.

1. People are most productive when: _____

2. People are most productive when: _____

3. People are most productive when: _____

4. People are most productive when: _____

5. People are most productive when: _____

Can you go on for a couple more? Now, what do you do that really motivates people?

6. People are most productive when I: _____

_____

_____

_____

7. People are most productive when I: _____

_____

_____

_____

If you have been honest, you have listed your theories of motivation. If you have completed the sentence "People are most productive when I . . . stand over them with a stick," this is your theory of motivation. If you have completed this same sentence with "provide them with interesting and challenging jobs," this is your theory of motivation. What remains, then, is to make sure that your practices and procedures reflect your ideas about motivation.

Your Assumptions Applied to You

Using your own ideas on what motivates people, which you have just identified, how could your boss bring these to bear on *your* job?

HOW MY BOSS COULD CHANGE MY JOB OR CONDITIONS TO REALLY MOTIVATE ME

Your Assumptions Applied to Your Subordinates

Now that you have identified your theories on motivation and have shown how these could be better brought to bear on your own job, let's look at how you could apply these ideas to your subordinates. If your "theories of motivation" include such things as "stand over them with a stick" or "raise hell with them when they get out of line," you might think we should now help you do those things more effectively—show you how you might carry a bigger stick or raise hell more effectively. But I can't help you. If you do these things now, everybody around you knows that you do, and you are now getting as much mileage out of them as you possibly can. So I have no suggestions to offer. If, on the other hand, your interest is in looking at the jobs of your subordinates and seeing what might be done to help them satisfy the needs of self-fulfillment, independence, esteem, etc., perhaps I do have some ways to help.

Many of the specific areas discussed in this book about your relations with subordinates have been concerned, at least indirectly, with enriching the jobs of subordinates and accomplishing the goals of the organization. If you and your people share a climate of trust which encourages open discussion, if you communicate well, if you get participation in decisions (because better decisions can be the result), if you are concerned with their development, if they have a clear picture of their jobs and goals (which they helped set), if you delegate appropriately, and so on, then your subordinates probably are having their higher order needs largely met now.

However, to help you focus particularly on making their jobs more meaningful, you might raise the following questions about the specific jobs under you. (These questions are meant to suggest approaches. You will raise more significant questions about the specific jobs.)

Job design

1. What can be done to make the person more self-sufficient?
2. What happens *before* he gets the assignment that might be included in the assignment? (For example, is some need determined first by someone else? Could he also determine the need? Etc.)
3. What happens *after* he finishes an assignment that might be included in the assignment? (For example, when he finishes a report, do you present it "upstairs"? Could he do this? Etc.)
4. Can larger segments of the job be given to him? Why is he handling only the parts he is?
5. What new things could be added to his job for him to learn? What new and different tasks could be assigned? What special assignments could be given to him? What problems could he be given to solve, either as a member of a task force or individually?
6. When someone leaves the organization, could he take over all or part of that job? Are there parts of *his* job which are routine to him but which would be challenging to others?

Planning and control

1. What part of the person's duties are planned for him now? What parts of the planning could he take over?
2. Can he participate more in the basic plans? In the implementing plans?
3. Is the person given assignments and due dates so that he can plan, determine priority, and schedule his own work?
4. How is performance according to plan measured now? Can these measures be made available directly to the individual? More immediately? More complete? More specific data?
5. Can some controls be removed with the person still being responsible?

Your direction

1. What do you do for the person in your supervision/administration that the person could do for himself?
2. What can he do in an emergency or in your absence that might be done all the time?
3. What additional authority can he be given to do or decide?
4. On what decision issues could his recommendations be sought which are not sought now? (Would making these recommendations ensure a better result as well as help him grow?)
5. What new things could the person learn? What training could he give to others on your staff?
6. How are his achievements recognized now? Can this be made more meaningful? Can the person's skills be spotlighted? Can he been seen by outsiders as the expert whom they can contact with a particular problem?

Remember that the person himself is your greatest resource for ideas on how his job could be enriched. Just raising the question with him will have an enriching impact. Now let's think about specific applications to subordinate's jobs.

List your subordinates' names in the left-hand column. Then think about what changes you could make to bring your theories to bear in each case. (Of course, you will also consider what your boss and the other people "upstairs" will permit, how willing you are to take risks, the people themselves, etc.)

People who report to me: How I can apply my motivation
                                theories to them:

_____ _____
_____ _____
_____ _____
_____ _____
_____ _____

280   Motivation Chap. 11

People who report to me: How I can apply my motivation
                            theories to them:

CHAPTER **12**

SOME IDEAS ABOUT ADMINISTRATION

In this chapter I'll present 13 "mini-essays" on as many topics in administration. Some of these essays are based on the ideas of others which I have found to be helpful. Some reflect my own ideas and experiences. The first several essays deal with our assumptive world in organizations, such as our ideas about authority; the next few deal with some aspects of the manager's job: delegation, indecision, and operating in a crisis. Toward the end of the chapter, the subjects are mostly about subordinates: how to think about them, develop them, and fire them when necessary.

Some administrative practices and procedures are not discussed here because they differ so widely, depending on the organization. Take your organization's practices in selection, for example. You will perform this function according to the established practices and resources of your organization. Some of you will, literally or almost, stand up on a crate at the gate and select by "looks." Others of you will have more elaborate "scientific" procedures. In some organizations, selections are made by some specialized group, such as the personnel department. Other organizations insist that the new person's manager make the selection. (He can't select people any better than *we* can, but at least he can't blame them on *us!*) Therefore, I shall not talk about selection, pay schemes, evaluation systems, and the like, for such practices can and do vary widely.

THE WORLD OF "AS IF"

To talk about the world of "as if," let's use the technique of having a man (Mr. Maa) from a "backward" nation try to get, among other things, an understanding of how we organize ourselves to get things done. His first call is on the Assistant to the President (Don) of an organization.

Don: I thought it would be helpful to begin with the organization manual to give you an overview of just how we are put together.
Maa: I'd like to know that.

Don: This is our top organization chart. Here, you'll see the President in this box, his personal staff (there I am) right there, and here are the vice-presidents who report to him. Now here are the general managers of the various operating units, and their key people are along this row.

Maa: They build and sell the product?

Don: No, of course not. We are still too high in the organization to see who does this.

Maa: High? You mean farther out in space?

Don: No, no, not that, exactly. These are upper-level jobs, the top jobs to which people can be promoted when they are selected for advancement. When a person has risen to one of these jobs, he passes orders and directives down. But these jobs are not really "up," if you see what I mean. It's just like maps of North America. Canada is always "up," and Mexico is always "down." But they aren't really "up"; we just say they are.

Maa: (Writes in notebook: "Top jobs not up.") I see that some of the boxes are larger than some of the others.

Don: Of course. You will note that the top boxes are larger and that the boxes get smaller as you go down on the chart. (It's not really up and down, remember.) The size of the box indicates the size of the job. The bigger the job, the bigger the box, and the bigger the people that have to fill them. Do you understand?

Maa: I think so. (Writes in notebook: "Fat people must have large boxes.")

Don: Well, I'm glad you get that. I should point out that some organization charts have equal-size boxes, but we haven't carried democracy quite that far yet. It might be a good gesture, though, and it would make a swell feature article in the company paper.

Maa: What are these lines that connect the boxes?

Don: I'm glad you asked about those. The lines indicate the flow of authority down through the organization. It all starts up here with the president, ignoring the board of directors and stockholders, for now. This is where all authority stems from, this box here. Authority flows down these lines to all these other boxes in the organization.

Maa: What materials flow this way?

Don: It's not a material. It's more like electrical power. When the president says that something must be done, then all the people in all these other boxes say it must be done, and then whoever has to do it, does it.

Maa: What if they don't?

Don: But they *do!* They do, that is, if they want to keep their jobs. As they used to say in the army, "We can't make you do anything, but we can make you wish you had." This power stemming from the top is passed down to these other people in the organization, and if the people under them don't do what they say, then the people in these boxes can remove them from the payroll.

Maa: Then, the higher up you go, the more power you have to remove people from the payroll? Is that what "authority" is?

Don: Well, you might put it like that, I guess. But it doesn't sound right.

Maa: (Writes in notebook: "President can remove everybody from the payroll. Doesn't sound right.") Some of the little boxes don't have lines from them. Your's doesn't. What does this mean?

Don: This means that we are staff. The other people whose lines continue downward are called "line." Staff people perform special services, but don't have any authority over the line. The staff thinks up things and advises the line people on what to do, but the line people don't have to do them, and often they don't.

Maa: (Writes in notebook: "Staff thinks up things, line doesn't do them.") All of the lines are of the same breadth. Does this mean that their power flowing down is all the same?

Don: Well, that's what it is supposed to mean, but that's not really true. Some people are just bound to be more influential than others. I suppose that you might say that some are paid very little attention to. This isn't the way it should be, of course.

Maa: What happens in the white spaces?

Don: What white spaces? Oh, you mean the spaces between the boxes and the lines? Why, nothing happens in the white spaces. Oh, I see that the man from public relations is here already to take you on a plant tour. I'm very sorry that we didn't have more time together. I would have liked to get into responsibility and accountability. But perhaps someone else will fill you in on these. Without knowing about them, you really won't be able to see how we get things done. Mr. Maa, it's been a pleasure to meet and talk with you.

Maa: Thank you. (Maa and his guide leave.)

Don and Maa (to themselves): What a strange fellow.

It would be interesting to follow them on the tour and see the guide try to explain why the board room is the best appointed and one of the largest rooms, but is used the least. And why the president has the largest desk and the smallest need for one. And why there is an inverse relation between assigned parking locations and people's need for exercise. And the hundreds of other curious things to be seen around our organizations.

It would be interesting to explain to Mr. Maa the many rules and regulations needed to prevent people from being disorderly. It would also be interesting to listen to an explanation of the many well-accepted assumptions behind our personnel policies and practices, which for the most part are based on memories of the Great Depression.

It would be interesting to explain to Mr. Maa the process of socialization through which all of the definitions, charts, rules of operating, ground rules, expected behavior, mores, etc., come to be accepted as "reality." Many of these are unwritten, some are unspoken, but all must be accepted before a person can be said to be "house-broken." Mr. Maa might note, even if we don't, the increasing difficulty we are having in getting these pictures of "reality" accepted by the new work force.

Most of the organizational "world" we live in is not real, although we act "as if" it were. This world is held together because all of us act "as if" it were real. If this agreement were not accepted and complied with by the vast majority of people in the organization, the organization would become unglued. All of us can tell stories about "leaders" in the system whose authority was either not understood or accepted and the interesting things that happened as a consequence. (In "T" group training, a specialized form of training group, people are taken out of their usual organizational context, placed with people like themselves but with whom there are none of these "agreements" about status, symbols, expected deference, and they must learn to be just themselves, all over again. Much, much more happens in this training, of course; this is just one aspect.)

On his return to his own country, I wonder what Mr. Maa would report about our organizational worlds. What would our organizational worlds be like if we really looked at them ourselves?

ARE WE TALKING ABOUT THE SAME JOB?

Even if your organization doesn't have a full-scale program of job descriptions, or management-by-objectives program, it makes sense to make sure that you and your subordinates have the same idea about what they are supposed to be doing. You might begin by asking them to make a list of their duties as they see them. Then get together with them individually and see how their list compares with yours. Next, ask them to list their duties, as agreed on, in order of importance or priority. Which are the most important? Which the least? Which in-between? (I have used what I call a "life-boat drill" for this. Which duty would be the first you would save? If some must "go down with the ship," which would they be?) Then, you list them in order of importance as *you* see them, and compare these lists. You might very well be surprised at how your perceptions differ from those of your subordinates (the "illusion of communication" again).

Another consideration is: How do you set the constraints, or "outer limits," of a person's job? Some will have the attitude of "I'm going to go as far as I can in doing this job until someone else tells me to stop." At the other end of this scale is the attitude of "I'm not going to do anything that might be overstepping my bounds unless the boss tells me to." Where are your people on this scale? Where would you like for them to be? Do they know of your expectations? Are you prepared to back them up if they go out on a limb?

After you reach agreement with each subordinate on what job is to be done, you can look at goals or objectives. Although this might seem to be going about it backwards, this is often the best way to approach an established, on-going job.

More and more organizations have embarked on an organizationwide program of management by objectives. Many of these programs are highly successful, but some are failures. (One company enthusiastically began a program, and at the end of the year each department head proudly reported that the subobjectives had been met or exceeded. But the company unexpectedly lost $17 million that year!)

We won't go into details of management by objectives here, since there are many excellent books on the subject. I would just note that building a team of the entire organization would seem to require that each individual define and relate his immediate, day-to-day activities to his own unit's goals and to the larger goals of the whole organization.

Despite the growing number of such programs, a more common condition faced by the manager is not to have any goals set and communicated by higher management, except in broad and general terms. If you haven't been given any goals from higher up, make a list of them anyway, as you see them. (You might want to discuss these with *your* boss.) Then share the goals with your people to make sure you are all working toward the same ends. Scott Myers has an appropriate analogy.* Consider a subordinate who is bowling. In one condition, a cloth curtain hides the pins from the bowler. Therefore, he can just keep on rolling the ball down the alley and hope, by the noise and activity down at the pins, that he is accomplishing something—hopefully the right things. In a second condition, his supervisor stands at the curtain, so he can see both the pins and the bowler. He can give encouragement or corrections after each ball has been sent down the alley. This is of more help to the subordinate, who now has some feedback from someone as to how well he is doing with each try. But how much better a third condition would be—to remove the curtain and let the subordinate see for himself what he is aiming for, how he does with each try, what he needs to do to get a better average, and so on. There is still a real place for coaching, but goals can help a subordinate track his own progress. Many studies have shown that real improvement can occur if the producer gets immediate feedback about his production, contributions, and accomplishments.

---

* Dr. M. Scott Myers was active in Texas Instruments Company's program in job enrichment for employees. This analogy was used in a talk I once heard him give.

ABOUT AUTHORITY

"I wasn't given enough authority to get that job done!" Does that sound familiar? It makes "authority" sound like something we collect in a sack; we can look in the sack and say, "No, that's not enough. A little more, please. There, that's enough." Bill Oncken points out that there are really four kinds of authority.* (We have argued about their titles, and I prefer to use mine. But the important distinctions are his.) They are:

1. The authority of *position,* which is what we usually mean when we talk about authority. Bascially, it's the ability to make things hard on someone if they won't do what you say. At one university where I once taught, the custodial staff was put to work directing traffic. But hardly anyone paid any attention. Whistles helped some. But when the staff was given guns (even though unloaded), people began to pay close attention.

This kind of authority can be delegated, and it's the only one of the four kinds that can. But you can help subordinates develop the other kinds.

All of us are familiar with having people "pull their rank" on us—and how we feel when they do. But someone with this kind of authority will be given deference.

2. The authority of *knowledge,* which stems from the competence and skill you have acquired. If you have this authority, people will seek you out because they have confidence in your judgment, and they will do what you say because they believe that you "know what you're talking about."

This kind of authority may or may not come from experience, and it may or may not come from formal education.

3. The authority of *behavior,* which comes from the social skill you have developed—skill in your interpersonal relations. The easier it is for the other fellow to talk with you, to listen to you, and to work with you, the harder it will be for him *not* to do what you ask.

On the other hand, if you try to manipulate people, or use them, or judge them, you will not develop this authority with them. But if it's easy to do business with you, it will be easier for the other fellow to respond to your wishes.

4. The authority of *trust,* which is a measure of the quality of the relationship you have with people and which grows out of behavior. If you have this authority, people trust your motives and commitments, and they trust you to have their best interests in mind. Once you have "lost" this authority, it is very, very difficult to regain. And some never develop it.

---

* William Oncken is a widely known lecturer on management subjects. It was my good fortune, some time ago, to attend a session which he conducted. Some of his ideas, such as these four classifications, are consciously used with his permission. Other illustrations and concepts I use probably came from him, even though I have forgotten their source. I would commend to you any of his "in-person" talks.

In order to accomplish his objectives, the manager must work with and through people in other departments over whom he has no authority of position. Also, the manager must depend on his boss and others at higher levels for special things which only they can provide. To work effectively with peers and superiors, the manager can depend on only the last three kinds of authority described. If the authority of "position" is the only kind of authority the manager has with subordinates, cooperation will probably be at a minimum level.

One of the reasons I feel it is very useful for a manager to work with volunteer groups outside of the organization (such as community agencies, church groups, political groups, etc.) is that he has no authority of position over the other volunteers. Rather, he must develop the other types of authority.

"I wasn't given enough authority to get that job done" becomes a rather silly statement when restated as "I wasn't given the power to fire enough people to get that job done." How much authority you really have depends on *you*.

HOW MUCH EFFORT?

Some years ago, Peter Drucker described a diagram which has been very helpful to me, and I thought it might be useful to you as well. Here is the diagram:*

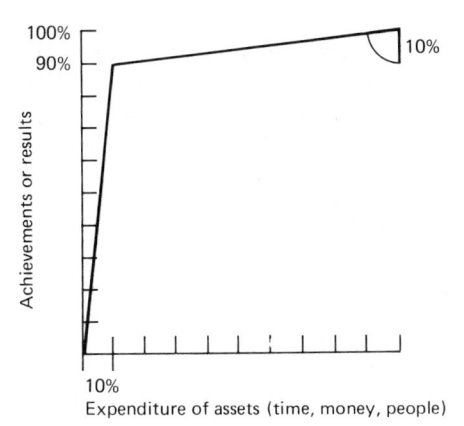

On the left-hand side of the diagram are the achievements or results to be attained. At the bottom is the needed expenditure of the asset to achieve the results. (The asset may be time, money, people, etc.) The chart shows that

---

* Peter Drucker, "Managing for Business Effectiveness," *Harvard Business Review*, May-June 1963, pp. 53–60.

with expenditure of 10 percent of the asset, 90 percent of the results are achieved. The remaining 90 percent of the asset is needed to achieve the remaining 10 percent of the result. Drucker says that this relationship has been verified whenever it has been studied. We can also see it working clearly in familiar things such as in the building of a house.

How might this be applied to your management job?

1. Do you really want *everyone* to have a *full* understanding of, say, a new policy? Or is 90 percent enough?
2. Do you *never* want to have a stock-out condition? Or is 90 percent of the time "in-stock" enough?
3. Do you really want your secretary to be able to find *everything* in the file when you ask her? Or is 90 percent enough?
4. Do you *never* want a complaint to arise from the service you provide? Or can a reasonable and expected complaint level be set?

Of course this doesn't mean that 90 percent of accomplishment is always enough. If I'm going to be sent to the moon *and brought back,* I want you to make sure that you have reached 150 percent of that goal. But for many goals and results, we can stop, deliberately, short of 100 percent achievement, with a tremendous saving in expenditures.

Which 10 percent of your activity is accounting for the 90 percent of your results?

DELEGATION

Delegation simply means assigning work to subordinates. For a manager with subordinates, delegation is one of the most important skills. You already know a great deal about delegation, so let's begin our discussion with some questions for you to answer. (This quiz is the trickiest one in the book, so watch yourself!)

Agree	Disagree	Statement
_____	_____	1. If it takes so long to explain a job that it's easier to do it yourself, then do it yourself.
_____	_____	2. A good manager can *not* know just "what's going on" and yet sleep like a baby.
_____	_____	3. As a manager, you want to be the first to know how a job comes out.
_____	_____	4. If you want a job done well, do it yourself.
_____	_____	5. Don't let a subordinate learn every part of your job. He can replace you!
_____	_____	6. If a subordinate comes to you with a solution to a problem you have given him and if you have a better solution, use yours.
_____	_____	7. If a subordinate recommends a poor solution, raising a little cain with him will show him you have high standards.

Agree	Disagree	Statement
_____	_____	8. If a subordinate prepares a letter for you to sign, there is nothing wrong with making a few minor changes before having it retyped for your signature.
_____	_____	9. There is no risk in passing down decision-making.
_____	_____	10. If a subordinate to whom you have delegated a job keeps coming back to you for more resources, information, or authority, you probably haven't done a proper job of delegating.

Now let's compare our answers and discuss each one.

1. *Disagree*. One of the big problems we have in delegating is our tendency to be impatient. And there is a good chance that we will be misinterpreted. It does take some effort to formulate instructions that are clear and concise and that will not result in errors. In the short run, it's easier to do the job yourself. But in the long run, to be a manager requires that you take the responsibility for directing others. We sometimes excuse our doing it because it's a "once-in-a-lifetime" job. But these have a way of returning weekly. Sometimes, we do it because we just *like* to. But this isn't managing.

2. *Agree*. It takes guts to give other people jobs to do and then leave them alone. How well you can sleep when you have done this is a measure of your confidence in yourself, your instructional skill, and your subordinates.

3. *Disagree*. The only way to be the first to know how a job comes out is to *do it yourself*.

4. *Disagree*. This is a popular statement, but it doesn't reflect management. The longer you continue to do a job well, the less you are managing and the less you are able to get on to more important business. Here, we see a familiar "chicken and egg" predicament: the "chicken" says, "I can't delegate as much as I want to because my subordinates aren't competent" while the "egg" says, "My boss doesn't delegate enough to me. How am I supposed to learn?"

5. *Disagree*. But the fear can be a real one, even if it's unconscious. A "bright young guy" can and eventually will replace you! But to *not* delegate because of this feeling is to limit the effectiveness of both your organization and two individuals—you *and* him.

6. Here, I both *agree and disagree*. You can probably think of examples when your judgment was better than the subordinate's recommendation, and you have probably had the experience of working for someone who always tried to "second guess" you. But the main point is: if you do, *make sure he knows why*. Nothing can kill a subordinate's desire to take on responsibility faster than having you make his decisions for him. After a very short time, he finds it "easier to ask." For example, one of my first assignments was to write a report. During the writing, I had many questions, but I thought that the boss would catch them later. When I handed the report in, he said, "Finished? Good. Now let's send it to printing." "But aren't you going to read it?" I

asked. "No." Then I took it back and *really* wrote a report. It was a good lesson for me. Do your subordinates seem to come to you with every little problem on an assignment? If so, they may be telling you something about what they have come to expect.

7. *Disagree.* If you agreed with this statement, it was probably because of your interpretation of what a "little cain" means. Sure, he needs to understand the need for improvement. But fear of criticism is one of the biggest obstacles to your successful delegation now. Criticism that is too harsh is the fastest way to discourage initiative, cause resentment, and reduce a subordinate's self-confidence. Do your subordinates ever say, "I don't want any more responsibility?" If so, they are telling you something about their level of self-confidence. What *you* do is a great determinant of that level of self-confidence.

8. *Disagree.* On two counts. The majority of changes we make are arbitrary, anyway. They don't *really* matter; they just fit our personal preference. Furthermore, why have the letter retyped? I know many managers who spend a lot of time being rewrite men for their subordinates. Since the subordinates know this, they gauge their level of effort to this fact. Who is working for whom?

9. *Agree.* Yes, I said I agree. Absolutely *no* risk. Impossible, you say. You could undoubtedly give me a lot of argument about why there is always risk. (But I told you these were trick questions.) There is no risk in passing down decision-making. The risk comes when *action is taken.* Therefore, control the action, and you control the risk!

Here are the "degrees of delegation" and some comments on each:

a) "Decide and take action. You need not check back with me." This is the freest rein we can give a subordinate. But we had better have a high degree of confidence in him, as well as good controls that will send up red flags all over the place if things get out of hand.

b) "Decide and take action, but let me know what you did." This is similar to the first degree, but gives you a faster reaction time, if needed, to correct a wrong course. The confidence level must still be high.

c) "Decide and let me know your decision. Then take action unless I say not to." Now we are beginning to control the action. This way of controlling action gives you a look at what is planned, but saves his time.

d) "Decide and let me know your decision. But wait for my 'go ahead.'" The distinction between this degree and the preceding one is small but important. Here, the subordinate must get definite approval before proceeding. If you do not have complete confidence in him, or if the stakes are high, this may be a useful course.

e) "Decide what you would do, but tell me your alternatives with the 'pros and cons' of each." This is asking for his analysis and recommendation. But you will review his thinking to assure yourself that his course of action is the best.

f) "Look into this problem and give me the facts you come up with. I will decide." This is asking for an investigation and some analysis. You are reserving the decision-making for yourself.

g) "Wait to be told." Here, there is no delegation, and he waits for your decisions and directions.

An inexperienced person just joining the organization might be started at the lower levels of this scale (delegation levels (e), (f), or (g)). As he gains experience and confidence, and you gain confidence in him, he would be moved upward to the other levels. Whichever level you would use at any given time would depend on the total situation.

10. *Agree*. The only exception I can think of is that of an assignment of unknown scope. How much he would need to do the job would unfold as he progressed. Aside from this, if subordinates have to return again and again, think through your original instructions. Delegation is a skill to be learned, and how your people react to your delegation can help you learn that skill.

To be a manager is to arrange for assignments to others. And delegating can be a powerful tool for developing others as well.

DON'T JUST DO SOMETHING, STAND THERE!

Lack of decisions can create more problems than decisions that are made. Frequently, a manager can put off for days and weeks a decision that needs to be made. This procrastination can take the form of a search and research for all the facts, a weighing of the facts on finer and finer measuring scales, and by ignoring the question after all the facts have been obtained. Here is Dr. Seuss' commentary on the malady of indecision:

Did I Ever Tell You..?
BY DR. SEUSS*

Did I ever tell you about the young Zode
Who came to two signs at the fork of a road?
One said: To PLACE ONE. And the other: PLACE TWO.
So the Zode had to make up his mind what to do.
Well... the Zode scratched his head. And his chin.
                        And his pants.   (cont. on next page)

---

* Copyright Dr. Seuss. (*Redbook Magazine*, February 1956.) Reproduced by permission.

And he said to himself, "I'll be taking a chance
"If I go to Place One. Now, that place may be hot!
"And, so, how do I know if I'll like it or not?
"On the other hand, though, I'll be sort of a fool
"If I go to Place Two and I find it too cool.
"In *that* case I may catch a chill and turn blue!
"So, maybe, Place One is the best. Not Place Two.
"On the *other* hand, though, if Place One is too **high**,
"I may catch a terrible earache and die!
"So Place *Two* may be best!
                        On the other hand, though . . .
"What might happen to me if Place Two is *too low* . . . ?
"I might get some very strange pain in my toe!
"So Place One may be best." And he started to go.
Then he stopped. And he said, "On the OTHER hand, though . .
"**On the other hand . . . other hand**
                             . . . other hand though . . . !"
And for 36 hours and ½, that poor Zode
Made starts and made stops at that fork in the road,
Saying, "Don't take a chance. No! You may not be right."
Then he got an idea that was wonderfully bright!
"Play safe!" cried the Zode. "I'll play safe! I'm no dunce!
"I'll simply start off for both places at once!"

And that's how the Zode, who would not take a chance,
Got to No Place at All, with a split in his pants.

We should always try to make the decision that will leave us the greatest flexibility in the future (that will leave the greatest number of options). Similarly, deciding to *not* make a decision can also be a useful strategic decision. But to not make a decision because of uncertainty, lack of confidence, personal vacillation, or other reasons can create many problems. How can you tell if a delayed decision is either one or the other? Here are some clues to each condition:

Clues pointing to a deliberate delay of a decision	Clues pointing to "just plain indecision"
Past track record in taking calculated risks is good	Alternatives seem equally desirable or undesirable, giving rise to a desire for "just a few more facts," and these new facts make the decision less clear
Specific awaited developments can be cited	
Planned and specified time for incubation can be cited	Sifting and resifting of the same facts without exploring new data or different facts
Willing to explain reasons for delay in decision	Decision-maker is annoyed at the clamor for a decision
Comfort with ambiguity caused by delay of decision	Advice of others continually sought but rejected
Calculated chance that changes in conditions will remove need for decision can be stated	Many reasons cited why someone else should make the decision
Consequences of no decision watched carefully	Unusual seeking of reassurance from superiors
Other decisions clearly have a higher priority	Strong wish that the need for the decision would "go away"
	Overconcern with the consequences of an unpopular decision
	Consequences of not making a decision greater than those of a wrong decision would be
	Unmade decision has had a high priority for some time
	Decision-maker keeps busy with low-priority jobs to keep from facing decision

A review of this list may help you decide which it is.

"GEE, ISN'T THIS CRISIS FUN!"

It was the late Pete Jansen, one of the great production men of my time, who taught me how to look at a shop or office and tell if its production operation is well planned. If it is well planned, it looks dull. If it is unplanned, it looks exciting! Then I began to learn that we really *have more fun* working in a crisis atmosphere. Everyone is interested, you get top management attention, and it's a lot more exciting than following the well-planned routine. Lyle Otterness describes the two conditions:

> The competent manager—who remains "cool under fire," who thinks clearly and acts decisively—will ordinarily move through the process of meeting a crisis with real (though unexpressed) satisfaction and pleasure. He enjoys the action, the challenge to his competency, the rapidly developing results of his decisions, and the clearly visible consequences of a job well done under pressure....
>
> Dealing with the future is not always a pleasant task and seldom an easy one. Planning for tomorrow or next year requires careful accumulation of information, painstaking evaluation and analysis, examination of external and uncontrollable variables, making a number of "good guesses," and a very large measure of concentrated thinking about the problems involved and the consequences of the risks that must be taken.
>
> It is a time-consuming job, often sinking to the level of drudgery and hardly ever as exciting as the minute-by-minute action that takes place in a crisis. The satisfaction of having done a good job is to a greater or lesser degree postponed, pending fruition of the plan.
>
> When tomorrow or next year comes, the results are likely to be accepted as routine in the midst of planning for a new future. Often the results are only barely tangible because of the changes and adjustments in plan and organization that have taken place through planned flexibility and the routine planned controls that affected them. Plans that fail, more likely, are the ones to get much attention after the fact.*

Otterness also points out the circular nature of the problem that soon develops: our crises take time from effective planning, and our lack of planning creates more crises.

What begins as a temporary solution to a crisis may become rapidly institutionalized as systems and procedures are developed. For example, in the story about the construction crew working in a remote site, the motor pool dispatcher sent a one-ton truck into town one Thursday morning to get the mail. As the truck passed over a quarter-ton capacity bridge, the bridge collapsed, and the truck fell into the river. This crisis caused a lot of excited running around until a 90-ton mobile crane was located in a distant town and

---

* Lyle Otterness is an experienced manager, as this view of crisis management suggests. Reprinted by permission from an unpublished paper.

brought to the scene. When the same thing happened the following Thursday, there was less running around, because there was a precedent to follow. The mobile crane was sent for, and maintenance carpenters were ordered 'round to make repairs. The planners, noting all the activity on Thursdays, brought their expertise to bear. After tracing on flow charts what had been happening, the planners arranged to have the mobile crane standing by the river every Thursday and the maintenance carpenters in position to go to work.

After several months of this, the rental bills on the mobile crane began to reach the accountants, who were outraged. "Renting this crane every week will break the company!" they said. "It's stupid to rent it every week. Buy one at once!" And they did. The next time materials were being assembled for another construction job, a mobile crane had been added to the list of essential equipment. "Getting their mail is important to the morale of the workers," said the personnel men. Over the next few years, so many cranes were being purchased that the capital assets group in finance at the home office began "make-or-buy" studies. Then. . . . We could go on and on with the story, but I'm sure you got the point.

Sure, working in a crisis situation is more fun. But it's usually a clear signal that you haven't done the planning that only you as a manager can do.

"THERE'S ONLY ONE LITTLE THING WRONG . . ."

We often wish for an inconsistency among our people without being aware of what we are doing. The same traits we applaud seem at other times to get in the way of the person's effectiveness, and we somehow wish they wouldn't. Here's what I mean:

- "Our finance man is just great. He says 'no' to all of our requests, and we have to fight to get what we want. But we have the best looking cash flow in the industry. There's only one little thing wrong. He's losing all of his good people because they can get more money at our competitors."

- "Our personnel manager is one of the finest men you would ever want to meet. All of the employees think he is just wonderful. There's only one little thing wrong. He would give away the store unless you keep a close eye on him."

- "Our security man is tops in his field. We have received top ratings from the government in every inspection they've made since he came. But I do wish he wasn't so suspicious of *us!*"

- "We have a very creative research guy. His innovations are the envy of his profession. But the trouble is that he's a loner. He doesn't work well with groups."

- "Our head computer man is a real genius. Take him any broad management-control system needed, and he can come up with a program to handle it beautifully. There's only one little thing wrong, though. He can't seem to make daily decisions on time. He keeps putting them off because he doesn't have enough facts."
- "Our chief engineer is an outstanding logician. But his department is usually in revolt. He just doesn't seem to understand the human element."

And so on.

These people are being consistent, and we would seem to have no right to demand inconsistency. Instead, we need to see that their strengths in one area may well be weaknesses in another. We must accept them as "total people" for what they can contribute.

In his book *The Effective Executive,* Peter Drucker states that the unique purpose of an organization is to make strength productive. Organization, in Drucker's words, "cannot, of course, overcome the weaknesses with which each of us is abundantly endowed. But it can make them irrelevant. Its task is to use the strengths of each man as a building block for joint performance."*

Regardless of a man's faults, can his strengths make the unique contribution needed by the organization? If so, keep your focus on these strengths. If his weaknesses present a severe problem to himself or to the organization, try "work-around" methods, or shoring, or make exceptions, so long as his strengths outweigh the problems created. But when the problems outweigh the person's contribution, remove the person. Where this balance point is will differ, depending on the strengths and weaknesses you perceive and your ability to live with the problems created.

"HE'S THE GUY THAT CUT THE CABLE, REMEMBER?"

That's what somebody would say whenever Joe was considered for a promotion with the telephone company. And he *had* accidentally cut a buried cable, 37 years earlier when he was a beginning lineman. Joe remained a lineman for all those years, while his associates went onward and upward with the company. How much Joe *might* have contributed to the company in all those years we will never know. Here is Parkinson on the same subject:

THE "X" FACTOR IN SELECTION

Organizations with every precaution against waste of time and money will often waste ability. One result of this is the preferment of the incompetent,

---
* Peter Drucker, *The Effective Executive,* New York: Harper & Row, 1966, p. 71.

which is to some extent inevitable. Where in fact avoidable, it comes about through the rejection of every candidate against whom anything can be said.

    A is proposed but he is said to be arty,
        B is suggested but he is too bold.
    C's name is mentioned but he is too hearty,
        D's dictatorial, E is too old.
    What about F? He is frankly too charming.
        And what about G? Gossip says he's queer.
    As for old H, he is much too alarming.
        And K—we must face it—drinks far too much beer.
    How if we settle for L? But he's ailing.
        M is too deaf, or so we hear tell.
    Forget about N—why his memory's failing!
        And that goes for O, who argues too well.
    Shall we have P? Too caustic and clever.
        Q is too quiet and R is too rude.
    S is so silent and T talks forever.
        U is efficient but horribly crude.
    And V? Irreplaceable! Capable! Valuable!
        Really too valuable just where he is.
    But W? W? He'll never trouble you.
        Let's turn him down and return to the quiz.
    Come now to X—does anyone know him?
        What does he look like? We can't just recall.
    He can't be too fat or we'd surely have noticed.
        He can't be too short and he can't be too tall.
    He can't be too stupid, but can't be too brilliant
        for no one remembers a word that he said.
    Is he hardworking and is he resilient?
        Perhaps he is neither. Perhaps he is dead.
    To X no one can offer the slightest objection.
        We are none of us sure that we know him by sight.
    He gives rise to no jealousy, hate or affection.
        Appoint him at once! For this post he is right!*

---

* C. Northcote Parkinson, *In-laws and Outlaws and Parkinson's Third Law*, Boston: Houghton Mifflin Co., 1962, pp. 133–134. Copyright © 1959, 1960, 1961, 1962 by S. A. Roturman. Reprinted by permission of John Murray, Ltd. and Houghton Mifflin Company.

SO, WHO NEEDS A GENIUS?

Here is a situation involving a man we shall call Jim Underwood. Read it over and decide what advice you would give to Jim's supervisor. You will have six choices to choose from.

JIM UNDERWOOD

Jim Underwood is an electronics engineer working at the Henderson Electronics Corporation. He has been employed for the past three years and has attracted widespread fame around the company for his innovations. This was not entirely unexpected, since Jim was an outstanding scholar in college and finished at the top of his class. On his graduation, he was considered a "prize" and was much sought after by many rival electronics firms. Underwood chose the Henderson Corporation as being the "kind of progressive firm he wished to make a career with." But there is evidence that the rival firms don't accept his decision as final and are continuing to make attractive offers to him. This isn't exactly considered ethical in the industry, but is sometimes done.

Jim Underwood's genius is far-ranging in the field of electronics. No problem seems to be beyond him, and he will solve the technical problems of others almost casually. When Jim would get involved in a particularly knotty problem, he wouldn't even go home for days in a row. What little sleep he got was on a couch in the reception area. Needless to say, during these periods his personal attire and grooming would suffer. The first time this happened, his wife called the police, and it created quite an uproar. Now, other personnel in the office make sure she knows when he is on one of these working "binges."

There were other problems with Underwood. He "suffered fools badly," even when these happened to be customers. One big account was lost when he told the president of the company that he was stupid. Jim was right, of course, but this didn't help keep the customer. Jim behaved the same way to people in the company, despite their rank or position. And he wouldn't follow the simplest company procedure or policy if its logic was not apparent. Most of these incidents were not too important, but unfortunately, some were.

Underwood was at the top of his salary grade for a nonsupervisory engineer. And it had been a year since his last raise. Jim stated in very clear terms that he is *not* interested in a management position. But his supervisor is concerned that Jim continue to get raises, particularly in view of the continuing offers from other companies. But a raise over the top of his grade would bring complaints from other engineers who work with him. Not that Jim isn't worth it. His problem-solving really makes money for the company.*

Jim's supervisor comes to you for advice. Which alternative approach would you recommend? Select the *one* best solution from the following:

1. Leave Jim completely alone to do whatever he wants to do. If any restriction is placed on him, he might quit.

---

* This case appeared in my book *Dynamic Management Education*, 3rd ed., Reading, Mass.: Addison-Wesley, 1971, pp. 70–71. Reprinted by permission.

2. Try to control his customer and internal contacts, but otherwise deal with him as the obvious exception he is in matters of pay, company conventions, policy, and procedures.
3. Explain to Jim that he must learn both to conform to accepted business behavior (with regard to hours, etc.) and to act more human.
4. Tell him that to get ahead in business, he must "straighten out" and take on a supervisory job; otherwise, he will only hurt his own career.
5. Insist that Jim "toe the line" in policies, procedures, and conventions. Allow no special privileges or exceptions. If he doesn't like it, he can quit.
6. Get rid of Jim. Obviously, he makes waves, and the company would be better off without him.

Write the number of your choice of the best approach here: _____ If you haven't made one yet, reread the statement of the case and the alternative choices.

Don't go on with your reading until you have made a selection.

In the space below, state why you selected the choice you did:

Choice 2 was, to us, the obvious alternative to select. If you did not pick this one, why didn't you? Did your choice reflect, instead, the "culture" of your particular organization—values about what is important and what isn't? Did your choice reflect your own values? Did our selection of choice 2 reflect our own values, which aren't necessarily shared by others? Let's talk about it.

We need, and usually have, compliant and conforming people working for us. Without compliance, the structure of the organization would come unglued. Without conformity, there would be no teamwork, and our systems wouldn't operate. But we also must have self-renewing innovation, or we are not going to meet our long-term objectives, and eventually we will fail.* But Great Scott, it's often hard to manage the movers and shakers and innovators of this world! Why?

1. We can't understand what they are talking about, at least some of the time. And this can be a blow to our ego.
2. They always have 16 different ways of doing it, with four reasons apiece why those ways are better than our way. (And they are usually right!)

---

* The notion of these three categories originated with Bill Oncken and is used here with his permission.

3. They often can't work well with "the team."
4. They often are abrasive to us, to others at higher levels, and to their co-workers.
5. They take more time to supervise, and they often cause more problems than everyone else in the group taken together.

But on the other hand, they can be worth their weight in gold, despite all of our problems with them!

So, if you have only compliant and conforming people working for you, you'd better throw in a live one, even though you are asking for problems. But make sure, before you put up with the temperament of a *prima donna,* that the person has the talent of one.

You may have more budding creative people in your organization than you realize. The climate you and your organization have developed has a great deal to do with whether or not these people show and develop their potential for being creative. As far as I can see, the main thrust in courses on "creativity" is to remove the inhibiting forces, primarily by establishing a nonjudgmental climate in which people's ideas are accepted without their being criticized. Then, more ideas are produced. (What happens when the participants go back to their own jobs following such a course is often something else again.)

If the climate is such that "total compliance" is regarded as a goal, the process of socialization of a new member to introduce it, and the controls to ensure it, may cause passivity or aggression, which I see as being closely related. (This often creates a cycle—excessive restraints cause passivity or aggression, and we see passivity and aggression as clearly showing the need for more restraints.)

What every organization needs is not merely people who can think up ideas, but also those who can think the ideas through and work out the details, sell the new ideas convincingly, and institute a concrete innovation as a result of their efforts.

DEVELOPMENT

When you think of the development of your people, what do you think of? Formal training, probably. If they need to be developed, you send them off somewhere to attend classes, courses, conferences, workshops, and seminars. But actually, their most significant development takes place *on the job.* (I haven't seen any research figures, so let me make some up.) About 87.6% of a person's development takes place on the job, and you are his most important teacher.

Opportunities for development come up often in the course of a normal day. But since they aren't labeled "Developmental experiences," we often don't think of them as such. Which of the following statements are developmental, and which are not? (Check one.)

Is	Is not	Statement
____	____	1. "What would you recommend?"
____	____	2. "Tell me only what you feel I should know about your operations, and also tell me why I should know it."
____	____	3. "I'm not going to make your decision for you, but I'll certainly talk your problem over with you whenever you wish."
____	____	4. "Here is a special project for you that will give you experience in a new area. When you finish a plan for accomplishing it, bring it in and show me what you are going to do."
____	____	5. "Please attend this planning meeting in my place. You know our goals. You have full authority to commit us to whatever course of action you feel is appropriate."
____	____	6. "The decision you made to cancel the project was not made soon enough. Let's review it together to see when it should have been halted in order to minimize our losses."
____	____	7. "I've got to make a policy decision on this matter. Please think about it and give me your recommendations."
____	____	8. "This morning after the staff meeting, the head of the finance department mentioned the fine cooperation he has been getting from you. Keep up the good work."
____	____	9. "I have decided *not* to take the course of action you have recommended. Let me tell you why I decided on a different course."
____	____	10. "Here is a new book on management I have just read. When you have had a chance to read it, let's get together and discuss it. We may find ways of improving our operations."
____	____	11. "Here's an announcement of an opening in another division. I think it would be a real challenge for you, and I think you could handle it. We would really miss you here, but think it over."
____	____	12. "At our next Friday's staff meeting, please plan to present a review of your immediate staff, their strengths and areas needing improvement, and your plans for their development."
____	____	13. "Make out a list of your duties and responsibilities as you see them, and let's set a date to go over them together."
____	____	14. "Next Tuesday at ten, let's get together to review our progress this year and make plans for next year. You might be thinking about areas in which you would like to gain experience."
____	____	15. "We have been asked to furnish a luncheon speaker to talk about our operations. If you would do it, I think it would give you an opportunity to think broadly about the whole operation, as well as about your segment."
____	____	16. "Here's a description of my job. Look it over and identify what parts of it you wouldn't know how to do if you were to take over."
____	____	17. "We have an opening in our company memberships in the Chamber of Commerce. I would like you to use it. It will give you a chance to meet and work with managers from many businesses."

Which statements did you see as developing people? We saw *every one* as developmental. Again, development is not something apart from getting the work of your organization done.

In any job of substance, a great deal of development will take place naturally, as the person just does his job—*if* he has a clear understanding of the job, knowledge of specific goals and results to be achieved, and can look forward to the reward of accomplishment. Beyond this, opportunities arise day after day which can be used to develop subordinates—if you are aware of this aspect of your job and consciously use the opportunities. Here are some possibilities:*

Related to present job
Expanded job assignment
Conducting meetings, conferences, forums
Preparing and making presentations
Key writing assignments
Performance reviews toward objectives
Exposure to upper management
Consultative assistance with the individual's managerial, leadership, and organizational problems
Personal developmental plans
Career coaching

Close to present job
Sick-leave replacement
Vacation replacement
"Acting" assignments
Task-force team member
Research assignments
Committee assignments
Teaching assignments
Proposal-team assignment
Recruiting experiences
Coordination assignments
Temporary assignments
Screening/selection board assignments
Evaluation and audit assignments
Assignment to internal drives (United Good Neighbors, savings bonds, etc.)
Consulting assignments
Problem-solving assignments

Requiring a job change
Understudy role
Cross-function transfer

---

* Adapted from a compilation by Jack Bookter, The Boeing Company.

Job rotation
Project assignments
Remote office or area assignment
Assignment to customer as representative
Line to staff transfers and staff to line
Assignment to managers with high developmental skills

Experiences outside the organization
Accepting positions of responsibility in civic, community, service, church, social, and political organizations
Service in professional associations
Selection as advisor to organizations such as Junior Achievement
Appointment to governmental overseeing bodies, study groups, etc.
Planned reading

These lists suggest the range of opportunities available to be used in development.

If you choose to use formal training—the other 12.4% of a person's development (from the figures we made up)—you will also play a key role in determining whether or not the training "sticks." All of us have had the experience, or know someone who has, of being told on returning from a course, "Okay, I don't care what they told you in 'charm' school, here we'll do it my way." If this is the reception to be given on his return, let's not send him in the first place.

Before any of your subordinates attend a course or meeting, do these things:

1. Read the brochure or course description carefully. While some are written by a Madison Avenue ad man, most consciously try to describe the session accurately, including what the participant will be expected to get out of it.
2. Investigate the sponsoring organization and speakers as best you can. See if the management development, training or personnel departments have any record of past attendees from your organization, and get their experiences.
3. Discuss it with the subordinate. Get agreement as to his developmental needs. See if he has alternative experiences in mind. Discuss with him what changes in general or specific knowledge or skills are reasonable to expect as a result of attending. (There is no greater waste than someone attending a conference and spending most of his time wondering "Why was I sent to this?")
4. Discuss what his absence will mean in terms of his job and his family.

On his return, ask for a report covering the session from the standpoint of item 3 above. Ask him how you can support him in applying his new skills and knowledge. During the next few weeks or months, ask him for his evaluation at that point.

Formal training experiences are usually available in a wide variety. Here are some possibilities:

Company training courses
College and university courses
Courses offered by other organizations and institutions
University advanced management programs
Sloan programs at M.I.T. and Stanford
Seminars, workshops, conferences, and symposiums
Programs offered by customers and suppliers
Correspondence courses

Correspondence courses would seem to offer an ideal solution to the problem of development for the busy manager. However, many managers have signed up for these at a considerable dollar commitment, but never go beyond the second or third lesson. (I've never seen the figures, but I would suppose that the vendors of these courses have 200,000 of the first lesson printed, 5000 of the second, 900 of the third, and 100 of the balance prepared.) The books and booklets furnished do have some questions to be answered and sent in, but otherwise the experience is a lonely one of reading material that often seems unrelated to the day-to-day pressures faced by the reader. At least the relation to *his* reality is not always obvious.

The same problem arises when the manager sets out on a program of reading selected books and articles. There is no way he can get an answer to the questions: "So what? What does all of this have to do with me and my life?" There are some real limits to the usual reading for "self-development." By the same token, many managers are just not oriented to reading for their own development; if they don't enjoy it and see little purpose in it, they won't do it. They will buy the books, of course, since this is a way of getting over their feelings of guilt that "we ought to be doing something about our own development." But they won't read them.

This is one reason why long lists of books are not included in this book. If you are interested in reading, you'll find book titles from your friends, from the book section of newspapers and magazines, from the library, and from other places. A list here would just make you feel guilty because you won't read them, even though a list might make *me* feel *less* guilty: "I told them what books to read to be expert managers. If they won't read them, that's *their* problem!"

There are quite a few approaches now being used to "change" people through education which I consider highly doubtful. These are largely based on the idea that you "change" people by exerting some outside force on them. You may recognize these approaches:

1. *Inspirational.* This approach is usually made by a "dynamic" speaker, who draws on all of the emotional ploys in the book and makes heavy use of humor. Typically, such a speaker points to his own success in making money.

(In one such "personality" course, the founder is said to have made his first million at a very tender age. His price for a franchise, times the number of franchises he sells for a given city, times the number of cities in which he operates make this earnings accomplishment entirely possible.)

2. *Auto-suggestion, self-hypnosis.* The outside force in this method usually consists of records or casette recordings which can be listened to while the individual is shaving or driving to work. The slogans and resolutions can then be repeated over and over by the person. The slogans and resolutions are usually of the "up-lift" kind such as: "I can be the world's best salesman!" and "I can make $50,000 this year!"

3. *Exhortation.* The outside force in this approach is a very strong urging, pleading, persuading, etc., through advice and warnings to behave in a certain way or follow a particular course of action. A change is spoken of as a conversion which, when internalized, becomes our "conscience."

4. *Techniques.* This approach involves giving a person some skills in interpersonal relations without providing an underlying insight about behavior. You have had contact with people, I'm sure, who have been exposed to this approach. When we are being "techniqued" by someone, we always know it and usually resent it because the lack of real interest and genuine feelings tells us that we are being *used* by someone who thinks we are too dumb to see through it. One woman who had the most popular course used to greet me with, "Hello, there, Mr. Zoll, how is your wife?" (Call him by name—it's the sweetest sound in the human language to him. Ask about something personal.) But I'm sure I could have responded, "I'm okay, and we got my wife's head back on all right" without any recognition on her part of anything unusual.

I'm sure that there are other categories of training which should be approached warily (if at all), but these four are currently the most popular.

"YOU'RE FIRED"

I've come to the conclusion that firing someone is one of the most avoided jobs in management. It is often delayed beyond all reasonable limits. It is put off, and put off, until one day the manager realizes: "We can't fire him. He's been with us for 17 years!"

When you have a problem serious enough to consider firing a person, you fret about it for months. Asking the advice of others is no help. When one doesn't have to prosecute or administer the outcome, one is always in favor of the militant approach. To the advisors, the answer to your problem is easy: "Fire him!" But you don't. Or if you do, you take one of the following evasive approaches:

1. *The "hatchet man" approach.* Find the person who has no qualms about doing the job. This is usually someone who isn't personally involved with the person. It helps if he is mean, anyway.

2. *The sanitary pink slip method.* Here, the individual receives notice of termination with his paycheck. The nice thing about this method is that you can be as surprised as he is!
3. *The budget reduction.* "Don't get me wrong, Charlie. I think you are tops. But unfortunately, they have cut my budget, and I can't keep you on." He is then usually given a "hunting license," which puts everyone on notice to watch our for this guy.
4. *The "let's make it uncomfortable for him until he quits" approach.* You know how this works—leave him off invitation lists, omit his name from the phone book, take his secretary away from him with one excuse or another, etc. This would seem to take more energy (and more sadism) than handling the problem directly, especially if the guy doesn't "get the message," and you have to keep thinking up other things to do to him.

There are probably other devious approaches which have been thought up and, worse, practiced.

If, in your best judgment, the person should be removed from the payroll, then remove him. Here's how:

1. Make sure that this is the best answer. It may be "best" because you can't think of anything else to do and the situation is intolerable. Sure, if you were more skilled, or had more patience, or could perform miracles, firing him might not be the best answer. But all you have to go on are your present skills and your perception of the current situation.
2. Be prepared to *stick to* your decision. If you haven't really decided that this is your best answer, and if you haven't touched all the bases, don't start the process. If more facts might change your mind, get them.
3. State to him your perception of his work, or whatever the circumstances which have brought you to your conclusions. State it clearly, even though you may not communicate the point.
4. State to him his qualities which you *have* appreciated—why you selected him in the first place, what you liked about his work, etc. But don't encourage him to think you are changing your decision.
5. Don't try to argue with his feelings. Usually, the maintenance of his self-concept demands a defense. This is understood and should be accepted. Just do a lot of listening. Expect to be the brunt of his feelings and understand these for what they are.
6. Do what you can to help him begin the process of thinking through what he will do in facing his new situation.
7. Know that you won't feel right in your stomach for a while. Being a manager requires making decisions about other people.

The person being "let go" (interesting way to put it) may find your decision a real shock because of the interruption in his plans and the sudden need to think along whole new lines. Or, the decision may come as a relief, since the situation had become intolerable for him and he was unable to bring himself to the point of initiating action. Or, this confrontation may encourage him to take the initiative: "You can't fire me, I quit."

I don't think it ever works out to give a person "notice" and have him stay around even part time. He is totally preoccupied with finding another situation, he may have growing feelings about you (to maintain his self-image, remember) which he expresses to others, and he is embarrassing to everybody to have around. (At worst, it is like having someone die but not yet be buried; at best, it is like being divorced but not separated.) Sure, keep him on the payroll for the specified time—or even more—but don't expect him to be even partially productive.

He still is a good guy in many ways, even when he doesn't fit your situation. So you don't have to get mad at him or "put him down." Help him as you can to redirect his life and get on with it.

If your situation is one in which firing is not a real alternative (because of rules, regulations, policies, or practices within the organization), heaven help you all.

HOW TO "TECHNIQUE" PEOPLE AND GIVE THEM THE FEELING OF PARTICIPATION WITHOUT THE FACT OF IT, THE FEELING OF BELONGING WITHOUT THE ACTUAL, AND A FEELING OF CONCERN FOR THEIR WELFARE WITHOUT REALLY BEING INTERESTED

Forget it.

CHAPTER **13**

MANAGING YOUR TIME

If a manager said to you, "I just don't know where my inventory went," you would regard him as some kind of a nut. If he said, "I just don't know where my budget money went," you would know for sure that he had better be replaced—and fast. If he said, "I just don't know where the factory and office buildings went," you would call for the men in the white coats to come and get him. But when he says, "I just don't know where the time went today," you say, "Welcome to the club, brother!" Yet time is an asset which must be budgeted and controlled like any other resource. Almost all of the assets managers have are distributed *un*equally. The one exception is time. Every manager has 24 hours in a day, and these hours cannot be stored or saved or stockpiled. Yet we somehow accept the lack of control of this asset.*

Parkinson's first law is "Work expands to fill the time available for its completion."† He illustrates this with the example of the little old lady who has only one job to do all day—to write a letter. This job consumes the entire day! She spends an hour finding the right stationery, another hour finding her spectacles, half an hour searching for the address, an hour and a quarter composing the letter, and 20 minutes deciding whether or not to take an umbrella when going to the mailbox down the block.

Although we may smile at the obviousness of this illustration of Parkinson's law, it's harder to see the same thing operating in ourselves. When you put in a hard, fast day and go home tired, it's difficult to see or admit that no *results* have been achieved. But all too often this is exactly the case. You don't need a plan to be busy, and you don't need to know what you're doing to be overworked and behind in it.

LOGGING YOUR TIME

To learn how to manage your time, the first thing to do is to find out how you are spending your time now (see the suggested form on p. 310). Sketch out

---

* This illustration is taken by permission from a talk by Bill Oncken, as are some of the headings used in the analysis.
† C. Northcote Parkinson, *Parkinson's Law*, Boston: Houghton Mifflin, 1957.

five of these for your own use in recording your activities for five consecutive work days. I would suggest half-hour increments, which will allow you to record incidents which you might miss with longer time periods. Then *keep the records for five days on your own activities*. Do this *before* you go on with your reading of this chapter. You could skip keeping the records on yourself, of course, and just go on and read the rest of the chapter. But to do so would be to miss 95 percent of the value to you. So if you are serious about learning to manage your time better, keep the logs for five days.

SUGGESTED TIME LOG

Day of week: _____ Date: _____

Keep a detailed record of *five consecutive days* of your activities. Describe the subject of conferences, phone calls, letters written, etc. Note the name and position of other persons. Include even casual conversations. Begin when you arrive in the morning, and note any company work done in the evening.

7:00
7:30

8:00
8:30

9:00
9:30

10:00
10:30

11:00
11:30

12:00
12:30

1:00
1:30

2:00
2:30

3:00
3:30

4:00
4:30

5:00
Evening:

ANALYSIS OF YOUR ACTIVITIES

Note: To get the most out of the experience of analyzing how you spend your time, *do not* look over this portion until you have kept a record of your activities for five consecutive days.

A suggested form for you to use in analyzing how you spent your time is given on p. 314. Sketch out five of these forms for your own use in making your analysis. The instructions for using the form, as well as the meaning of each column heading, follow. Read through these instructions, and then make a beginning breakdown of your recorded activities in the appropriate columns.

Instructions—Analysis of Your Time Logs

A. Nature

The first column on the form allows you to analyze the nature of the work —whether it was management work or vocational work.

A. Nature	
Mgt	Voc

Management activity refers to such activities as planning, organizing, controlling, and directing the work of others. *Vocational activity* refers to the exercise of your special knowledge and skills that comprise your primary occupation, such as accounting, engineering, sales, manufacturing, etc.

There is certainly nothing "wrong" when a manager performs vocational activities from time to time. The president is expected to help out on an important sale; the treasurer wants to make his own analysis of the quarterly report; the production superintendent can bring special know-how to production problems; the general foreman wants to oversee the installation of the new, expensive machine, and so on.

B. Imposed from where?

The next major heading, with its five subheadings, provides a place for you to identify where the work you did during the period came from.

B. Imposed from where?				
Boss	Sys	Sub	Self	Out

From the boss (Boss). Check this column if the job came from the boss and was *outside* of the operation of the organization's systems. (In the breakdown of your job, much of it would be assigned from the overall job the boss is responsible for getting done. Most of these duties involve the operation of the systems and belong in the next category.) Include special duties and assignments of a nonroutine nature, such as questions, requests for special information, and sudden problems and needs which arise. Your work on these activities often uses your special skills and helps the boss and those at higher levels perform their assignments. These activities often involve only *internal* operations.

From the systems (Sys). Rather than consider each function of an organization separately, the systems view considers all related facets and their interrelations as a whole. A marketing system, for example, includes such related efforts as market research, selection and compensation of salesmen, inventory, finance, credit considerations, delivery, service, etc. A production system includes related efforts in design, engineering, procuring and financing raw materials, production planning, purchase and maintenance of machinery and equipment, providing for a trained work force, transportation, storage, etc.

When work comes to us from the various systems of the organization, we are working on the prescribed routines and activities (subsystems established by you or others) which make all these related activities a whole. It includes coordination with interface groups, approvals, service, communication, supply, support, etc., and often involves printed forms. Systems allow a team effort which enables all parts of the organization to meet their objectives and serve the goals of the total organization.

From subordinates (Sub). Much of your job will be concerned with the administration of subordinates. This includes such activities as coaching, counseling, directing, supervising, delegating, etc. You are a resource to your subordinates and get requests for help and support which are quite legitimate. However, some requests for help may simply be "upward delegation," when the subordinates, in effect, ask you to do their jobs for them.

From yourself (Self). These are the self-imposed tasks which you decide to do to better your organization or operations. (If the situation is bad enough, these tasks may be imposed from the boss or someone higher up. Hopefully, if you take on these tasks yourself, they won't come from others.) Such self-imposed tasks include putting your feet up on the desk and thinking about and planning for the future, rearranging the resources assigned to you (changing your organization, layout, flow, budget allocations, assignments, etc.), defining the problems you are now having and arranging for work on solutions, thinking about how relations with other groups can be improved, refining your present systems, clarifying your objectives, etc. Work on problems usually comes from elsewhere. Work on future opportunities comes from yourself.

From outside (Out). These activities include handling requests to serve, speak, and participate in the on-going life of the larger community. We all have our share of requests for information, for assistance, and for service which come in each day's mail.

C. Results obtained

The third major heading on the form allows you to briefly list the outcome of the activity.

C. Results obtained

If a problem was solved, note this. (However, solving problems usually just restores normalcy, without gains toward your goals.) If a step was achieved toward your objectives, state this. If a key part of your job (whether formally described or assumed) was accomplished, write this in this column.

D. Could have been delegated?

The last major heading allows you to think about and record whether or not you were the one who should have performed the activity.

D. Could have been delegated?			
Yes	No	If no, why not?

Just use your best judgment in choosing an answer and state why it could not have been delegated, if you feel it could not have.

SUGGESTED FORM FOR THE ANALYSIS OF YOUR TIME

(Construct five of these to match the days logged.)

Day of the week:_____ Date:_____

Analyze each activity of each period to determine if your activity represented management or vocational work, where the job came from, the results obtained, and whether or not the activity could have been delegated. (Refer back to the descriptions of each column.)

A. Nature		B. Imposed from where?					C. Results obtained	D. Could have been delegated?		
Mgt	Voc	Boss	Sys	Sub	Self	Out		Yes	No	If no, why not?

TIME IS THE ONE RESOURCE THAT CANNOT BE STOCKPILED!

Analysis of the Form

When you have filled out the "Analysis of Your Time" forms for each of the five days you kept a time log, you can take a closer look to see what it all means.

A. *Nature of your activities*

As mentioned earlier, there is nothing "wrong" when you perform vocational work. But what percent of your time is spent doing this? In your judgment, are you spending too much time in this? People newly appointed to a management job have difficulty "letting go" of the vocational work they had been doing. Other times, it's just fun to go back and "get your hands dirty." After all, doing vocational work was the source of our satisfactions for a long time. When we perform vocational work, we usually do it at the expense of our management duties.

B. *Where your work comes from*

1. From the boss. Many of these activities would be shown on your job description, if you have one. Job descriptions have some uses as well as limitations. If you don't have one, why don't you try to list your duties and see what you come up with? You won't be able to list some of your most significant contributions, though. (I once spent several weeks helping to write a job description for a very creative vice-president of engineering. We were quite proud of the results until we showed it to the vice-president. He studied it for a while, then said, "If this is what I'm being paid for, I'm not interested in the job!")

Special requests from the boss can become a burden, particularly if he considers you someone who will really deliver when he needs it. (And these special jobs are usually more fun than doing what you are supposed to be doing!) One way to keep numerous special requests under some limits is to list them, along with the things you are supposed to be doing, and ask your boss to help in determining priority. This way, he will see that his special requests are preventing you from doing other things. If he still wants the special jobs done, fine. But at least he knows that "something's got to give."

2. From the systems. We all create systems for one another to follow because these systems help us accomplish our objectives. These systems are the forms we must fill out, the vouchers we must submit, the people we must check with before doing something, etc. We understand perfectly why it is necessary for others to follow the orderly procedures we have established to prevent chaos. At the same time, we can't stand the "red tape" that other units have created just to bedevil us.

Parkinson says that in an organization of 1000 people, enough systems will be created to enable those in the organization to work hard without any need for reference to goals or results. Sometimes I think the number is closer to three people.

Time to play your role in the systems established in your organization is necessary, but how much time do you find you are spending at this? If too much, what can you do about it?

3. From subordinates. We are a resource to our subordinates, but we can also have them *too* dependent on us in getting their job done. Sometimes I think that there is more "upward" than downward delegation going on in organizations.

How much time are you spending in doing jobs which came to you from subordinates? Are they waiting for you to decide, initiate, move, etc.? Or, are you looking to them for this?

4. From yourself. Self-imposed jobs are the easiest to leave undone, because nobody but us knows that we should be doing them! Also, they are the easiest to overlook in our daily firefighting.

In the week during which you kept the time logs, did any of the activities come from yourself? Did you set aside time to think about your organization and how it was doing and how it could be improved? Did you wonder about all of the "symptom" problems and try to understand if there was a big underlying problem causing them all? Did you wonder about how your operations might be rearranged for greater effectiveness? Did you think about how your budget might be allocated for greater emphasis on the really important activities? Did you wonder about what really *are* the important activities?

These are all self-imposed jobs and are perhaps your most important duties. Did they get any time in your busy week?

5. From outside. Some of us have outside contacts as an important part of our assigned duties. But all of us probably get requests to perform some service, provide some information, or to participate in something. Outside activities can make an important contribution to the community, to government, to our profession, and so on. But having too many outside activities may become a burden. How much time did you spend in this area?

C. Results you achieved

The important thing in management is effectiveness, not just efficiency—not just to do things right, but to figure out what are the right things to do and then to concentrate resources and energy on them.

Managers in one large company were asked to list their duties in three categories:

"A" items: their major duties, the real reason they were being paid as managers

"B" items: their next most important duties

"C" items: their least important duties

A leading management consulting firm determined that in these three categories, efforts should be apportioned as follows:

"A" 65%   "B" 20%   "C" 15%

But when a record was kept on the amount of time each manager spent on duties in the three categories, it looked like this:

"A" 15%   "B" 20%   "C" 65%

Managers were spending only 15% of their time on their major duties, 20% on the next most important duties, and a whopping 65% on their least important duties. They were dealing with their least important duties *at the expense of their major duties.*

What would the same analysis of how you spent your time during that week recorded show? What results were you able to record? Were there decisions made, information shared, controls checked, agreements reached, approvals obtained, understanding and accord cemented, problems solved, plans laid, or a movement made toward your goals and objectives? Or did you have to record "general housekeeping," goodwill and socializing, or "just another meeting"?

Are you satisfied with the kind and amount of results you were able to list for the week? If not, what can you do about it?

For some people, one week may not be a fair period for which to expect results. As one moves up in management, the results may be more significant on a monthly or even quarterly basis. Therefore, set the period which is right for you and your job. (But don't let this be an excuse for not paying attention to how you spent the week you logged.)

Having a longer period to concentrate on can also place momentary problems in perspective. But the two or three goals you set for the month should be accomplished.

D. Could you have delegated this? If not, why not?

Your analysis in this area can have a real payoff. When you really start to look closely at what you do, you will see that much of it could be done as well (if not better) by a subordinate. If you delegated such tasks, you would have the time to do some of the other things that only you can do.

The "If not, why not?" part of your analysis will take some real soul-searching.

"Because they aren't ready for it yet." Why aren't they? How can they be made "ready"?

"Because they don't understand it well enough." Why don't they? How will you help them to understand it well enough?

"Because I'm the only one who sees the whole picture." Has this got to be the case?

"Because I'm the one who has been following this." Oh, I see. You didn't delegate it then, so you can't now.

There are some things which only you can do, such as approve plans, sign things, give a "go ahead" to actions, and so on. But you might want to make sure that you are really the only one who can.

Making this kind of analysis of how you spent the week can be embarrassing! I have required this exercise for some years in training middle managers. If there are 30 people in the group, about 29 of them will come up to me at the break or at lunch and say something like, "You know, that week I kept a log for was a *very* unusual week. I usually don't spend my time fussing around like that." So I give them five more log sheets and ask them to find a "typical" week and keep a log of *that*. If you have taken a close look at how you spent your time, you probably feel much the same as they did. But that's how you spent your time!

If making this analysis of your time was a useful experience, how often should you do it? Is this once enough, or could you plan on doing it at periodic intervals? At what intervals? How will you remind yourself to do it?

You can use the questionnaire that follows to summarize your thinking about your time management and what you might do differently. The questionnaire is followed by a checklist which gives some ideas on time management.

QUESTIONNAIRE

"How Do You Manage Your Time?"

Now that you have made an analysis of how you spent five consecutive work days, answer the questions below. Be frank—no one else need see the answers but you.

1. What did you discover about the *nature* of your activities over those five days? Were you spending *too* much or too little time on *vocational* activities? Too much or too little time on management activities? (Have a good talk with yourself.)

2. Where did your management activities come from (boss, system, subordinates, self, outside)? How many "self-imposed" activities could you list? Do you want to change this "mix"?

3. What did your analysis of your *results* show you? Are you really getting something done? Are there changes you want to make in this area?

4. What did your "delegation" analysis show you? (This can be a real "facing-up-to" talk with yourself. We hope it is fruitful.) What will you do differently next week?

5. Other new ideas about how you will spend your time?

Ideas on time management

_____

_____

_____

TIME IS THE ONE RESOURCE THAT CANNOT BE STOCKPILED!

IDEAS ON TIME MANAGEMENT

The habitual ways of operating you have developed can add to your effectiveness. But in time management, you have to adopt methods which suit you and your job. The following are ideas collected from many managers. They might be useful guidelines for your own management of time. They show a respect for the value of your time and that of your subordinates and superiors.

For each statement below, place a check mark in the appropriate column: "I do this now," "I should try this," or "Does not apply to me."

	I do this now	I should try this	Does not apply to me
1. Schedule unpleasant or difficult jobs for the time of day you work best.			
2. Handle the important problems first. Some people can hide from these for days by working hard at little problems.			
3. Have a plan for the day. Don't let your day be planned for you by the mail, by the telephone, and by drop-in callers.			
4. Try three lists: "Must do," "Should do," and "Nice to do." Throw the third one away, file the second, and do the first.			
5. Group similar activities in a given time period. Set aside an hour for dictating letters, another for returning phone calls, etc.			
6. Assign certain time blocks for major, unscheduled duties.			
7. Time for study, creative effort, and planning need to be scheduled in large blocks, not left to chance in a succession of seven- to ten-minute units.			

322 Managing your time   Chap. 13

	I do this now	I should try this	Does not apply to me

8. Be creative about the job, but seek out ideas that others have come up with. Beware the "not invented here" attitude.

9. Handle correspondence once or delegate it. Learn to dictate if you can't now.

10. Make better use of your secretary to answer letters. She is probably more able and creative than you give her an opportunity to be.

11. If outside requests are similar, devise standard paragraphs for use in the reply. Then merely indicate which ones to use for a reply.

12. Develop a simple follow-up system using your secretary. If you treat assigned due dates seriously, subordinates will, too.

13. For an "in-office" meeting, ask your secretary to hold the calls. Shut off the conveyor belt.

14. Don't call a meeting unless it can be made very clear what purpose is to be accomplished by it.

15. Tell those invited to the meeting the purpose, what is expected from them, what information to bring, and the intended outcome.

16. If a meeting ends in an assignment, document it and put it in your follow-up system.

17. Most meetings are one-third too long, due to some resistance to the death of the group. Kill it off.

18. Try "stand-up" conferences.

19. When you operate slightly understaffed, your people must place their tasks in a priority order.

20. Share your new approach to the management of your time with subordinates. They can help and give you additional suggestions.

Were your check marks in the "Does not apply to me" column really true statements?

How can and will you follow up to see later if you have done anything you checked in the "I should try this" column?

It's not the force or energy behind efforts which determine results. It's the way we channel them.

CHAPTER **14**

PROBLEM-SOLVING

Problem-solving is one of the principal skills needed by the manager. He is called on hourly, daily, monthly, and yearly to solve or help solve small, large, or very large problems which affect the organization's life.

The nature of the problem to be solved or the decision to be made will vary depending, in large part, on the level in the organization in which it arises. At lower levels, solutions to problems tend to be of the either black-or-white, go/no-go variety. They tend to be clearcut, are often technical problems, and can be solved on the basis of fact. They are in immediate need of solution, and often the "best" solution consists of "slapping a band-aid on it" and keeping the operation rolling. Decisions about problems at the lower levels can frequently be "programed." (When this occurs, do this.) Some managers use a "decision table" that lists problems down one side and conditions across the top. The point where the two columns join states the solution.

As problems come into view in upper levels, they tend to change considerably. Both the problems and their solutions become more "gray." These problems are often large and complex, nontechnical, or a mixture of technical and nontechnical; judgment and intuition play a large part in the decisions reached. Probabilistic, tentative, approximate answers are sought to long-range, far-reaching problems.

We will use a case illustration to walk you through the steps we will use in the problem-solving process. Later on, you will be asked to identify in some detail a problem you face or an objective you would like to reach.

AN ILLUSTRATIVE CASE IN PROBLEM-SOLVING

Bill Harold was the manager of the Proofing, Reproduction, and Registration Section for the Mathews Corporation. His section, though small, was a key one in the organization because all orders had to come into it before being confirmed to the customer and the agreement sold to the customer being placed into effect.

The letters of agreement signed by the customers after being filled out by the sales agents were first checked for accuracy and completeness, then reproduced, registered (a formal legal requirement), and confirmed to the customer. The sales agents working in a large metropolitan area usually brought the letters of agreement in themselves. The normal procedure was to assign each letter a number on receipt by the section; they were then handled in the order indicated by the number.

There were no seasonal changes; the total number of entries for each month tended to be about the same. If the letters of agreement came in "bunches," it was because the sales agents waited until they had a batch rather than deliver them for processing as they were received.

The receptionist for the section had adopted the practice some time before of putting "urgent" orders on top of the daily piles of materials awaiting processing. This informal practice worked well as long as there were few of an urgent nature. But more and more orders became "urgent" when the sales agents saw that having this priority would get their letters special attention. Finally, there were more orders "on top of the pile" than there were in it. At this point, the receptionist had asked for help, whereupon Bill Harold established a new system of granting formal priority. An "A" priority, signed by the zone manager on a special form, was given immediate attention; all other orders were to be handled routinely in their order of arrival.

This new procedure, which was strictly enforced, worked well for a time and took the "heat" off of the receptionist. There was some grumbling about it at the time, but this subsided after a short while. Note that it "worked well for a time." In what seemed to be an astonishing short period, however, 85 percent of all orders for processing came in with an "A" priority request. Under such conditions, as before, the truly urgent cases were delayed. In a few cases this had caused highly visible problems and an expressed concern by the top management as to the operations of the section.

To meet one of these emergency problems and to placate criticism of the existing procedures, Bill Harold installed a modification of the priority system, whereby an "AAA" priority was allowed when so requested by the district managers. This soon had to be changed to "the District Manager or his specified deputy," when the district managers complained about handling this detail themselves.

Bill Harold noted, with some alarm, that these "AAA" priority requests were also beginning to rise. Practically all of the other orders were now "A" priority; nothing came in for routine handling any more. Bill thought that this would, no doubt, soon lead to the need for a "super-super" priority, and eventually to a "super-super-dooper" priority system, which probably would lead to the same result as past efforts.

The system was clearly getting out of hand and promised to get worse. Bill Harold was distressed at the future prospects. At this point, he decided to analyze this problem, using the design given here. Bill's progress in working on it will be used to illustrate each step in the problem-solving process.

(Choosing this particular problem to serve as an illustration should in no way guide or limit your selection of your own problem to work on. It is merely used to make each step clearer to you.)

A MODEL FOR PROBLEM-SOLVING

To help you think through the steps in problem-solving* and to guide your efforts on your own problem, we will go through eight steps you should take:

1. State the problem
2. Set your objectives
3. List the known facts
4. Make a force-field analysis of the situation
5. List alternative solutions
6. Make a value analysis of the most promising alternatives
7. Make your decision and test it
8. Make an action plan

Whenever a list of the broad steps to be taken is given like this, there is the implication that such a process is linear—that it is followed step by step from beginning to end. But this is not so. Problem-solving is a dynamic process during which you go back and forth, retracing your previous steps, moving on only to go back to a previous step once again. When we list the known facts, for example, we may find that we have to go back and restate the problem differently. When we try and make a value analysis of alternatives, we may have to go back and get more facts. Therefore, when we talk about these steps in the process, and when you go through them in the analysis of your problem, expect to be dealing with a dynamic process.

An example of a form which you can sketch out and use in laying out your analysis is shown on the next page. Using such a form keeps your efforts on one sheet of paper in front of you. Alternatively, you can work on each step here in the book or on separate sheets of paper. We will follow the form in our discussion. Now let's look at the steps in detail. (If you decide to work on an objective you wish to reach rather than a problem, start with step 2.)

1. State the Problem

Try writing down the problem in simple language first. Then write down every assumption you can think of that you are making in the problem-statement. What are you taking for granted? What if this is not so? (If you need more space, use a separate sheet of paper for your responses.)

---

* This variation of steps in the process and the form for recording them have been adapted from a model developed by Max Canterbury, a very creative management teacher at The Boeing Company.

PROBLEM-ANALYSIS WORK GUIDE

1. State the problem	2. Objective. State the goal that is jeopardized by this problem. (If you had no problem, describe a key end-result you very much hope to accomplish.)	3. List the known facts. Note the pertinent facts about the problem. Write a brief history that would help account for your present dilemma.

4. Force-field analysis	5. List alternative solutions. Brainstorm with yourself (or with others) all the possible things you might do to solve this problem. Then list the most promising here.	6. Value analysis of alternatives						
		Failure risk: probability, cause, and remedy	Reduce restraint barriers	Contributes to goal	Least effort and cost	Least time	Least risk	Check alternatives most desirable
Driving forces → ← Restraining forces								
↑ ↓								
↑ ↓								
↑ ↓								
Lengthen arrows where force should be strengthened. Shorten arrows where force can be decreased								

7. Decision. Think of several ways of checking the decision out. Bounce it off a friend. Try it out on a sample basis.	8. Action plan. Lay out the steps for carrying out the decision.

A suggested layout for individual problem-solving (This form is followed in the text.)

Can the problem be stated in even simpler words? Does that change the problem?

Is the stated problem a small symptom of an even larger problem? Is that the one you should be working on?

Restate the problem. (You will probably rework the statement several times during your analysis.)

Step 1 in illustrative case

Bill Harold tried to write down the problem, stating it simply. The statement he arrived at did reflect the immediate problem he saw.

"To keep the present priority system from getting out of hand."

Bill then tried to think about all of the assumptions he was making. He saw three:

1. A system for establishing priorities is needed.
2. Emergency situations and special problems arise which require special handling.
3. A priority system can be made to work.

He felt that all of these assumptions were true, and he didn't see the need for restating the problem differently at this time.

2. Set Your Objectives

State the goal that is jeopardized by this problem. (If you had no problem, describe a key end-result you very much hope to accomplish.)

State your objectives as simply as you can. What will occur if the problem is solved or the objective is reached? What is bothersome about not being there now? How will you know when you have reached it? When? How much improvement? What will be the probable cost in time, money, and energy in reaching it? Is the objective really worth reaching?

What would make the problem disappear entirely instead of being solved? What giant steps could be taken to eliminate it? Why don't you take those steps?

Defining your objectives will help you to keep the problem in focus as you try to solve it. You may well come back to this step and redefine the key end-results you hope to accomplish.

Should you go back and restate the problem at this point? Should the problem be restated by being subdivided into several parts? By being combined with other small problems?

Step 2 in illustrative case

In his first attempt to define his objectives, Bill came up with the following:

"Objective: To make the priority system work."

As Bill thought about the key end-result his section was trying to reach, his objective became broader. The priority system was important, but it was only one facet of the section's operations—a troublesome facet, but only one. Bill rewrote his objective:

"Objective: To adopt a system for the efficient handling of proofing, reproduction, and registration which makes provision for the occasional special case."

This statement seemed to Bill to place the priority problem in perspective. Then he looked back over his statement of the problem. It now seemed to Bill that he had stated but a sympton of the larger problem, which he restated this way:

"The current system for handling proofing, reproduction, and registration (hereafter called PR & R) is not working effectively."

3. List the Known Facts

Note the pertinent facts about the problem. Write a brief history that would help account for your present dilemma. List in detail what you know about the situation and what you don't know, but need to. Make comparisons of what is wrong and what is right; of what has changed and what has not; of where the problem is and where it is not; of when the problem is happening and when it is not. How did it begin (gradually or suddenly)? Who first noticed it? What are the possible causes? What are the probable causes? Single or multiple causes?

Describe the present situation in some detail. What are the road blocks that are keeping you from getting to where you want to be?

What are the key unknowns about the situation? How could these become known? Through studies, statistical gathering of data and analysis, experiments, interviews, and other sources? Who will search for these unknowns? When?

A model for problem-solving

_____

_____

_____

_____

In light of this fact-gathering step, should the problem-statement or your objectives be restated?

Step 3 in illustrative case

Bill reviewed the situation as presented to you earlier. One thing about it caught his attention—the informal system of granting priority had worked well for a long time, but now wasn't. What had happened to cause this to be a problem?

Bill decided to gather more facts by examining records of production of the section and by interviewing a sample of people within the office and a few of the sales agents. Bill quickly discovered that the records of production were not kept in any methodical way. (Bill made arrangements to have a final count of submissions by agents and confirmations to customers kept on a weekly basis. These entry and exit figures for the system would give a much better feel for what the operations were handling.) As sketchy as the records were now, they did seem to show an increase of about 15 percent per year for the past three years. This was confirmed by the sales records for the firm. There had been no increase in staff of the section.

In following the progress of orders being processed within the section, and by talking to people at each step, Bill realized several points. First, many of the people within the section were new, due to normal attrition over the past several years. Second, in talking to the proofing unit, he learned that the sales agents were expecting more and more corrections and supply of missing data to be performed by the PR & R staff. Missing data were obtained from reference books (which were also available to sales agents). Some of the missing and incorrect data had to be obtained from the customers, which took much effort and was time-consuming. The attitude of the PR & R staff was that this was just part of their job to ensure correct information.

From interviews with the sales agents, Bill learned that many of them, too, were new. On joining the firm, they had assessed the existing situation, which included the necessity for obtaining priority status on all orders, and had therefore followed this practice. The sales agents generally didn't like the detail required in filling out the paperwork to submit, and they found that problems with incomplete data would be handled by the proofing staff (nonperformance was rewarded). Filling out all of the required details took time away from making other sales calls. (Proper performance was punished.)

When customers contacted the sales agents about delays in receiving their confirmations, the agents could and did blame "those bureaucrats doing the paperwork for the firm." These contacts again stressed to the agents the need for obtaining a priority on work they turned in. They were able to make a convincing case for this need to the person responsible for making the formal request for the priority.

Bill then stepped away from the function and raised some searching questions about it. If this section didn't perform its assigned duties, what would happen? Who would do them, or would they be done at all? Are all of the duties really necessary? How could they be modified or eliminated?

This analysis provided little in new insights as to how their problems might be overcome through elimination, primarily because of the legal requirements for proofing accuracy and for registration of each request before confirmation. It seemed most efficient to handle these centrally and together. The reproduction activity could be organizationally reassigned, but this did not seem useful at this time.

After getting these additional facts, Bill Harold went back and took another look at the statement of the problem and his objectives. He decided that the problem-statement was still okay, but decided to add to the objective:

"Objective: To adopt a system for the efficient handling of proofing, reproduction, and registration which makes provision for the occasional special case, *and in which both the PR & R Section and the sales agents perform their assigned tasks to make the system work.*"

4. Make a Force-Field Analysis of the Situation

This is probably a new idea to you, so let me explain it. Some years ago, Kurt Lewin and others became interested in what came to be called "the field theory" in sociology.* One of their ideas, that of doing a force-field analysis, is a simple, but extremely useful, idea for all managers. A sample force-field analysis follows.

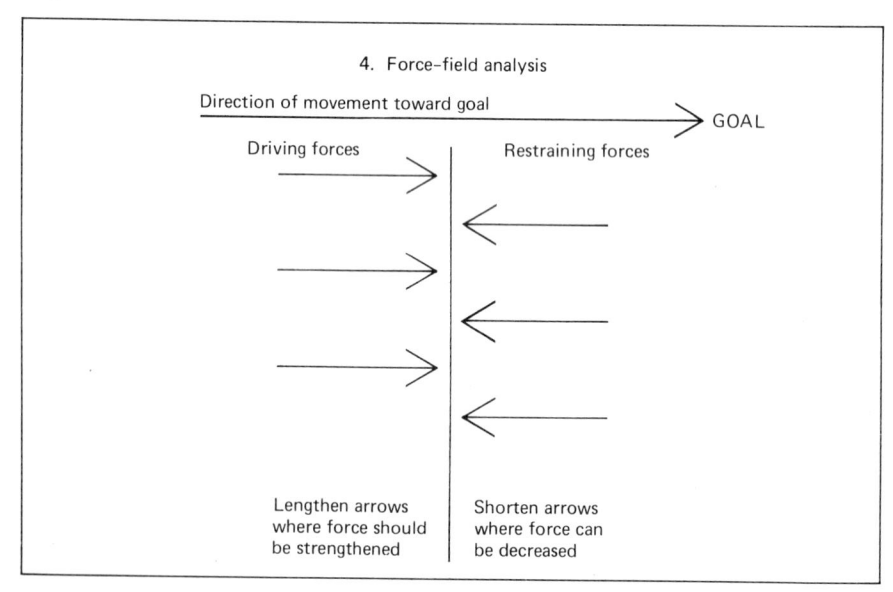

```
                    4. Force-field analysis
        Direction of movement toward goal
        ─────────────────────────────────────────>  GOAL

           Driving forces        Restraining forces
                  ──>             <──
                  ──>             <──
                  ──>             <──

        Lengthen arrows       Shorten arrows
        where force should    where force can
        be strengthened       be decreased
```

---

* Kurt Lewin in Dorwin Cartwright, ed., *Field Theory in Social Science,* New York: Harper & Row, 1951.

A force-field analysis lets us analyze the situation we face when we introduce change, lay plans to reach some goal or objective, or otherwise wish to alter the present state of things. A case example follows.

JOE WILSON

Joe Wilson is one of your subordinates and has been with you for eight months. His work is well above your expectations, and he seems to get along well with the others on the staff and with those in related units with whom he is in contact. But Joe has one way of behaving which is a little annoying to you. Whenever he is around you, he "clams up" and will not be free and open in his relations with you. This has caused no serious problem as yet, but it might if he withholds from you things you should know about.

You have tried to work on this problem by encouraging him to speak up and be more open with you, and you have even made a special note on his coaching form and have discussed this with him at his last coaching session. You feel sure that he wants to do a good job and live up to your expectations. You have pointed out how others are frank and open and how this has helped them get ahead. But somehow, you can't seem to push the right button with Joe.

This is certainly not an unusual situation or an unusual posture for a boss to take. The situation seems simple enough—we have a goal in mind for Joe (to act more openly), and we are exerting our influence on him to move him toward this goal. The forces that act as pressure on him to move in this direction are: (1) Joe's desire to do what you expect, (2) criticism for not being frank and open, (3) stress on how important it is, (4) inspiration examples of others moving ahead. All of these forces are "pushing" to move Joe, but he doesn't budge. Does this situation sound familiar?

The notion behind a force-field analysis is to examine not only the forces driving toward the goal, but also the restraining forces which are holding movement back. In Joe's case, the force-field analysis might look like this:

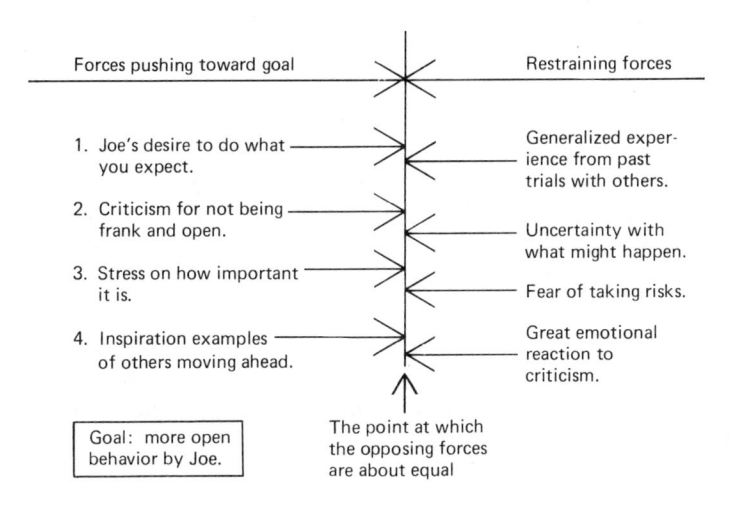

Forces pushing toward goal	Restraining forces
1. Joe's desire to do what you expect.	Generalized experience from past trials with others.
2. Criticism for not being frank and open.	Uncertainty with what might happen.
3. Stress on how important it is.	Fear of taking risks.
4. Inspiration examples of others moving ahead.	Great emotional reaction to criticism.

Goal: more open behavior by Joe.

The point at which the opposing forces are about equal

Without an analysis of the forces driving toward and forces restraining movement toward the goal, we would tend to think that to make the change come about, we need only to push harder. But when we only increase the driving forces, what happens? Right! The restraining forces build in strength as well, and little movement occurs. It would be more helpful to understand the restraining forces and see what might be done to reduce or remove them. Then, movement toward the goal is more possible. How could you reduce the restraining forces in Joe's case?

Now let's take a larger example. Let's say that your goal is "to increase the productivity of the work force." A diagram of the driving and restraining forces in this case might look something like this:

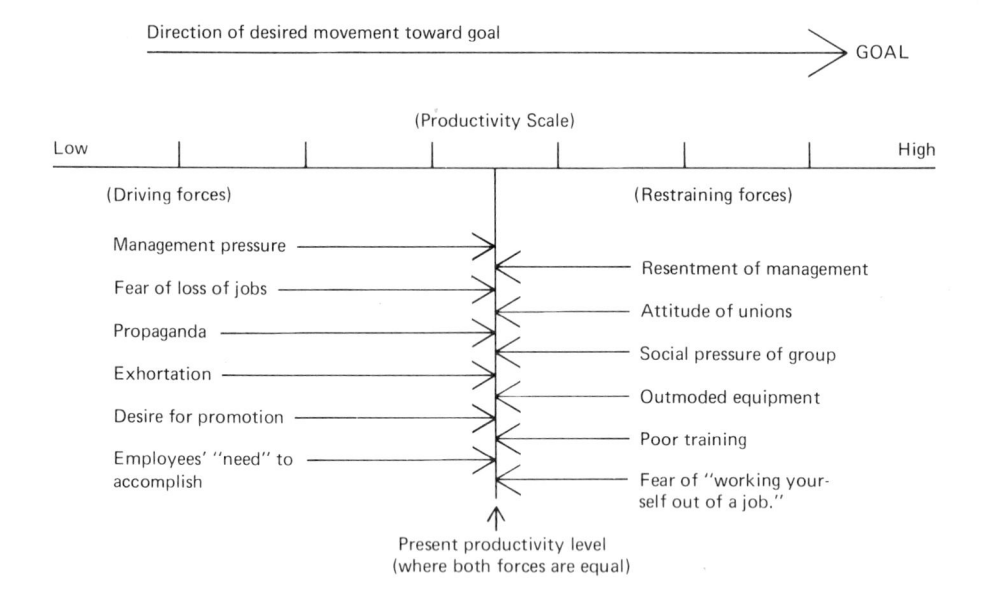

```
       Direction of desired movement toward goal
       ──────────────────────────────────────────────────────>  GOAL

                          (Productivity Scale)
Low    |          |          |          |          |          |     High
       ────────────────────────────────────────────────────────────────
       (Driving forces)              (Restraining forces)

       Management pressure ──────>
                              <────── Resentment of management
       Fear of loss of jobs ─────>
                              <────── Attitude of unions
       Propaganda ──────────────>
                              <────── Social pressure of group
       Exhortation ─────────────>
                              <────── Outmoded equipment
       Desire for promotion ────>
                              <────── Poor training
       Employees' "need" to ────>
       accomplish             <────── Fear of "working your-
                                      self out of a job."
                                ↑
                     Present productivity level
                   (where both forces are equal)
```

In technical terms, the "line" comes to a stop when the driving and restraining forces are about equal; this is called "a quasistationary equilibrium," which simply means that there is a temporary balance of forces on each side.

When managers strive to increase only the driving forces, they may move a bit toward their objective, but at the same time the restraining forces also begin to build up. This is shown on p. 333 (the heavier lines indicate increased pressure).

The diagram shows that, although you may move a short way toward your objective, the build-up of the restraining forces creates greater tension in the situation than was present before. In other words, it's like driving with your brakes on.

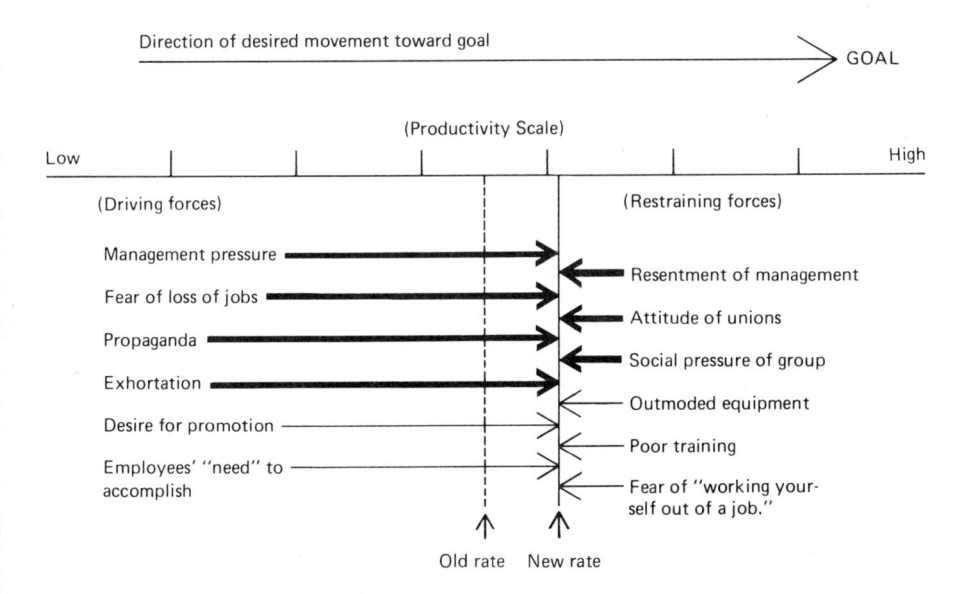

```
Direction of desired movement toward goal
                                              ──────> GOAL

                        (Productivity Scale)
Low    |      |      |      |      |      |      |    High

       (Driving forces)         (Restraining forces)

  Management pressure ━━━━━━━━━▶◀━━ Resentment of management
  Fear of loss of jobs ━━━━━━━━▶◀━━ Attitude of unions
  Propaganda ━━━━━━━━━━━━━━━━━━▶◀━━ Social pressure of group
  Exhortation ━━━━━━━━━━━━━━━━━▶◀━━ Outmoded equipment
  Desire for promotion ─────────▶◀── Poor training
  Employees' "need" to ─────────▶◀── Fear of "working your-
  accomplish                          self out of a job."

                         ↑    ↑
                      Old rate  New rate
```

Therefore, the smart thing to do is to analyze both sets of forces at work and see what you can do about reducing the restraining forces. Then, you will be able to move toward your objective with greater ease. In the example given above, what could be done about reducing resentment, building a better relation with the unions, reducing the social pressure on the group, up-dating the equipment, providing better training, and reassuring employees about the organization's future? Remember, reducing the restraining forces will greatly help to move you toward your objective. The normal driving forces will then become more effective. (The force-field analysis can be used for almost any problem you can think of—marketing, production, organizational, personal, etc.)

This problem-solving step, then, consists of making a force-field analysis of the factors driving toward your objective and those factors that restrain movement toward the goal. After you have made such an analysis, you can ask some questions about the problem you are trying to solve. If the restraining forces are reduced, are any more driving forces necessary? How would you go about reducing the restraining forces? Which forces cannot be reduced—ever or at this time? Which driving forces can be increased without a corresponding increase in the opposing restraining forces? After you have completed this step, should you go back and restate the problem or the objective; should you get some more or different facts?

Step 4 in illustrative case
In making a force-field analysis of his stated problem, Bill Harold first stated his objective and hen made a list of the things which were driving toward that objec-

334 Problem-solving Chap. 14

tive and the things which were restraining movement toward that stated objective.

Objective (or goal): To adopt a system for the efficient handling of proofing, reproduction, and registration which makes provision for the occasional special case, and in which both the PR & R section and the sales agents perform their assigned tasks to make the system work.

Bill's force-field analysis is shown below.

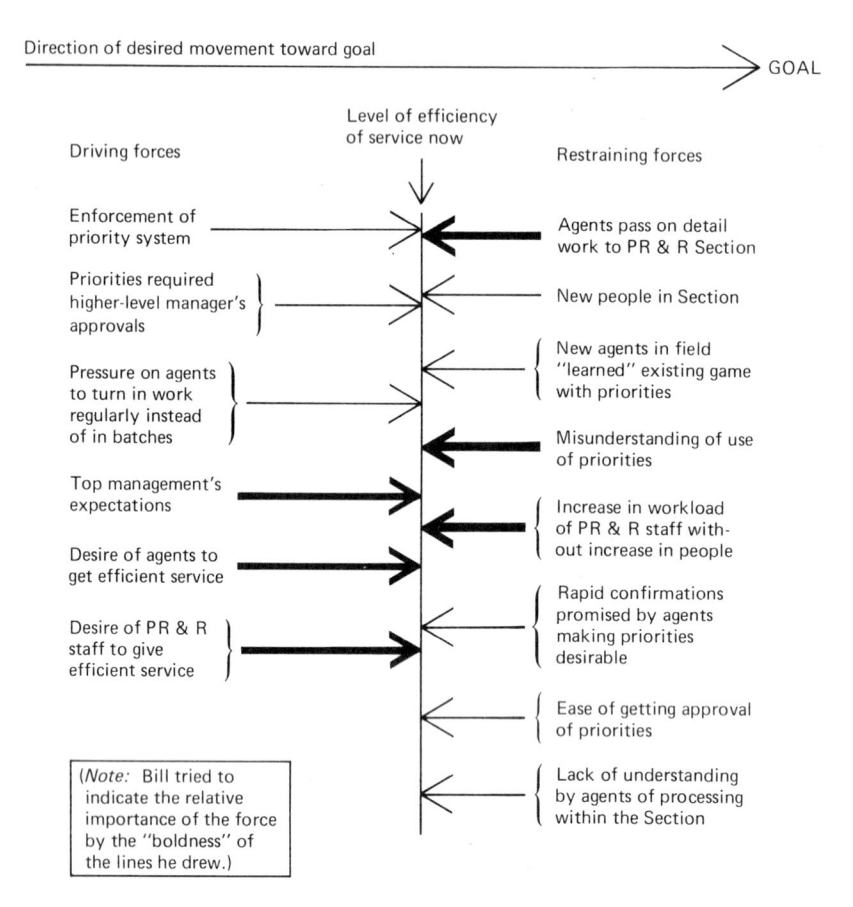

```
Direction of desired movement toward goal ─────────────────────────► GOAL

                              Level of efficiency
                              of service now
    Driving forces                  │              Restraining forces
                                    ▼

Enforcement of                                    Agents pass on detail
priority system         ──────────►◄──────────    work to PR & R Section

Priorities required     ┐
higher-level manager's  ├─────────►◄──────────    New people in Section
approvals               ┘
                                                  ┌ New agents in field
Pressure on agents      ┐                         │ "learned" existing game
to turn in work         ├─────────►◄──────────    └ with priorities
regularly instead       │
of in batches           ┘         ◄──────────     Misunderstanding of use
                                                  of priorities

Top management's
expectations            ──────────►               ┌ Increase in workload
                                  ◄──────────     │ of PR & R staff with-
Desire of agents to                               └ out increase in people
get efficient service   ──────────►
                                                  ┌ Rapid confirmations
Desire of PR & R        ┐                         │ promised by agents
staff to give           ├─────────►◄──────────    │ making priorities
efficient service       ┘                         └ desirable

                                  ◄──────────     ┌ Ease of getting approval
                                                  └ of priorities

(Note: Bill tried to                              ┌ Lack of understanding
indicate the relative             ◄──────────     │ by agents of processing
importance of the force                           └ within the Section
by the "boldness" of
the lines he drew.)
```

After making this force-field analysis, Bill saw two things more clearly. First, he realized that the forces pushing for more effective service were coming from top management and the PR & R staff almost exclusively. Second, it was apparent that these efforts were being overwhelmed by the restraining forces operating against reaching the goal.

5. List Alternative Solutions

Brainstorm with yourself all the possible things you might do to solve this problem. In "brainstorming" this step, you might also want to get others involved; sometimes imaginative ideas spark other good ideas. However, the "imagineering" people would tell us to withhold critical judgments at this point, because judgments will restrain us from getting all possible ideas out.

Make your lists of all the possible solutions on slips of paper, the blackboard, etc. Then write your alternatives in the space below.

a) _____
b) _____
c) _____
d) _____
e) _____
f) _____
g) _____
h) _____

After you have listed all the possibilities, use your critical judgment to select the most reasonable alternatives for further analysis.

Step 5 in illustrative case

At this point, Bill thought it was time to get the thinking of others on possible actions to be taken. He got three of his key people together and reviewed his findings so far. Then he asked for their help in listing alternative actions. Fifty-seven ideas were listed in all, but when each was looked at critically, there seemed to be eight best alternatives toward a solution. These were:

a) The section should either refuse to handle or turn back incomplete submissions from the sales agents.
b) The section staff should be increased by 20% immediately.
c) The basis of establishing priorities should be changed. Selected members of the section staff would assign priorities after hearing the request and deciding on its legitimacy.
d) Suggest training for the sales agents as to:
   1) What is a reasonable time for obtaining confirmation (such as seven to ten working days).
   2) How to fill in data accurately on letter agreements.
   3) Appropriate use of priorities for defined special cases.
e) Provide training for the section staff—particularly in proofing—to help them understand that they were not to do the sales agents' jobs for them.
f) Persuade and encourage the sales staff to turn in letters of agreements as received instead of waiting until they have a batch of them.
g) Begin rewarding sales agents who turn in their letters promptly and accurately. Provide recognition back to their boss for good work.
h) Get prompter feedback from the sales agents when service is taking too long. Feedback now is being given in the form of seeking priorities for everything, which clearly meant that the system wasn't working.

6. Make a Value Analysis of the Most Promising Alternatives

Now that you have selected some possible alternatives, step back from the analysis. Take time out to question your whole approach. What makes you think that this problem really needs solving or that the stated objective need be met? What makes you think you have the needed facts in this situation? What assumptions are you making which limit your view of the problem? The following form can be used to further analyze the best alternatives. (Note that lines (a) through (h) refer to the alternative solutions listed in step 5.)

6. Value analysis of alternatives						Check alternatives most desirable
Failure risk: probability, cause, and remedy	Check favorability factors					
	Reduce restraint barriers	Contributes to goal	Least effort and cost	Least time	Least risk	
a)						
b)						
c)						
d)						
e)						
f)						
g)						
h)						

As you go through this form, first think of all the negative points to each alternative. What is the risk of failure? What would be the impact of failure of this solution (cost, delays, look foolish, etc.)? What is the probability of failure? What would be the cause of failure? What could be done to prevent failure? What argument would probably be used to resist this solution? How sound would the argument be? Who would resist this solution? Why?

Next, think through the factors that made the solution desirable. Would the solution reduce restraints and barriers? Would it contribute to meeting your goals? Would it require the least effort and cost? The least time? The least risk?

When you have looked at all of the plus and minus factors, the most desirable alternative should be readily apparent. Perhaps there are two, or even three, desirable alternatives to choose from.

A model for problem-solving 337

Step 6 in illustrative case

Bill's small group then began to look carefully at each of the eight proposals to analyze their real value in meeting the stated objective. Here are some notes on their discussion.

a) (Either refuse or turn back incomplete submissions.) This move would certainly get attention (probably all the way to the President's office) if it were to be started suddenly. But having more accurate submittals would certainly improve the quality of service being given and would lessen the need for additional staff. Once the idea was accepted, little extra time and effort would be required on the part of the agents. If the idea was properly introduced, and if the agents know how to do what was expected of them, the risk of failure of this course of action should be small.

b) (Increase the section staff by 20 percent.) An increase would certainly be justified, based on the increased volume of work handled. But adding people should probably be the last resort. If the system operated as it was meant to, the need for additional people would certainly be smaller than it seems to be now. Asking for a 20 percent increase would probably not be approved; therefore, this alternative is risky. Also, it would be a costly alternative.

c) (Have section staff assign priorities.) The staff all agreed that this would not contribute toward the objective. The plan sounded good at first, but in discussing it, the group began to see that they would just be going back to the original system—which hadn't worked. Without other changes, the staff would be in a continual "hassle" with the sales agents.

d) (Suggested training.) This alternative seemed to contribute the most to the objective, with a low risk of failure—*if* the training was conducted properly. However, the staff finally agreed that it was not their responsibility to require or conduct training. This was the responsibility of the managers of the sales agents. The staff's responsibility was to point out the need for following a new, agreed upon system; to point out in detail what the new system would require on the part of the sales agents; and then to leave it up to the managers of the sales agents how they were going to implement the new approach. If the managers wished to draw on the resources of the PR & R group, this was fine.

e) (Training for the section staff, particularly in the proofing unit.) Rather than institute a formal training program, the group agreed that once the new procedures were formulated, they should be explained down through each level of the section. This would minimize the risk of failure, be less costly, and would take the least effort. The group felt it important that everyone in the section understand the new arrangement.

f) (Encourage the sales agents to turn in letters as received.) When the group began discussing this idea, they realized that they didn't know—and Bill hadn't investigated—why the agents were turning in their letters in this manner. Why did they do this now? Was it inconvenient for them to turn them in more regularly? Did they just like to have a stack accumulate to give them a feeling of accomplishment? Or why? There was some reason why this was occurring, and they needed to get some clues as to what this was. Bill made a note to investigate this point.

g) (Positive reinforcement for good work.) This was seen as a neglected area. The group saw that they were so busy dealing with things which weren't going right, they had no time to reinforce what was going well. Only crises got attention. The group agreed that this approach should be included in any final plan. It would help to accomplish their objective, with a small risk of failure, it was not costly, and it required little effort and time to accomplish.

h) (Feedback from the sales agents.) The group agreed that the section should provide more feedback about problems and difficulties being encountered by the sales group. There was no deliberate way now used to get information directly. This move was regarded as necessary to head off future situations like the one that had finally got out of hand.

Following this discussion, the group agreed on the decision to include a combination and modification of several of the alternatives discussed. Their decision will be presented after a discussion of the next step.

7. Make Your Decision and Test It

At this point, you should be able to select the one most desirable alternative and decide to go that way. Can you think of several ways your decision can be checked out to ensure that it will do what you hope? Should it be discussed with others? Can it be tried on a sample basis? What reaction or results from a test will you accept as a "go/no-go" signal? Write your answers in the space provided.

_____
_____
_____
_____
_____
_____
_____

Step 7 in illustrative case

The new procedures to be followed were:
1. The proofing section would establish standards of acceptance for letters of agreement, indicating which details they would supply and which *must* be included when the letters are received. If the required information was not included, the letter would be turned back to the sales agent for correction.
2. Each sales agent would be responsible for asking for priority to be assigned to any of his letters. This priority would be respected.
3. Information would be obtained for each sales agent about steady deliveries versus batch deliveries for processing. (The reason for the use of batch deliveries would be explored, and obstacles would be removed.)

A model for problem-solving

4. Information about the record of each sales agent in the number of turn-backs, priorities, and steady deliveries would be sent back to the agent and his manager, with special recognition for good work.

Once the new procedures were approved by higher management, the staff of the PR & R section would get a complete briefing on how the procedures would be followed. This would take place as a special effort, but within the regular contacts with people down through the organization. The sales managers would have the new system explained to them, and an agreement would be reached on an effective date (two or three weeks away). An offer would be made by the section staff to be used in any way the sales managers wished to communicate the new procedures.

A budget increase would be requested from higher management in order to permit an increase of five percent to the staff of the PR & R section.

The key staff of the PR & R section would plan a defined contact system with sales managers and sales agents on a regular check-off basis and would report back on developing problems with the new procedures or in any other areas of their operations.

Bill Harold agreed to discuss the proposed plan with three of the sales managers to get their reaction. They would be encouraged to discuss it with several of their sales agents and provide information back to Bill. If no serious objections turned up, the plan would be submitted for approval.

8. Make an Action Plan

Lay out the specific steps needed to be taken to implement the proposed action. Who needs to be "sold"? Who needs to approve it? What assets will be needed? Who will be affected? How will the change be introduced? What level of support and agreement can you expect? How will you deal with opposition? Write out your action plan in the space provided.

_____

_____

_____

_____

_____

_____

_____

Hopefully, you have involved those directly affected as you went along. Now, carry out the action plan.

Step 8 in illustrative case

Bill's steps to test the plan with the sales managers turned up no problems. As a matter of fact, the sales managers generally felt that something had to be done with the current priority system and were glad to see a new plan. They particularly liked placing the responsibility on the agents to determine their own priorities and to get reports on how their men were doing. "This is putting the responsibility where it belongs," one manager said, "instead of creating more and more rules which would fall of their own weight." The managers reported no problems in the reactions of the agents.

Bill's action plan was as follows:

1. To get approval from his department head through either an informal discussion or a formal presentation, whichever his boss wished.
2. A presentation on the new plan would be made to the General Manager of Sales on his boss's level, and to the head of the legal group, which was responsible for the legal aspects of the section's operations. With their concurrence, a presentation will be made the following week to those reporting to the General Manager of Sales. At this point, the plan would be explained further down through their organization as they desired—providing notes for subsequent meetings, published materials explaining the plan, or further presentations by the staff of the PR & R section.
3. The effective date would be set in the meeting with the General Manager of Sales (step 2).

Bill Harold asked for an appointment with his department head to arrange the first meeting.

How well do you think Bill Harold has handled his problem? Will his action solve it, in your view? Why or why not?

SOLVING YOUR OWN PROBLEM

Now that the steps in the problem-solving process have been discussed and illustrated, it's time that you tried one yourself. The problem you select to work on can be either an organizational problem, such as the illustration given, or a personal one. The problem you select for your first attempt at using the model shouldn't be too large or complex or have too many unknowns, which would take much research. Nor should the problem you select be too small and insignificant. These are rather vague limits, I know, but go ahead and select one and take it through the steps.

Begin with a statement of the problem—which will undergo some reworking, of course—and go on through the model to specific plans to implement the action. You will become well aware that problem-solving isn't a linear, step-by-step process; rather, as you progress you return over and over again to rework previous steps.

I certainly don't expect you to follow these eight steps all the time, or even continue to use this particular model. But doing so, at least in the beginning, will assure you that everything is considered in its approximate sequence.

Before we leave our discussion of problem-solving, let's consider two other aspects: first, how "people" problems may differ from technical problems; and second, the manager's role in managing the problem-solving process through effective delegation. These considerations may help you with the problems you face.

People Problems Are Often Different

You may have selected a "people" problem to work through as your problem-solving case. If so, you may have found that you were able to work the problem out through the model, even though the model may not have quite "fit" your problem. But Alvar Elbing reminds us that the "logics" of the technical problem-solving model can be a block to the development of a model more appropriate to real-life, "human" situations. Here are some important differences he notes:

1. In technical problem-solving, the "cue" which calls our attention to the problem in the first place *is the problem*. Something is wrong, and what is wrong is probably obvious to all. But in human problems, the relationship between the fact that *something* is wrong and just what *is* wrong is not at all obvious.

We may work away at surface problems only to find that as fast as we deal with one symptom, another arises to take its place. Thus, the step of "defining the problem" is often not simple and can be very complex.

2. Technical problems lend themselves to more precise definition because of specialized terms, precise measurements available, and specific standards which can be applied. But this is rarely the case with human problems.

3. The step of "getting the facts" can also be complex. There are a great many "unknowns" in dealing with people problems, and some of these are even unknown to the people who are having the problem.

4. The choice from among alternative solutions must involve a perceptive and realistic prediction of the probable feelings and reactions of the individuals involved. It must also take into account some rather nebulous factors of extreme importance, such as the quality of relationships and the level of trust.

5. Implementation of the decision also becomes quite different and can become a challenging problem in itself. Unlike a technical solution, which can often be mechanically carried out, the people involved in a decision to a human problem must understand the decision and how it will affect them, and they must see how their human needs will be met through participating in the solution. Therefore, unless attention is paid to these factors, implementing a decision which is meant to solve a human problem may create more problems, perhaps bigger than the one meant to be solved.

Problems involving behavior often cannot be solved directly, as can problems about things. The proposed solution can only attempt to *stimulate* the behavior desired to overcome or reduce the problem.*

---

* Adapted by permission from Alvar O. Elbing, "The Danger of Applying a 'Technical' Mind to Human Decisions," *European Business*, (Spring 1973): 48–52. (*European Business*, 28, bd. Raspail, Paris, published by the Société Européenne d'Edition et de Diffusion)

The main difference between "technical" problem-solving and "human" problem-solving is in the nature of the resource. The human resource is the only resource that cares how it is used.

Managing the Problem-Solving Process

Even more important than helping you as a manager learn how to solve problems would be helping you learn to better manage the problem-solving process. The "doers"—planners, designers, workers, etc.—should be doing the problem-solving.

To manage the process sounds like a simple procedure. And sometimes it is. The steps involved are:

The manager's role

1. *Define the problem.* As you perhaps saw in working your problem through the model earlier, this step is not necessarily a simple one. Determining what results are required is another way of defining the problem.
2. *Describe the objective to be gained from a solution.* What will be considered to constitute a successful solution? What would be a reasonable achievement? What is essential to have happen? Can desired "global" results be spelled out in detail?
3. *Assign responsibility, resources, review dates, and deadlines.* This is the act of delegation. (Note that we do not ask for solutions at this point, but *proposals for a solution.*)

The "doers" role

a) Figure out different ways it might be fixed.
b) Determine the best plan for fixing it.
c) Develop details and methods to be used.
d) Determine resources required.
e) Present findings and recommendations to the manager.

The manager's role, again

4. *Make management decision to proceed or not.* If the proposed direction seems feasible and reasonable as to cost and effort, obtain other approvals as necessary, etc.
5. *Assign resources and obtain commitments to the planned approach.*
6. *Review progress at appropriate intervals.**

By managing the process rather than trying to solve all of the problems that arise, you can extend your abilities and get more problems solved. Some of the

---

* Adapted from the basic idea of Joe Lindsley, a skilled problem-solving manager at The Boeing Company.

major problems must be solved by you personally, but many others can be delegated.

In the problem-solving case presented earlier about the runaway priority system, after you had worked the problem enough in its initial stages to be able to define the problem and your objectives in solving it, you might have given it to someone on your staff to carry out the remaining steps. In so doing you would be both developing people and getting a lot more problems solved. A manager must look for ways to extend his capabilities. Delegation of the problem-solving activity is one way to do so.

CHAPTER **15**

YOUR MANAGEMENT PHILOSOPHY

It may seem a little strange to you to consider such a topic at the end of this book. So far, I hope, the discussion has been very concrete and practical. Yet, here we are with a theoretical topic like this. Why? Because the philosophy you hold is important to you and is becoming increasingly important to your organization.*

In the early history of organizations in our culture, people were regarded as a commodity; they exchanged their labor for money. The money paid them for their tedium and isolation; in return, they were to passively accept any methods management might use to organize their work, direct them, and regulate and discipline them. If workers were not productive, it was their own fault; the solution was simple: replace them.

Then, many organizations began to adopt a different point of view. Since people have only 24 hours in a day, the organization "contracted" with individuals to spend a stated portion of their lifetime within the constraints specified by the organization. It was up to the organization to give enough attention to guidance, instruction, support, and maintenance of working conditions to maximize workers' productivity. Such a situation made it difficult for arbitrary, capricious, and inept managers to cover up their shortcomings.

Today, more and more organizations define their role as twofold: to meet their primary objectives, and to maintain and enhance the quality of life within the total organizational environment. By "total environment" I mean not only the ecological environment—cleaner air, less pollution, etc.—but also the human environment, a concern with the quality of life of the members of the organization. As organizations redefine their relationships with their members, the role of the organization's managers changes. Now, in considering the ap-

---

* This subject is not often treated directly in the literature or in management education courses. In exploring this relatively new area, I am indebted to Norman Allen, the long-time director of management development in The Boeing Company, for stressing the importance of this subject in management education; to Robert Boroughs, who urged its inclusion here and made helpful suggestions; and to Peter Yensen, who is on the staff of Addison-Wesley Publishing Company.

345

pointment of a manager, attention is given not only to his skills, but also his philosophy.

ELEMENTS OF A MANAGEMENT PHILOSOPHY

I use the term "philosophy" broadly, to mean all of the notions (maxims) you have about appropriate management behavior, the theories you hold about cause-and-effect relationships, and your values. Some of these maxims, theories, and values you are aware of; some you are not aware of, but could be. All reflect certain assumptions you make.

Most of our self-directed activities (planning, decision-making, direction of subordinates, etc.) are based on our own personal philosophies. When a problem arises, we handle it one way or another. We may or may not have any well-thought-out reason behind the action; it may be more or less spontaneous and based largely on our past experience. When something *really* new arises, we often handle it by pretending that it is identical with some situation we have handled in the past, and thus we *know* what to do. (But all too frequently this gets us into trouble, because the present situation isn't really like the one we handled in the past.) But whether our actions appear to be spontaneous, or whether we stop and think about them first, our maxims, our theories, and our values usually guide our actions. These are implicit in our behavior, even when we have never tried to make them explicit. Let me explain further what these three elements of our philosophy are.

Maxims

If your behavior is reasonably consistent, it may be based on certain *maxims* you hold. (The word "maxim" is somewhat old-fashioned, I guess, but it expresses the precise meaning I want.) Maxims are concise statements of principles or rules of conduct. They represent the notions you have about useful practices.

Can I be more specific? I'll try, by giving examples. But in giving examples, I feel the need to remind you that these views aren't necessarily mine.

As you look over the examples given, do you agree or disagree with them? Then consider whether your *actions* agree or disagree with each maxim.

1. A manager should take the time to work on the development of subordinates even when this activity is not directly rewarded by the organization.
   _____ Agree   _____ My actions agree
   _____ Disagree   _____ My actions disagree

2. Group in-puts to decisions should be obtained when it will result in better decisions and better implementation of decisions. But it should not be used as an insincere technique.
   _____ Agree   _____ My actions agree
   _____ Disagree   _____ My actions disagree

3. What people don't know won't hurt them.
   ____ Agree   ____ My actions agree
   ____ Disagree   ____ My actions disagree

4. A manager must control his time to make time available to work on jobs from himself. These include changes and improvements which help his organization do a better job.
   ____ Agree   ____ My actions agree
   ____ Disagree   ____ My actions disagree

5. When you have defined objectives to be reached by subordinates (with their participation in the decision), formulate and write down what will occur when their performance is satisfactory so that they will know exactly what is expected of them.
   ____ Agree   ____ My actions agree
   ____ Disagree   ____ My actions disagree

In these examples, you may have found some differences in your "agree-disagree" answers and your answers as shown by your actions. The acid test is whether or not you *act* this way. If you say one thing, but your behavior says another, your behavior tells the truth. "Yes, but if I just had more time . . ." "Yes, but I intend to start doing this as soon as. . ." "Yes, but I will when the budget lets me . . ." Forget the "yes, buts"; you don't really believe these things, you merely use them for their public relations effect and to build a false self-concept. The old farmer who said, "I'm only farming half as well as I know how to now!" was really only half the farmer he thought he was.

Our maxims, or rules of conduct for ourselves, come largely from our direct experiences in our lives. But they can also be formed by our formal and informal education, tried out on the job, and adopted if they prove successful for us. In talking about experience alone being the best teacher, Henry Ford is supposed to have said, "The school of 'hard-knocks' is the best one. But when you graduate, you're too old to go to work!"

Theories

Some of the notions we have in our heads explain for us the relationships of causes and effects. These ideas I will call *theories*. As we discussed in the chapter on motivation, everyone has a whole set of theories on which he bases his actions. (But note again that action may sometimes be taken without being based on either maxims or theories.) Our theories help us to organize our thinking about the world, help us to take some action now to reach some later goal. Without theories, the world would present a picture of chaotic randomness, and taking any action would be difficult.

On the next page are some examples of *theories;* indicate how you feel about them.

1. When a change is seen by people as being ambiguous in its impact on them, a great deal of energy is spent trying to learn of its potential impact. Therefore, one should try to give full explanations about changes to those who might see themselves as possibly affected.
   _____ Agree   _____ My actions agree
   _____ Disagree   _____ My actions disagree

2. In conserving our energy (which we all try to do), we tend to spend our time on things that are going wrong and disregard things that are going well. But a manager must go against this natural inclination and reinforce the behavior of people who are doing well. This is important in keeping operations on the track.
   _____ Agree   _____ My actions agree
   _____ Disagree   _____ My actions disagree

3. Subordinates will often take their cue from the behavior of their manager. Therefore, the manager should conduct himself as he wishes subordinates to. This makes the excuse that "rank has it privileges" highly questionable.
   _____ Agree   _____ My actions agree
   _____ Disagree   _____ My actions disagree

4. Since "people respect what the boss inspects," a manager's follow-up and expressions of interest and concern should deliberately pinpoint the key issues and not be random or unpredictable.
   _____ Agree   _____ My actions agree
   _____ Disagree   _____ My actions disagree

5. The way to prevent a union from coming in is to do such things as air condition the plant, pay higher wages than the surrounding firms, and have better benefits than the union is asking for elsewhere.
   _____ Agree   _____ My actions agree
   _____ Disagree   _____ My actions disagree

I won't again stress that it's your actions that show what your theories really are. By now, you know it's true.

Our theories may come from our generalizations about our direct experiences or may be based on formal or informal research by others. Some of our theories might be proved to be completely wrong if we obtained any systematic data to test them. But lacking any proof to the contrary, we act on the assumptions we have.

Values

The third element in a person's philosophy is his *values,* the set of basic principles which he uses as guideposts in his life. Values include beliefs about what is "right," "correct," and "ethical." For example, if your job is to set up

Elements of a management philosophy 349

rules or laws, these will reflect your values. Your values determine what you *will* do and what you will *not* do in the absence of laws, rules, precedents, or directions. Your values are subtly defined by the compromises you are willing to make.

For each of the values that follow, indicate whether you do or do not accept the stated value; also indicate whether or not you might make the statement, given the right set of circumstances.

1. "He just isn't working out on that job. But they don't know this. So, let's transfer him to them."
   _____I accept this   _____I might say this
   _____I don't accept this   _____I would never say this

2. "Why not? There's nothing illegal about it."
   _____I accept this   _____I might say this
   _____I don't accept this   _____I would never say this

3. "Go ahead, but don't let anybody find out about it. And remember, if I'm ever asked, I don't know anything about it."
   _____I accept this   _____I might say this
   _____I don't accept this   _____I would never say this

4. "Well, it may be illegal, but the law is wrong."
   _____I accept this   _____I might say this
   _____I don't accept this   _____I would never say this

5. "I know I promised to have it for you, but don't you see, something came up." (Having an excuse is just as good as meeting the commitment.)
   _____I accept this   _____I might say this
   _____I don't accept this   _____I would never say this

6. "Sure, we could help the other unit out; we have exactly what they need. But what have they ever done for *us*?"
   _____I accept this   _____I might say this
   _____I don't accept this   _____I would never say this

7. "When the well-being of the organization is at stake, individuals must sometimes be sacrificed."
   _____I accept this   _____I might say this
   _____I don't accept this   _____I would never say this

8. "I know this course of action is right, and I tried to tell them so. If they won't let me take it, then that's their problem."
   _____I accept this   _____I might say this
   _____I don't accept this   _____I would never say this

9. "Well, we have decided to settle your claim. But we must ask you never to tell anyone about it."
   _____I accept this _____I might say this
   _____I don't accept this _____I would never say this

10. "The adaptable manager in today's modern organizations must select the expedient, the opportunistic course of action in order for his organization to prosper in today's rapidly changing world."
    _____I accept this _____I might say this
    _____I don't accept this _____I would never say this

Here again, the values you *really* hold are shown by your actions rather than by your statements. If you can think of circumstances in which you might make an exception to your stated value, these circumstances help you to define what your value really is.

Where your values come from is too complex for us to explore. You may or may not associate your values with a religious institution. You may or may not have formed them by adoption from (or reaction to) those held by your parents. You may or may not be able to trace them back to groups you belong to, or people who have influenced you.* Today, more and more values are imposed on the organization from outside—from government laws and regulations, unions, and other social groups that bring pressure to bear. But, as other research has shown, once actions are changed, an attitude change tends to follow, and the new value is accepted.

We all have values. Even though you may find it difficult to clearly spell them out, you have them. Your values come to light in your judgments and in many of your actions. They play a major role in your decision-making because through them, you decide on desirable or undesirable goals. In many ways your values govern the conduct of your affairs.

Your philosophy of management, then, is made up of the maxims, theories, and values you hold. But just because we have been able to define these components and to give an example of each, that doesn't mean that they normally appear separately. They frequently appear in rather mixed form. Here is a statement containing all three:

> People don't "tick." They are motivated by complex inner needs that they strive to satisfy. A manager should know his people well enough to know something about their motives. Then, he can manage in a way that satisfies the needs of each in the process of accomplishing the work of the organization. It is important that he accomplish both, not one or the other exclusively.
>   _____I agree _____I disagree

---

* Some years ago, in his book *The Lonely Crowd* (New Haven: Yale University Press, 1950), David Riesman traced the change of values from tradition-directed to inner-directed ("gyroscope man") to other-directed ("radar man"). His descriptions of these societal tendencies are thought-provoking.

If you agree with the statement, how do you manage people? If you disagree, what do you believe?

When you go through the experience of trying to identify your own philosophy, as I will ask you to do shortly, don't expect to be able to define neat categories of maxims, theories, and values; it really isn't important that you define your philosophy neatly. But these three elements will probably be present in what you do identify.

IDENTIFYING YOUR MANAGEMENT PHILOSOPHY

Your experience with this book so far has been largely an introspective exploration—looking at yourself and your practices over a wide range of topics. Hopefully, the experience has given you a better idea of who you are, how you act, what you believe, and what you value. (I don't think it possible to decide and choose what you *would* be unless you know what you are now.)

I think you will discover that trying to state your philosophy is an important experience for you. As hard as this may be, stating your maxims, theories, and values—what you believe in and practice as a manager—will help you to understand better how you have organized your experience. When we can make these maxims, theories, and values explicit, we can question them, probe them, weigh them, and decide if they are really the ones we want.

So, let's try it. I'll present some questions based on the experiences provided in the preceding chapters of the book. These questions are meant to suggest areas you might think about in formulating your philosophy. Do try to make the distinction between what you believe (and do) now, and what you will consciously try to do in the future. These intentions should be listed on the page headed "My Resolutions," and here you should indicate the additions and changes you wish to make and apply.

I would urge you to write down your philosophy rather than merely think about it. You will find that writing requires a discipline in your thinking. It's not an easy task. Expect to ponder over your ideas, come back and make changes, and do some real "soul-searching" in the process.

Let me restate your next assignment. Following are some questions about your experiences in each chapter for you to use in thinking about your philosophy in the area covered. Then come two pages labeled "My Management Philosophy." Using the questions, and others you may think of, write down a sentence or two about your own philosophy. When these are put together, collating and combining when you can, you will develop a statement of your own philosophy. There is also a page headed "My Resolutions." These resolutions should be prepared as your philosophy is emerging from your statements.

The questions on pp. 352–354 are meant to spark your thinking about the philosophy you hold now and resolutions you might make.

Chapter 1

What personal philosophy have you demonstrated by reading this book or by attending a course in which it is used? (Consider what motivated you, what your own needs were, what assumptions you made about your own growth, and your own values about education.)

Chapter 2

What is your philosophy about management practices? (Consider your stated action on each in-basket item. What does your action show you? Consider your answers to the questions at the end of the chapter. What do these tell you?)

Chapter 3

What is your philosophy about yourself? (Consider your personal answers to the questions posed and the plans you formulated about the future.)

Chapter 4

What is your philosophy about your relationships, up and down? (Consider your reactions to your boss, as well as being a boss over others. What do you believe about developing a trust climate? About taking risks? About getting feedback and using it? About applying the idea of positive reinforcement?)

Chapter 5

What is your philosophy about communication? (Consider your expectations about "the illusion of communication." Think about your practices in this area. What guidelines do you try to follow? What are your expectations and practices in two-way communication?)

Chapter 6

What is your philosophy about effective thinking in yourself and others? (Consider your notions about what effective thinking is and what it results in. Consider your present habits and approaches. What steps do you take in getting help on your thinking? What do you feel and practice about giving help to others in this area?)

Chapter 7

What is your philosophy about managing change? (Consider your generalizations in the area of change and its impact on people. Also consider your practices in providing information to those affected by change, your ideas about the importance of trust, getting participation, seeing the points of view of those affected by change, and managing change to encourage easy accommodation to it.)

Chapter 8

What is your philosophy about groups at work? (Consider when you choose to use groups and when you won't use them. Consider your feelings about work and emotionality in the life of a group. Consider your notions about effective actions as a manager in working with groups.)

Chapter 9

What is your present philosophy about getting participation in decision-making? (Consider what you now do and what you say you believe. When do you think it is important to get participation? Why? How important, generally, is it for you to get commitment by subordinates to the decision or to its implementation? Why?)

Chapter 10

What is your philosophy about handling organizational conflict? (Consider your beliefs, usual anxiety level when it occurs, present practices. Look over each of your actions on the in-basket items. What do these actions show about your beliefs? Consider your answers to the questions at the end of the chapter. What do these tell you about your maxims, theories, and values?)

Chapter 11

What is your philosophy about motivation? (Consider the assumptions you now hold about people in general. Do these apply to yourself? Consider your assumptions about specific individuals who work for you. Where do you think motivation comes from—outside or inside the person? Consider ways in which you might get data to confirm or change your theories. What do your theories tell you about your values about people? Consider the policies and practices of your organization which you accept or tolerate.)

Chapter 12

What is your philosophy of administration? (Consider your reactions to, and agreement or disagreement with, the ideas presented. What does this tell you about your maxims, theories, and values? What is your philosophy in the many areas not covered in this chapter, such as your organization's existing policies and practices in pay, selection, promotion, transfer, and the many other administrative areas with which you are concerned daily?)

Chapter 13

What is your philosophy about managing your time? (Consider how you presently spend your time—your priorities, your use of delegation, and your reactions to the maxims given in the checklist.)

Chapter 14

What is your philosophy about problem-solving? (Consider the "level" of the problem you selected to work on. Is this a typical problem you handle? Should it be? What values are shown by your statement of objectives? What theories do you show in your search for causes? What is shown by your value analysis of alternatives? By your planning for action? Implementation?)

Chapter 15

What is your philosophy about having and stating your management philosophy? (Consider your reaction to the experience of trying to make them explicit. What, if anything, do you feel this might help you accomplish? What is your feeling about doing what is of immediate use, or advantage, depending on each set of circumstances faced, *versus* taking action based on your own basic principles you have decided are right or just?)

In the space provided, make notes as you formulate and write down your philosophy. After looking over the questions about each chapter and going back to the chapter as you search for some answers, jot down a sentence or two summing up your philosophy in each area. As you progress, you will see where you can collate and combine related ideas. The result will be a statement of your management philosophy now. Then, note your resolutions for changes you wish to make.

MY MANAGEMENT PHILOSOPHY

MY MANAGEMENT PHILOSOPHY (cont.)

MY RESOLUTIONS

(Use this space to note changes you would make, differences you would like to see, and other resolves for the future.)

NOW THAT YOU KNOW YOUR PHILOSOPHY OF MANAGEMENT . . .

How did you find the experience of trying to make explicit your philosophy of management? Probably not easy, as I predicted. But as I've said before, without trying to spell out the statements making up your philosophy, you cannot question them, probe them, weigh them, and decide if you want them.

Let's talk for a minute about the resolutions you made, if you did so. Changing the patterns of our behavior is no simple chore, as you may have discovered with perennial New Year's resolutions. What specific steps can you plan to make these changes effective? (Significant changes are made slowly, step by step.) What obstacles will you probably run into? How can these be overcome? What follow-up will you plan in order to check on how you are doing?

After taking a good look at what your philosophy is now, you can be different if you wish. But these changes can come only from inside you.

When you have stated your philosophy, you have a more conscious guide to your actions as you face the varied, unlabeled confusion of demands from your daily job. You can believe in yourself more. And you can consciously assimilate new ideas you wish to add.

The Psychological Contract

There is one more use possible when you have formulated your philosophy of management—that is in negotiating a psychological contract concerning your job. The notion of a psychological contract between an organization and its members is a relatively new idea.* Briefly, a psychological contract consists of the expectations an organization has of a member and the expectations a member has of the organization. This psychological contract is not a written document; indeed, it is hardly ever made explicit and discussed. If I work for your organization, for example, you expect me to accept the authority structure and obey the rules you set forth. In return, I expect to be treated fairly by the organization. Perhaps both sets of expectations can be set forth in more detail. If you expect a commitment on my part to the goals of the organization, I may expect to have an influence on the goals set. If you expect loyalty from me, I expect status and job security from the organization. In other words, there should be a fair exchange. The organization enforces its expectations through the use of its power; the member enforces his expectations either overtly, through leaving the organization or going on strike, or covertly, through withholding or minimizing his involvement and productivity.

---

* A valuable book dealing in small part with the psychological contract is Edgar H. Schein's *Organizational Psychology*, 2nd ed., Englewood Cliffs, N.J.: Prentice-Hall, 1970. This is a very readable small book, and I commend it to those of you interested in further explorations in managing.

Now that you know your philosophy of management... 359

Now that you have come to know yourself better by identifying your philosophy, you have available some ideas to use in making your contract with the organization more explicit. This contract is not legal and binding, of course; we wouldn't expect you to sue the organization for violating the terms of your psychological contract with it. But there would be the basis for a discussion if one has been agreed to and the terms are not being met.

Since you can't make a contract with the whole organization, you will need to make one with the representative of the organization who is most influential in your life with the organization—your boss. Let me give you an example of some of the terms and conditions you might present at a negotiating session with your boss, either at the start of your assignment to him, or during the course of an assignment. (As you read these examples, can you picture yourself discussing items such as these with your present boss? Can you picture one of your subordinates coming to you to discuss such a list?)

What You Can Expect of Me

1. To give you my skills wholeheartedly and to do each assigned job to the best of my ability; to practice my developing philosophy as I understand it.

2. My conscious efforts to increase the skills I have and to formulate and practice a more useful management philosophy.

3. To try to advance the total organization, taking the larger view over that of my assigned segment when the aims conflict.

4. I will take risks with you and others in the organization in giving feedback and in saying what I really think and feel.

5. To tell you of actual conditions—as good or as bad as they are—to make sure you have no surprises.

6. I shall dissent when I think it important; if very important, I shall do whatever I can to advise, persuade, and convince you and others to the course I would recommend up until the point the decision is made. Then I will treat the decision as if it were my own.

What I Expect of You

1. Mutual creation of a situation whereby my own needs and strivings can be met—primarily through the challenge of the job itself.

2. Your guidance and creation of opportunities for my growth at a reasonable pace.

3. To be judged on cooperation with and advancement of other parts of the organization as well as individual accomplishment in my assigned areas.

4. A respect for my openness and an expectation of it, an understanding of my intent, and your openness with me in giving me feedback and answering the questions I might have.

5. To accept my straightforward communication and not punish me for it, but to correct my actions when this is needed.

6. To accept the spirit of my dissent—to tell me when it is being misunderstood or when I am overlooking something that others are taking into account.

What You Can Expect of Me

7. To allow people over whom I have responsibility to develop their own potential and satisfy their own varying needs through their work experience. This will require more than the usual attention to self-actualization, independence, and esteem.

8. Not to bother you with unnecessary social visits when you are occupied or to ask you to do my job for me.

9. To be honest in everything I do, acting from my principles and values.

10. To be accepting and supportive of you and to be ready to "clear the air" through discussion with you when I feel I cannot be supportive.

What I Expect of You

7. To support my efforts in the development of people and in creating opportunities for their need satisfaction —to expect, accept, and counsel with me on new approaches.

8. To see me when I ask you to; to give me a decision when needed or an explanation why you can't.

9. To expect honesty, to create a climate in which compromise of my values is not expected or required.

10. To be accepting and supportive of me and to be ready to "clear the air" through discussion with me when you feel you cannot be supportive.

These items are given as the sorts of things you might wish to negotiate with your boss. What was your reaction as you read the list? Would an agreement on such a list provide both parties with a way to approach a discussion if there was an actual or imagined violation of one of the "contract" items? What would such an agreed upon list do in the relationship between you and your boss? Between you and your subordinates?

By now, you should know that you won't get off so easily by merely looking at a list of items which I have created. In the space provided, create your own items which you could use in negotiating a psychological contract with your superior.

What My Boss Can Expect of Me

What I Will Expect of the Boss

Now that you know your philosophy of management . . .

_____   _____
_____   _____
_____   _____
_____   _____
_____   _____
_____   _____
_____   _____
_____   _____
_____   _____
_____   _____

Such an approach may require you to take quite a risk on some items and little risk on others, depending on the relationship perceived. But the tool can be valuable in establishing sound, growing relationships.

EPILOGUE

One cannot go through the sorts of introspections as provided by the experiences you have been through without being changed in the process. You were a certain person when you began your explorations in this book; you are another person now. Some of the changes may have been subtle, so that it might be difficult for you to point out the differences in you now. Other changes may have been triggered by great insights which you were about ready to understand now. These you might be able to point to as specific learnings. Although we wouldn't expect you to change into a completely different person after reading this book, we would expect that you would begin (or probably have begun) experimenting with slightly different ways of observing, thinking, and behaving. As these are successful (you are reinforced), you will gain more confidence in their use. If some fail, you will, hopefully, do some diagnostic thinking to determine what went wrong and have another go at it, with some improvements. Or, you may react otherwise, as is discussed by two of our social philosophers:

PEANUTS

WHEN YOU'VE LOST AT SOMETHING, YOU CAN REACT IN TWO WAYS...

ONE WAY IS TO ANALYZE JUST WHY YOU LOST...TRY TO FIGURE OUT WHAT YOUR WEAKNESSES WERE, AND THEN TRY TO IMPROVE SO THAT NEXT TIME YOU CAN WIN..

BLEAH!

THAT'S THE OTHER WAY!

© United Feature Syndicate, Inc.

No one expects you to operate at peak effectiveness as a manager *all* the time. There will be times when you, like the rest of us, do not listen or care much what others think or feel, or feel like taking responsibility, or be an effective manager, or even be a manager at all! But at other times you will, and we hope that you will find that your "batting average" will improve through your new insights and skills.

The whole point in improving your effectiveness is to accomplish the organization's objectives through your increased abilities to work cooperatively with others and to provide opportunities to others for satisfying relations and meaningful work in order for them to grow as tall as they can grow. This is a value of mine, which I hope you share.

ABOUT THE AUTHOR

Allen Zoll is the principal in the firm Management Education Associates. His firm specializes in management education, training of trainers, conference design and administration, and organization development. Clients range across the United States and Canada.

Before forming the company in 1970, he was with The Boeing Company for almost 14 years. Various titles held include Corporate Management Education Advisor; Management Education Chief; Management Development Advisor, Vertol Division; Manager of Management Development, Pilotless Aircraft Division. He was also assigned as a working consultant in organization, policy formation, and management surveys.

Dr. Zoll received his B.B.A. degree from Southern Methodist University, his M.S. in business from Columbia University, and his Ph.D. from the University of Washington, where he served on the faculty of the College of Business Administration for seven years. During this time he also served as a consultant to businesses in the Northwest, and in 1955 was retained by The Boeing Company. A year later, he joined Boeing full time.

Dr. Zoll spent four years in the infantry in World War II, rising from enlisted private to combat platoon leader, and received the bronze star, and purple heart with cluster. Before the war he worked as a machine operator for a metal products company.

He is most widely known for his participative methods in adult education. He is the author of *Dynamic Management Education* (2d ed., Addison-Wesley, 1969), *The In-Basket Kit* (Addison-Wesley, 1971), and various articles.

Allen and his wife, Lucille, reside in Seattle, Washington.